YOUR PSYCHOLOGY PROJECT HANDBOOK

Visit the *Your Psychology Project Handbook, second edition* Companion Website at **www.pearsoned.co.uk/wood-psychproject** to find valuable **student** learning material including:

- Downloadable forms, checklists, templates and worksheets to help you in the different stages of your project work
- Annotated examples of good and bad reports
- Guidance on how to organise a literature review
- Self-test questions to check your understanding
- Annotated links to relevant sites on the web

YOUR PSYCHOLOGY PROJECT HANDBOOK

BECOMING A RESEARCHER

Second Edition

Clare Wood
David Giles
Carol Percy

PEARSON

Harlow, England • London • New York • Boston • San Francisco • Toronto • Sydney
Auckland • Singapore • Hong Kong • Tokyo • Seoul • Taipei • New Delhi
Cape Town • São Paulo • Mexico City • Madrid • Amsterdam • Munich • Paris • Milan

Pearson Education Limited
Edinburgh Gate
Harlow
Essex CM20 2JE
England

and Associated Companies throughout the world

Visit us on the World Wide Web at:
www.pearson.com/uk

First published 2009
Second edition published 2012

ISBN: 978-0-273-75980-5

British Library Cataloguing-in-Publication Data
A catalogue record for this book is available from the British Library

Library of Congress Cataloging-in-Publication Data
Wood, Clare Patricia.
  Your psychology project handbook: becoming a researcher / Clare Wood, David Giles,
Carol Percy. – 2nd ed.
      p. cm.
  Includes bibliographical references and index.
  ISBN 978-0-273-75980-5 (pbk.)
  1. Psychology–Research–Methodology.   I. Giles, David, 1964– II. Percy, Carol.   III. Title.
  BF76.5.W64 2012
  150.72–dc23

                                                                            2011049349

ARP impression 98

Typeset in 9/12pt Giovanni Book by 71
Printed and bound in Great Britain by Ashford Colour Press Ltd

BRIEF CONTENTS

About the Authors   x
Publisher's Acknowledgements   xi
Guided Tour   xii

1   COMING UP WITH THE IDEA   1

2   MANAGING YOUR SUPERVISOR   11

3   THE LITERATURE REVIEW: IDENTIFYING YOUR RESEARCH QUESTION   38

4   DESIGNING YOUR STUDY   52

5   PROJECT PLANNING AND MANAGEMENT   75

6   ONLINE RESOURCES   86

7   RESEARCH ETHICS   94

8   DATA COLLECTION   120

9   DATA ANALYSIS AND PRESENTATION   142

10   PREPARING THE REPORT   170

11   DISSEMINATING YOUR RESULTS   190

12   EMPLOYABILITY AND YOUR PROJECT   202

References   209
Appendix – Answers to the Ethical Scenarios   211
Index   213

DETAILED CONTENTS

About the Authors   x
Publisher's Acknowledgements   xi
Guided Tour   xii

1 COMING UP WITH THE IDEA   1

1.1   What Makes a Good Project Idea?   2
1.2   So, Where Do you Begin?   3
1.3   Doing Projects as a Team   7
1.4   Projects to Avoid   8
1.5   A Word on Career Aspirations   9
1.6   What Next?   9
      Chapter Summary   10
      Further Reading   10

2 MANAGING YOUR SUPERVISOR   11

2.1   Why 'Manage' the Relationship with your Supervisor?   12
2.2   What to Expect from your Supervisory Relationship   14
2.3   Allocations to Supervisors   15
2.4   First Meeting with your Supervisor   20
2.5   The Literature Review and Design Phase   22
2.6   Data Collection Phase   25
2.7   Data Analysis Phase   27
2.8   Report Writing Phase   28
2.9   After you Have Submitted your Report   31
2.10 Troubleshooting your Supervisory Relationship   32
      Chapter Summary   37
      Further Reading   37

3 THE LITERATURE REVIEW: IDENTIFYING YOUR RESEARCH QUESTION   38

3.1   Conducting a Literature Search   39
3.2   The Research Question   45
3.3   Building a Theoretical Framework   47
      Chapter Summary   51
      Further Reading   51

4 DESIGNING YOUR STUDY   52

4.1   Initial Decisions About Study Design   53
4.2   Issues in Experimental Design   53
4.3   Correlational Design   59

4.4	Observations	61
4.5	Designs Based on Interviews, Focus Groups and Other Interactions	62
4.6	Analysing Archival Data	63
4.7	Design Decisions Relating to the Analysis of Qualitative Data	63
4.8	Phenomenological Designs	67
4.9	Designs Using Interpretative Phenomenological Analysis	68
4.10	Designs Using Discourse Analysis	69
4.11	Narrative Designs	70
4.12	Designs Using Conversation Analysis	72
4.13	Designs Using Thematic Analysis	72
4.14	Grounded Theory Designs	73
	Chapter Summary	74
	Further Reading	74

5 PROJECT PLANNING AND MANAGEMENT — 75

5.1	Ownership and Stakeholders	76
5.2	Resources	79
5.3	Planning your Project Schedule: Gantt Charts	80
5.4	Risks	83
5.5	Monitoring and Maintaining Progress	83
5.6	Planning a Local Dissemination Strategy	84
	Chapter Summary	85

6 ONLINE RESOURCES — 86

6.1	Introduction	87
6.2	The Literature Review	87
6.3	Recruitment and Project Management	88
6.4	Experimental Work	89
6.5	Surveys and Interviews	90
6.6	Data Analysis	91
6.7	Data Storage, Backup and Sharing	92
6.8	Writing Up	92
	Chapter Summary	92

7 RESEARCH ETHICS — 94

7.1	The Principle of 'No Harm'	95
7.2	How to Prepare your Essential Documentation	99
7.3	Preserving Anonymity and Confidentiality	106
7.4	Recruitment	106
7.5	Your Materials	110
7.6	Research with Children and Other Vulnerable Groups	111
7.7	Data Protection Issues	114
7.8	The Right to Withdraw	116
7.9	A Checklist for Scrutinising your Proposal	117
7.10	Some Ethical Scenarios	118
	Chapter Summary	119
	Further Reading	119

8 DATA COLLECTION   120

8.1   Interviews and Focus Groups   121
8.2   Not Just a 'Big Interview': Distinctive Features of Focus Groups   125
8.3   Transcribing the Tape: Reality Bites!   126
8.4   Using Questionnaires and Scales   128
8.5   Experiments   134
8.6   Using Archival Data   135
8.7   Observation   137
8.8   Working Off Campus   139
     Chapter Summary   140
     Further Reading   141

9 DATA ANALYSIS AND PRESENTATION   142

9.1   Statistical Methods   143
9.2   Qualitative Methods   152
     Chapter Summary   168
     Further Reading   168

10 PREPARING THE REPORT   170

10.1   Report Writing Style   171
10.2   The Main Body of the Report   172
10.3   Sundries   183
     Chapter Summary   188
     Further Reading   189

11 DISSEMINATING YOUR RESULTS   190

11.1   Dissemination Outlets   191
11.2   Publishing in an Academic Journal   192
11.3   Preparing and Submitting a Poster or Oral Conference Presentation   197
11.4   The Media   199
     Chapter Summary   201
     Further Reading   201

12 EMPLOYABILITY AND YOUR PROJECT   202

12.1   Applying for Jobs   203
12.2   Shortlisting   204
12.3   Transferable Skills from Your Project   205
12.4   Mapping Your Skills onto a Person Specification   205
12.5   Your Project and the Job Interview   207
     Chapter Summary   207

References   209
Appendix – Answers to the Ethical Scenarios   211
Index   213

ABOUT THE AUTHORS

CLARE WOOD (BA Kent, 1993; PhD Bristol, 1997) is Professor of Psychology in Education at Coventry University. Her main research interests are concerned with understanding how children learn to read and why some children struggle to achieve this, as well as how technology may help children to acquire literacy. She originally aspired to be a professional artist and, after a brief period working as a studio assistant at Madame Tussaud's in Windsor, she decided that painting wax was not a transferable skill, and decided to study psychology at university instead. However, her ability to paint wax, fibreglass and scenery successfully funded both her undergraduate and postgraduate career, and resulted in her inhaling large amounts of solvents on a daily basis, which she believes may have fundamentally changed her brain structure for the good. Clare taught psychology at University College Northampton (now the University of Northampton) before working at the Open University in Milton Keynes, among the concrete cows and bearded folk. While there she co-edited *Psychological Development and Early Childhood* (Blackwell, 2005) and *Developmental Psychology in Action* (Blackwell, 2006). She has since also co-edited *Contemporary Perspectives on Reading and Spelling* (Routledge, 2009), and the *International Handbook of Psychology in Education* (Emerald, 2010), and co-wrote the second edition of *The Psychology of Education* (Routledge, 2011). She is currently Editor in Chief of the *Journal of Research in Reading* and Associate Editor of the *British Journal of Educational Psychology*. In 2006 she received the Award for Excellence in the Teaching of Psychology. Her students are demanding an inquest …

Clare first met David and Carol at Cheltenham and Gloucester College of Higher Education (now University of Gloucestershire) during her first teaching post, when they were all fresh–faced and keen. Academia is a small world, however, and they later reunited at Coventry University, when they were older and marginally wiser. One source of wisdom came from the fact that all three of them had been the module leader for the dissertation module and had a turn at chairing the undergraduate ethics committee in the psychology department. Based on these experiences, they decided to write a book to help students through their dissertation.

DAVID C. GILES (BSc Manchester, 1993; PhD Bristol, 1996) is Reader in Media Psychology at the University of Winchester. His main research interest is in the psychology of media influence, and he has published papers on topics such as media framing, parasocial interaction and online mental health communities. Despite spending a lot of his time teaching advanced statistics, he is a founding editor of the Taylor & Francis journal *Qualitative Research in Psychology*. After failing to scale the heights of popstardom in his youth, he worked in his early 20s as a freelance music journalist, writing for a host of publications (although *Music Week* and *NME* are the only ones to survive the last recession). During this time he became curious about the mysterious workings of the entertainment industry and, after finishing his PhD (on the role of visual memory in children's spelling), wrote *Illusions of Immortality: A Psychology of Fame and Celebrity* (Macmillan, 2000). He followed this with the rather less media-friendly *Advanced Research Methods in Psychology* (Routledge, 2002) while teaching a module at Coventry University that provided the inspiration for *Media Psychology* (Lawrence Erlbaum, 2003) and *Psychology of the Media* (Palgrave, 2010). He also tried his hand at writing a couple of novels that now reside on a dusty shelf somewhere.

CAROL PERCY (BSc 1990, PhD 1994, Queen's University Belfast) is a Senior Lecturer in Psychology at Coventry University. Her main research interest is in people's experiences of health and illness. After completing a PhD in feminist social psychology, Carol briefly considered running away to be a cabin crew member for a well known middle eastern airline. Uncertain of her ability to meet the company's stringent requirements for appropriate feminine demeanour, she opted instead for an academic post developing a master's degree for students in Hong Kong. Carol has taught qualitative research methods for 16 years, and has provided methods training to various groups including the Higher Education Academy and Her Majesty's Prison Service. She particularly enjoys supervising dissertation students, and encouraging them to present their work at conferences. Carol has co-authored numerous student conference presentations on projects ranging from the discursive analysis of media crime reports, to the lived experience of people whose homes have been flooded. Thanks to a 'Leading Practice Through Research' award from the Health Foundation, Carol recently spent a year setting up and evaluating a self-management intervention for women with polycystic ovary syndrome. Carol cannot paint or write novels, although she did have a number of poems published in the school magazine when she was aged nine.

PUBLISHER'S ACKNOWLEDGEMENTS

We are grateful to the following for permission to reproduce copyright material:

Table 4.3 from *The Psychologist* Vol.18 No.10 (Madill, A., Gough, B., Lawton, R., & Stratton, P.) reproduced with permission from *The Psychologist*, © The British Psychological Society.

In some instances we have been unable to trace the owners of copyright material, and we would appreciate any information that would enable us to do so.

GUIDED TOUR

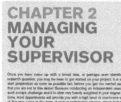

By the end of this chapter you will: Each chapter begins with a handy set of bullet points outlining the topics covered.

Common pitfalls: Identify some of the easiest mistakes that can be made when working on your final-year project, from the initial ideas to the conclusion.

Common confusions: Help to distinguish between concepts and methods which can be easily mixed up.

Maximising Marks: Help you to get the full potential out of your project, with advice about easily-avoidable errors and ideas for how to improve your marks.

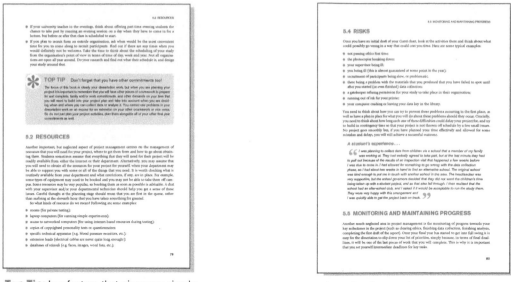

Top Tip: Is a feature that gives you simple suggestions that can help you get the most out of every stage of your project, and generally make the process as smooth as possible.

A student's experience: Useful, real-life anecdotes and advice from people who've been where you are now.

A supervisor's experience: Genuine project supervisors talk about their own experiences, and what you – and they – can learn from them.

Chapter summary: Recaps the main points of the chapter, and is useful when flicking back through the book for hints and tips when you come to each stage of your project.

Further reading: Directs you to books, journals and websites which can help you gain a deeper understanding of what you need to do to make your project a resounding success!

CHAPTER 1
COMING UP
WITH THE IDEA

Coming up with an idea for a project is often the hardest part of designing a piece of research, whether you are an undergraduate student, a postgraduate or an established researcher. In this chapter we will give you some ideas for strategies that you can use to get started on this important first step of the research journey.

BY THE END OF THIS CHAPTER YOU WILL:

- Know what makes a good research project idea.
- Know some strategies for getting started on the process of developing an idea for a research project.
- Understand some of the issues related to team-based projects.
- Have an idea of the kinds of projects that are best avoided.

1.1 WHAT MAKES A GOOD PROJECT IDEA?

A good project is always one that is **rooted in the psychological literature.** In other words, resist the temptation to think of something so novel that you are going to struggle to find any background literature to relate it to, or where the only literature that exists on it is from a discipline other than psychology. Your research question should be located in an area of psychological literature, and ideally the question should be interesting and valuable in its own right (i.e. it is under researched as a topic), so that it does not matter what results you eventually find.

A good project idea is also **one that will result in something new being added to the literature.** Novelty and originality can come in a variety of forms. The most obvious form of novelty is to ask a question that the current literature on the topic has yet to address. However, you could also think about this in modest terms, such as 'has this question been addressed *in this way* before?', or 'has this topic been explored *with these types of participants* before?' In other words, it is enough to build your project around a change to the methodological approach taken to a topic area, or a change in the population that a task or idea has been applied to.

It may well be the case that you have found a topic that is very under researched and will present you with the opportunity to look at a question that has not been considered previously. That can be quite a challenge, as it will be down to you to locate appropriate literature to ground your study in, drawing on ideas from related areas of psychology. There may also be the temptation to try to answer all the unanswered questions on that topic! Remember to keep to a simple idea that is feasible for you to do.

On that note, a good project idea is also **something that is achievable** by you in the time that you have available, given the resources and the populations that you have access to. For example, many undergraduate students are interested in forensic psychology but, for practical reasons, it is not possible or appropriate for them to have access to offenders. However, it is perfectly possible to develop an idea that is relevant to forensic theories and issues that can be conducted with other students or other people you do have access to. For example, you could look at aggression and emotion, or fear of crime, in an undergraduate population.

Similarly, some students wish to engage in intervention research or longitudinal designs (see Chapter 4), but often the timescale needed to implement such designs is too long to be accommodated in the time that you have available to conduct and write up your project. If you think that you are interested in this kind of design, you are advised to put a lot of careful thought into the time needed to really achieve the outcomes of your project (see Chapter 5).

In terms of resources, psychology departments differ in the extent to which they have equipment that they are willing to loan to students, in their policies regarding allowing students to book rooms for research purposes, and the extent to which they are able to support students who need computer software to be programmed for them. You are advised to find out early on what resources your department has for your use, and what other resources you have legitimate access to. Also find out how to go about requesting them, how long you can book them for, and how much advanced notice you need to give to technical staff.

Something else that makes for a good project idea is to work on **something that you understand.** This is not intended to be a glib remark. Often students will ask their supervisor to help them formulate a research idea that is novel so that they are maximising their chances of getting a really good grade. However, often supervisors can get a little carried away and the result can be a project that is too challenging in terms of the theories and ideas that need to be understood in order to write it up effectively. Similarly, it is also possible that you may come up with an idea, but the theories that you need to engage with in order to ground that idea in the literature are ones that you do not fully understand. This is often the case in cognitive psychology; for example, this area often uses deceptively simple tasks that can be appealing to students, but the ideas behind the tasks may be rooted in concepts and theories taken from advanced cognitive psychology or neuropsychology, which can be challenging to write about effectively if you only have a limited knowledge of them. You will find that you will lose a lot of marks at the writing up stage if you are unable to articulate clearly the ideas behind your study.

1.2 SO, WHERE DO YOU BEGIN?

We have outlined below four different strategies for selecting a topic. These are not exhaustive: you may have your own way of doing this, but use these as guidelines for the kind of activities you could engage in when beginning on this journey.

1.2.1 Approach 1: What interests you?

You may decide to base your project around a psychological topic with which you have some personal experience, or that is prevalent in the media at the time. There is absolutely nothing wrong with doing this. However, it may require more background research on your part in order to work it up into a researchable idea. For instance, you might have an interest in the phenomenon of *road rage*. Below we have illustrated how you might go about developing your interest in this idea.

- Start by focusing on *psychological aspects* of road rage. So you would need to consider individual differences (e.g. personality types), social or environmental factors and any other concepts from your degree course that might impact on the topic, such as biological 'arousal'.

- This project would require a large literature search from the outset. Start with keywords such as 'road rage' (there may be some recent literature). If this gets you nowhere, try some likely combinations such as 'aggression' and 'driver/driving'. If you know of some related terms from the literature, this is always a good place to start. For instance, enter 'driver behaviour' as a search term into a research database such as PsycINFO, Scopus or Web of Science, and that might identify some literature that will provide you with relevant theoretical ideas, and may contain references to aggressive driving behaviour. However, if your topic is very novel, you may be forced to combine two or more literatures. For example, a study of the personalities of internet shoppers might require you to combine literatures on human-computer interaction and consumer behaviour.

- *Read something!* A trawl through the abstracts might give you an idea of the types of questions asked in the literature or of the methodologies employed, but there is no substitute for getting hold of one or two papers, or a book, that are relevant to your topic and trying to come up with some inspiration. It could be, after all, that you find some interesting literature on the evolution of aggression and this will give you some ideas for studying road rage.

COMMON PITFALLS

There are pitfalls associated with this type of approach. The most serious of these is that you generate a topic idea without taking the time to read around it, only to find that there is no psychological literature related to it that you could use to construct a rationale and theoretical framework for your study. (Chapter 3 explains what a theoretical framework is in more detail and why it is important that you construct one in the introduction to your dissertation).

You should also be aware that, in researching a topic that is personally significant to you, it may raise some ethical issues in terms of whether you are going to be able to cope with researching the topic on an emotional level. It is easy to overestimate how well you may have come to terms with something that has affected you personally, especially if it is psychological in nature. Topics that are very personally salient are best avoided as dissertation topics for this reason.

A student's experience . . .

> When I started my dissertation I was determined to conduct a study into people's experiences of losing a parent to cancer. I had lost my own mother to cancer when I was younger, and I thought it would be a nice idea and something that my family would be proud of. When I submitted my ethics application, the committee suggested that I come up with an alternative topic because there were ethical issues associated with interviewing people about losing a relative to cancer when I was not trained to counsel them if they became distressed. They were also concerned that I might be unprepared for my own emotional reaction to people's accounts of this, given my own experiences. Initially I was disappointed, but I later chose to write an essay about cancer for another module I was taking and I was surprised to find how difficult I found it to write, and how emotional I became just reading the literature on the topic. I realised the ethics committee was right to be concerned as I would not have been able to control my reactions to the accounts of cancer that people would tell me about during the interviews. I found a way of reframing my idea around asking people more generally about the importance of having a mother figure in early childhood.

1.2.2 What have you found interesting on your course?

It may be useful to track back through your old lecture notes to find an interesting topic that you could explore further. This might be a topic covered in a lecture or seminar, or a piece of practical work that you carried out. This is a safer strategy than the 'what interests you' approach because, if a topic has been covered on your course, there must be an academic literature on that topic, and you will already be familiar with some key theoretical ideas in that field that you could base your research question around.

If you are adopting this approach, we would suggest that you approach your background research in the following way:

- Return to your notes and reading list for that module. Look up some of the sources in the library. You could also contact the person who is currently the module leader for that module to ask for the latest version of the module guide so that you have a more up-to-date reading list to work from.

- Think of some further research that could be done in this area. It may be that some of the theories could be modified, or elements of the studies changed slightly. Or it might be that a phenomenon from one area could be applied to a different context. For instance, health psychologists are constantly applying the theory of planned behaviour to different health behaviours. Is there anything they have missed in terms of trying to explain people's behaviour – what other factors might contribute to intentions and explain failure to perform intended actions (e.g. giving up smoking)? Could the theory of planned behaviour be usefully applied to understanding non-health related behaviours?

- Perhaps there are obvious flaws in some of these studies. You might like to apply a different methodology from one that has been used before, or design some new test materials that might produce different results, or even think of new populations to test. Perhaps a particular phenomenon has only been studied using undergraduates, and it might be interesting to apply it to older adults or children. In developmental psychology, there is often mileage in just varying the age of the children studied (say, produce a simplified version of a test designed for 7 to 8-year-olds and run it on nursery age children). The modification of tests and tasks to make them suitable for use with new populations is something that is valuable and novel in itself.

● You might also like to combine ideas from different literatures – for example, you could look at autobiographical memory and how it is related to aspects of a person's self-concept, or consider performance on theory of mind tasks in relation to some aspect of children's drawings. This is often the way new literatures begin to open up.

COMMON PITFALLS

An easy trap to fall into when using this 'course based' approach to generating research ideas is that you may design something that does not reflect the most up-to-date thinking on a topic. This is because lectures are designed to introduce you to a topic and orient you to classic research and ideas in that area. Level 1 lectures, especially, may not always represent the most recent development in a particular field. It is your responsibility to conduct a search around your proposed topic and get a sense of what recent studies look like and what theories are being cited in those papers, to complement your more general knowledge from the lecture notes and reading list.

1.2.3 What is a 'hot' research area at the moment?

If you are considering research as a career, or even just going on to do further study at postgraduate level, then a good strategy is to try and tap into some current research that is going on in the discipline. There are three ways you might do this:

● *Look at the personal web pages of psychologists.* Many psychology lecturers have their own web pages with varying amounts of detail concerning their current research interests. Visit the homepage of any university department, and you should find an overview of research in the department and profiles of staff members' own research interests. Often these pages will also include downloadable versions of their publications, or email addresses for you to contact them on, in order to request copies of papers that they have written. If you do email an academic to request copies of their research, do remember to write your email respectfully, using standard English, as if you were contacting them by letter. Informal email requests from students can come across the wrong way.

● *Look at some current journals.* In the current journals section of the library there will be a number of psychology journals worth looking through. Identify a general area of interest, see what is being published in that area at the moment, and decide if there is anything that you think might be worth following up.

● *Read a copy of 'The Psychologist'. The Psychologist* is the magazine that the British Psychological Society produces for its members (*APA Monitor* is the equivalent journal for the American Psychological Association). If you are a student member of the Society you will receive this, but if you are not you should be able to find copies of this journal in your university library. The articles in it are written in an accessible way and often represent the research going on at the moment, and all articles provide some starter references for the topic at the end.

COMMON PITFALLS

Always be careful when beginning your literature review by engaging with recent empirical journal articles first. The reason for this is that, as a general rule, it is better to get familiar with a research area by reading a book chapter or review article on that topic before looking at specific studies. A common difficulty is that, without the background knowledge of an area of research, some very recent empirical papers can come across as too difficult to understand. By locating some background literature and reading that before engaging with the journal articles you have found, you should avoid feeling overwhelmed by the level of detail or discussion presented in the paper, and it will help you to build your theoretical framework in your introduction to your dissertation later on (see Chapter 3).

1.2.4 What research is going on in your psychology department?

Most potential project supervisors will have a number of specialist areas that they would be keen to supervise projects in. This is because these may be areas that they have a history of conducting research in themselves, or at least have a good knowledge of the literature in those areas. They may even have research projects that you can get involved in, with a view to you taking a small element of the research, designing your own question around it, and writing up that particular part. This may be a useful option if you or they have already arranged access to a specific participant group. However, you should not necessarily expect a potential supervisor to design your project for you or be willing to include you as a researcher in a piece of research that is ongoing.

- *Begin by looking at the staff web pages for the lecturers in your department* (it is worth checking which lecturers are eligible for project supervision at this stage, as not all staff listed on the website will necessarily be involved in this). Each person's web page will include references to their research activities and interests and a few publications that they have produced. Identify from this exercise which members of staff are conducting research that interests you.

- *Attend the research seminar series in your department.* Most psychology departments have a research seminar series in which members of staff report on the results of their most recent work in an area. Attendance at such events not only impresses potential supervisors, but it also gives you the chance to ask them questions about their work.

- *Go to the library and access copies of their papers.* Be proactive and find some of their work and read around it. In some cases you may be surprised to learn that you have some very well known and respected researchers in your department, whose work is widely cited by others in the area. Plus, most academics will be very pleased (and flattered) that you have found their work interesting enough to locate and read it.

- *Arrange a meeting to discuss ideas.* Having done your homework, it is a good idea to arrange a time to talk to the member of staff whose work interests you the most, to explain what you find interesting about the area and find out more about that topic. At this point your lecturer may suggest some ideas for you to follow up that would be suitable for you to do.

COMMON PITFALLS

!

A common pitfall from this type of approach is where students engage in this kind of discussion not because they are interested in a research topic, but because they like a particular member of staff who seems friendly or approachable. You can end up researching a topic that holds no interest for you just because you lack the confidence to explore the viability of a relationship with another member of staff who is sterner or more demanding of you. Always be guided by your level of interest and understanding, and not by how well you think you will get on. Members of staff that you may have previously disliked or found intimidating are often entirely different in the context of one-to-one research supervision.

1.3 DOING PROJECTS AS A TEAM

Although not all psychology departments will permit students to do this, it is becoming increasingly common for some student researchers to pair up or even form small teams that together will enable them to conduct a larger-scale piece of research with more variables. This may be suggested to you by a project supervisor because they have an idea for a study that would be too large for a single student to manage. The intention of the supervisor may well be to combine the data that all the students obtain, to produce a study that is large enough in scope to warrant publication. However, the expectation would be that individual students will decide at the outset what part of the study they plan to write up for their project, and each student will need to have a research question that is unique to them.

There are a number of advantages to such teamwork. Clearly the burden of data collection is shared, but also the preparation of materials and ethics paperwork relating to the project can also be produced as a result of team discussion and negotiation. Team skills are highly valued by employers who may also be impressed to see that you have worked on such a project (see Chapter 12). Plus there is also the possibility of co-publishing the work if all goes well (see Chapter 11).

However, there are also a number of difficulties associated with team-based project work. First of all, team working does not suit all students, and is best avoided by students with a competitive nature who may be reluctant to share literature and materials. Students who work on this kind of project must have extremely good communication skills and time management practices in order to coordinate effectively with what the other students on the project are doing. You should not expect the supervisor to project manage the research – it is your project, and you need to take collective responsibility for ensuring that all goes well. There is also the risk of one of the students in the team becoming dependent on the rest of the team to look after them and make sure that they have some data for their dissertation. For this reason, it is best that research questions are agreed at the outset and the study is designed so that, if one student fails to commit to the project, it is possible to remove their contribution from it in a way that will not impact on the quality of the other students' work. You and your supervisor may even consider drawing up a formal agreement that everyone in the team signs up to, so that there is an explicit understanding about who is responsible for what, and who will be writing about which aspects of the project.

The trick to effective team-based research is to find a student or a group of students to work with that you like and who are mature enough to understand when it is appropriate to work collectively, and at what point you should all be working alone (i.e. at the writing up stage). Steps should be taken at the outset to ensure that, while materials and even some reading matter may be shared between students, drafts of each other's work should not be circulated around the group in case plagiarism occurs. Similarly, the contribution of other students to the project should be formally acknowledged in your report.

1.4 PROJECTS TO AVOID

Most project ideas can be developed into a feasible research project, but there are some kinds of project that are best avoided.

- Projects that are **simply replicating well-established effects** (e.g. Stroop). There is always a way to come up with a slightly different take on a well-established task or phenomenon. Straightforward replications of existing studies signal a lack of effort to your marker. Chapter 4 will give you some ideas for how to add value to the design of your study and avoid such criticisms.

- Projects that are **unethical** (i.e. will cause harm to either your participants, yourself or your university's reputation). Chapter 7 gives advice on this.

- Projects **where you are not entirely sure what you are doing, or why you are doing it.** This can happen if you have an enthusiastic supervisor who persuades you to do a project in their research area, without realising that it may be outside of your comfort zone! Always make sure your supervisor fully explains their ideas to you and make sure you have done the background reading that they suggest. Do not rush this part of the process. Chapter 2 will support you with this.

- Projects that you have **not sufficiently researched before you begin collecting data.** It is tempting to begin data collection as soon as possible and often students rush into projects without having taken the time to think carefully about the advantages and disadvantages of different kinds of methodological approach, or without doing a sufficiently wide review of the literature. This can result in a flawed or poorly justified design, or answering a research question that has already been addressed elsewhere in the literature. Chapter 3 will help you work through the justification of your research question from a review of the literature.

- Projects that are **overambitious.** These are typically the kinds of projects that students design because they believe that the work is desperately needed, and are therefore reluctant to focus on a single research question, or stick to a manageable set of variables (see Chapter 4 for detailed advice on this). Similarly, some students are determined to work with a 'real world' sample of participants, and this too can cause difficulties.

A student's experience . . .

" *My original dissertation proposal was an interesting and novel idea but, in hindsight, it may have been too ambitious for an undergraduate project. Originally I hoped to recruit a sample of 30 blind children between the ages of 8 and 10 years. I anticipated that recruitment would be difficult, so I began the process early and by the end of my second year I had written letters to all the schools and organisations that I could find in my area. As time went on I decided to extend my search, so I began contacting schools and organisations throughout the UK. Unfortunately, after months of trying and even after lifting the age range, I was only able to secure two participants. Although I knew the project was ambitious, I didn't realise the difficulty of securing a specialised population as an undergraduate. I lost months of research time and in the end had to change my whole project proposal. I would advise dissertation students to consider the difficulties of securing a specialised population. In hindsight, my project was too ambitious and was more suited to postgraduate studies. If I was in the same position again I would definitely choose a less specialised population and save myself from months of added stress!* "

1.5 A WORD ON CAREER ASPIRATIONS

One last consideration that you may wish to bear in mind is how well your project topic or activities reflect your career plans. That is, prospective employers are very interested in what you chose to do for your final year project, not just in terms of knowledge of a topic area but also with respect to skills demonstrated and responsibilities undertaken (see Chapter 12).

> ✳ **TOP TIP**   Obtaining person specifications
>
> Depending on what you want to do next, you may wish to build into your project activities that can demonstrate to a prospective employer that you can liaise with external agencies, or write for different audiences, or undertake numerical or qualitative analysis, or develop simple tests. It is therefore worth taking the opportunity at this point to view some job descriptions or person specifications for the types of jobs that you are interested in getting into. This is best achieved by looking for such posts when they are advertised and then requesting 'further details', as if you were a potential applicant (which, in a sense, you are!). You will see that there are specific skills that employers will list as essential for applicants to demonstrate. It is worth seeing a list of these skills before you finish your degree so that, if your final year is not going to give you those skills, you can engage in voluntary or part-time work that will.

Many of you will be interested in careers in psychology, and these will inevitably require you to undertake postgraduate study. These courses are highly competitive and it can be useful to show that you are serious about your career by undertaking a project in a related area. However, it is not always necessary – the main thing that they will be interested in is how well you did in your degree and what marks you achieved across your course. It may be more appropriate for you to focus on a sensible and manageable project and undertake voluntary work in your area of interest, rather than to push yourself into an ambitious or even unrealistic project area. You may even find that your department will set some limits on what topic areas they can supervise, so it is not uncommon to do your dissertation in a slightly different area from the one you wish to specialise in later. The best thing is to take some advice from a member of staff who is familiar with the area that you wish to specialise in, and to discuss possible topic areas with them with a view to your longer term aspirations.

1.6 WHAT NEXT?

So, by the end of this stage of the process you will have identified a general topic idea, but you will not have much more than this. This is a good time to organise a meeting with your supervisor, and the next chapter takes you through some advice on how to manage this crucial relationship and what you can expect to get out of it. Chapter 3 will then take you through the best way of narrowing your general topic into a reasonable research question, through a systematic review of what literature has gone before. Some practical advice at this stage is not to rush to start your research project. This handbook is designed to take you through the process in a logical sequence. You will see that data collection does not begin until Chapter 8, and that other things need to be considered before you get to that point.

A student's experience . . .

> " I was really concerned about making an early start on my data collection. I knew I had some time over the summer before my final year, and I had the opportunity to go into somewhere I had worked in the past to get a lot of data relatively easily. I also thought that it would make the project better if I avoided using undergraduate students like everyone else would be doing. So I quickly designed a questionnaire study, got ethical clearance for it at the end of my second year, and collected all my data before I returned to university in October. Then I started to attend lectures in my final year that gave me ideas for ways to improve the study I had just conducted. The more I saw what other students were doing for their projects, the more I wished I had waited just a little longer and had thought carefully about the limitations of using a self-report design and had come up with ways to counter those problems in how I had developed my questionnaires. I got an OK mark, but I realise that I could have made it a lot better if I had just waited until the beginning of my final year before starting my study. "

CHAPTER SUMMARY

- A good project idea is one that is rooted in the psychological literature, is novel and is achievable by you in the time you have, using the resources and populations that you have access to. It is also a topic that you understand well.

- We have suggested four ways of thinking about how to identify a topic area: you can consider something that you are already interested in through personal experience; something you have found interesting from your psychology lectures; something that is a topic of contemporary interest; or something that is related to an area of research currently undertaken by an academic in your psychology department.

- You can think about doing a piece of research with another student or students, but this needs to be carefully thought through and each student should have their own research question that is not dependent upon the activities of the other student in any significant way, in case something does go wrong. There is an increased risk of plagiarism on such projects, and it is your responsibility to ensure that this does not occur in your work and that your work is not copied by another student.

- You should avoid projects that are simply replicating well established effects, are unethical, that you do not understand, that you have not properly researched before you begin data collection, and that are overambitious.

FURTHER READING

For some really good advice on how to approach a search of the literature, read:
Hart, C. (2001). *Doing a Literature Search: A Comprehensive Guide for the Social Sciences.* London: Sage.

For a discussion of some really interesting research ideas, and the various reasons why the research has not yet been done on them, read:
'The most important psychology experiment *never* done.' *The Psychologist*, 20, 658–659 (2007).

CHAPTER 2
MANAGING YOUR SUPERVISOR

Once you have come up with a broad idea, or perhaps even identified a possible research question, you may be keen to get started on your project. It is a good idea to start preparation as soon as possible but, before you get too carried away, remember that you are not in this alone! Because conducting an independent research project is such a major challenge and it is often very heavily weighted in your degree result calculations, most departments will provide you with a high level of one-to-one support. Some of this may come in the form of project preparation classes, group lectures and online support, but a large part of it will come from the close working relationship you will have with one member of academic staff. This relationship is often the key to the success or failure of your project, so it is well worth thinking about it even before you settle on your topic or methodology.

BY THE END OF THIS CHAPTER YOU WILL:

- Understand why it is important to manage your relationship with your supervisor.
- Know how to prepare for (and follow up on) a meeting with a prospective supervisor.
- Have an idea of what level of supervisor support you can expect.
- Understand what your supervisor is likely to expect from you and why.
- Be able to set an agenda for a typical supervision meeting and record agreed tasks that arise from it.
- Be able to seek and respond positively to constructive criticisms of your work.
- Have some ideas for solutions to problems that may arise in your supervisory relationship.

2.1 WHY 'MANAGE' THE RELATIONSHIP WITH YOUR SUPERVISOR?

One very immediate reason for managing your relationship is simply personal comfort. Most of us prefer to spend time with people we get on well with, rather than being forced to work with those who really irritate or upset us. As a student of psychology, you will be aware that, while we often take relationships for granted, they actually involve quite a bit of effort on both sides to keep them running smoothly. Sometimes we only become aware of this when either partner in the relationship falls short of the other person's expectations in some way. We have all had the experience of feeling let down by someone we thought we could rely on, and perhaps we have also felt surprised or guilty when a friend or colleague has made it clear that they are disappointed in our behaviour. So putting in a bit of effort to get on well with your supervisor may help to make the whole process of working together much more pleasant.

One thing that can sometimes get in the way of a comfortable working relationship is the power imbalance that you may feel between you and your supervisor. When you began your university studies, depending on the kind of school you attended, you may have found lecturer–student relationships refreshingly informal, in comparison to those between teachers and pupils at school. However, you may still be aware of a difference in status between you and your supervisor. It is perfectly rational for you to feel that you have less power in the supervisory relationship, since your supervisor is an experienced, established academic and is likely to have a major say in the mark you are awarded. However, that does not mean you should never question your supervisor's judgement, or that you must simply follow their 'orders'. This is *your* research project, on which *you* will be assessed for many of the decisions taken. Early on in your supervisory relationship, you need to take responsibility for the direction of each meeting and for your work in general. So how do you do this when you are not 'the boss'?

You might find it helpful to consider the multiple roles we all occupy, and the different domains in which we hold expertise. Your supervisor may be an expert in a particular research methodology, but not in the precise subject of your project. You might, for example, choose to research psychological aspects of a pastime in which you have personal experience, be that martial arts, equestrian eventing or skydiving. Unless your supervisor is an experienced devotee of that particular activity, you may find that you are the expert on that aspect of your work. On a more serious level, your own personal background may be a source of expertise, where your research involves people from a gender, or cultural or ethnic background to which you belong and your supervisor does not.

Another way to make sure that you hold your own in discussions with your supervisor, is to develop your skills in assertive communication. A little later in this chapter we will discuss some basic techniques for planning and organising supervisory meetings, but you also may want to have a look at some readings on assertive communication techniques. At the end of the chapter, in the further reading, we suggest sources where you may find out more about redressing the power imbalance in conversation.

Even if you are already happy with your skills in assertive communication, and you are not bothered about the level of personal warmth between you and your supervisor, it is still worth thinking about the nature of the relationship. If you manage it successfully, your supervisor will be able to:

- help you to refine and develop your idea;
- point you towards relevant literature that you were not aware of;
- help you to gain access to participants;

- give you constructive feedback on your design and materials;
- help you to get going with your data analysis;
- give you constructive feedback on your work before you hand it in for assessment.

This level of individualised support is pretty much unique in undergraduate student experience these days, and is something that many students and supervisors really value and enjoy. The key to making sure that you benefit from what is on offer is to cultivate a good working relationship from the early stages right up to submission of the final report, and even afterwards.

COMMON CONFUSION

My responsibility or my supervisor's responsibility?

Although we are discussing the importance of managing your working relationship with your supervisor, it is worth getting clear a fundamental point: this is your project, not your supervisor's. You should be taking the lead throughout the process. To hammer home this point, many departments use the word 'independent' in the project module title, and/or refer to supervisors as 'advisors'. This reflects the distinctive aspect of the final year project: that it is an opportunity for you to show that you can work independently, and how much you can achieve on your own. A good piece of advice is not to expect your supervisor to do anything for you or instead of you (e.g. locating literature or negotiating access to participants). Try to do these tasks for yourself, but be mature and organised enough to seek out and take the advice of your supervisor, especially where you are unsure or if you encounter difficulties.

This brings us to another key distinction: working independently versus working alone.

COMMON CONFUSION

Working independently versus working alone

If you were expected to work entirely alone on your project there would not really be any need for supervision, and your project would be a high-risk endeavour. Very few researchers work entirely alone, and many professional researchers work as part of a collaborative team. Even the most single-minded people often draw on the support of others to give them constructive feedback and an additional perspective on their work. Your project is an opportunity to develop this skill. You are expected to initiate the project and take the lead in progressing it. You are also expected to keep in regular contact with your supervisor, in order to ask for advice and follow up on their support.

In many departments, your supervisor is the person who first marks the project report. In the interests of fairness and objectivity, final year projects are typically double marked, and agreement has to be reached between the supervisor and another member of staff not directly involved with the project. However, the mark awarded can be influenced by the extent to which you worked independently, were proactive in driving the project forward, and responded positively to feedback from your supervisor (check the assessment criteria used in your department). As the person who worked most closely with you, your supervisor is seen as the best person to assess this aspect of your project. It follows that by demonstrating these qualities in the supervisory relationship you will give yourself the chance to maximise your mark.

Once the project has been completed and the final report submitted for assessment, you might expect the supervisory relationship to finish. However, many students and supervisors stay in contact for months and even years after graduation, so the supervisory relationship may have an influence far beyond the few months you spend working together directly on your research project. In some cases students and supervisors will go on to become co-authors of conference presentations or journal articles based on student project research (see Chapter 11). The seeds sown in your undergraduate project could even grow into a postgraduate research degree or a funded project that might provide you with employment. If you are interested in working in academia, a good relationship with your supervisor could pave the way for future research posts, or recommendations to other academic staff and universities.

Even if you are not interested in pursuing academic research after graduation, there are other good reasons for managing the relationship with your supervisor. The time you spend working with this one member of staff is a chance to make yourself known as a unique individual, to stand out from what may be dozens or even hundreds of other undergraduates studying in the same department. Your supervisor is often the member of staff who knows you best, and is well placed to write academic references for you pre- and post-graduation. Future employers will be interested in your working relationship since this may be a key to how good an employee you will be in the future. It is therefore important that you make the most of your chance to shine as a responsible and cooperative co-worker.

COMMON CONFUSION ?

'I have to be superhuman or my supervisor will think I am a loser'

All this talk of being proactive and 'shining' may sound a bit daunting. It is important to remember that your supervisor does not expect you to be perfect, totally together or capable of working entirely alone. If you were, then there would not be much left for a supervisor to do! Essentially all a supervisor is looking for is evidence that you have prepared for meetings, that you listen and ask questions effectively, and that you follow up on any advice or tasks agreed at the meeting. What is likely to impress tutors, colleagues and employers is your willingness to take on board and learn from constructive criticism.

2.2 WHAT TO EXPECT FROM YOUR SUPERVISORY RELATIONSHIP

Although you may have studied research methods and conducted small scale group or individual projects of some kind before, the dissertation project is usually the first time in your studies when you will work closely with one individual member of staff for an extended period of time. You may already have some ideas about what to expect, but two valuable sources of information on this are the experiences and perspectives of past students and experienced supervisors. We have collated some of the key points from these to give you some sense of what happens in most departments. However, bear in mind that these can and do vary from university to university, so do find out what *you* can expect from *your* supervisor in *your* department.

To address the question of what you can expect, it does help to consider your supervisor's point of view. Supervisors, like all human beings, vary considerably in their motivations, but some of the objectives that your supervisor will have could include the following:

- To help you achieve the best possible mark for your project.
- To offer you an opportunity for a rewarding project experience.
- To stretch you to achieve your full potential as a researcher.
- To get some data collected for a project that fits their own research profile.
- To keep you/them/the department/university from getting into trouble – ethically or legally.
- To produce a conference poster, paper or journal article with you from your research.

The priority given to each of these possible objectives may vary from person to person so, if you have the opportunity to choose a prospective supervisor, you might like to ask them what they see as the most important objectives for supervision. Be aware, though, that the question may well be bounced back and you may be asked what you are hoping to get out of the process!

MAXIMISING MARKS

Identifying your objectives

Before setting out on any significant work activity, it is worth getting clear what your objectives are, as well as the resources you will need to meet these. Early on in the process, you may find it helpful to think of answers to the following questions:

- What do you want to get out of this project?
- Which parts of the project do you think will be the easiest for you?
- Why?
- Which parts of the project do you think will be the most difficult?
- Why?

Answering these questions may help you to identify potential problems early, so that you can talk to your supervisor about how to solve them.

2.3 ALLOCATIONS TO SUPERVISORS

Some university departments allow students to select the supervisor of their choice, whether on a first come first served basis, or through a more complicated allocation system. Other departments allocate students purely on the basis of the proposed topic and methodology they have stated on a *project proposal*.

MAXIMISING MARKS
Completing a project proposal

Even if you are not required to complete a project proposal in order to be allocated to a supervisor, you may find it useful to write one, to clarify your ideas and to get the most from a first meeting with your supervisor. As a rough guide, the following sections should be completed:

- project title;
- aims and/or research question and/or hypothesis;
- summary of background research you have conducted: what we already know about this topic;
- proposed methodology, with rationale;
- proposed recruitment/sample;
- proposed analysis;
- proposed timeline.

There is no need for lots of detail in each section. A short paragraph would typically suffice for each. Remember to give full references for any published work you cite.

Often the final decision on supervision is made using a combination of student and staff preferences, based on both personal and academic grounds. To facilitate this process of matching staff and students, it sometimes helps if you arrange to meet a potential supervisor to discuss your ideas before any allocations are made. You may also find it extremely valuable to talk to students who are already working with the member of staff you are considering. You may get to meet such students if you are recruited to take part in their data collection. Some departments have specific arrangements, such as weekly research seminars, to which dissertation students are invited to present their work to other undergraduates. Make sure that you attend these seminars if they are open to you and, if no such arrangements exist in your department, why not ask for one to be made available, or better still, volunteer to arrange it yourself?

There are various criteria on which you might choose your supervisor:

- Because you like or admire them.
- Because they have expertise in your topic and/or the methodology you would like to use.
- Because you feel they will be reliable in attending meetings, being contactable, responding to emails, etc.
- Because you feel you can understand them well when they explain things to you.
- Because you feel they are likely to give you clear and useful feedback on your work.
- Because they have an established reputation/status as a researcher.
- Because you think they are pretty laid back and will not push you too much to work.
- Because you think they are a hard task master and will make sure you get your work done in time.
- Because you have the impression they are a generous marker, or a bit of a 'soft touch'.

You may well have some more criteria of your own that are influencing your decision. Which of these criteria do you think are the wisest to base your choice on? And which ones are the least wise?

Having a supervisor that you like or admire may make the process of meeting and communicating more pleasant, at least at first, but it is not a guarantee of success. You may find that it is hard to accept criticism from someone you feel you have become close to, or that the distinction between friendship and supervision gets a bit blurred at times.

Having a supervisor who is an established or high status researcher may offer some advantages. Your supervisor knows how to do research well, and how to get published. They may have contacts that will be useful to you in the course of your study or in your career after graduation. On the other hand, they may be so expert at research that they find it difficult to explain things to a novice researcher. Alternatively, they may be so busy with their own data collection, analysis, writing up or conferences that they are not as readily contactable or available as a less research-active member of staff would be.

If you choose a supervisor for their apparent laid back attitude, this may help you to feel less pressured in the early stages of your study, but it will not guarantee a stress-free time for the whole of the process. Unless you are very self-motivated and have excellent time management, you may find that you fall behind with your work and suffer great pressure to catch up and submit the project report on time.

On the other hand, if your choice of supervisor is based on the perception that they are tough and demanding, it may be that you have a slightly distorted view of what the dissertation is about. Most universities require honours students to conduct a project to demonstrate that they are able to work independently to meet targets and deadlines. If you rely too heavily on your supervisor to manage your time and your outputs, you are denying yourself the opportunity to show that you have these skills.

If you choose on the basis that your prospective supervisor might be a generous marker, this may be a misconception. University departments monitor and maintain marking standards across different members of staff, so any rumours about generous and 'hard' markers are usually urban myths. As mentioned earlier, dissertation reports are typically double marked, and the second marker will have had no previous connection with your study. The two markers discuss your work before arriving at the final mark, so that any 'halo effect' you may have induced in your supervisor is likely to be counterbalanced by the dispassionate judgement of the other member of staff.

Choosing a supervisor with expertise in your topic or chosen methodology is usually a pretty good idea, when this is possible. Indeed many departments who allocate students to supervisors often make the allocations on just this basis. That is why it is important to be as clear as possible on any proposals or outlines that you may be asked to submit as part of the project planning process. A supervisor whose topic interests and methodological skills match your planned project will be in a good position to provide you with guidance on every aspect, from literature review and design to data collection and analysis. However, that does not mean that you cannot do a good project if you are supervised by someone who is not a subject expert. Many academics have a broad range of interests, and are happy to support students who want to research something unusual. If students only ever conducted projects that fitted the interests of staff in their department, many great ideas for research would simply not get done. Some lecturers relish the challenge of broadening their topic knowledge or methodological skills by supervising well-motivated students in a relationship where both parties learn alongside each other.

In deciding how important these criteria are to you in your choice of supervisor, consider where else you might find information and support on your topic or methodology. If your literature searching skills are already good, you may well be able to research the topic very effectively and impress your supervisor with what you have found. Your supervisor may struggle to advise you on a method they have never used before, and may recommend that you seek support from another member of staff for this aspect of your work. The extent to which this outsourcing of supervision is acceptable varies from one department to another, so this is something else that you need to ask about. Some academics are unwilling to help students who are not on their supervisory list, and this is usually because of their other teaching or research commitments. Particular lecturers are often inundated with enquiries from project students, especially if they have particular expertise, e.g. in qualitative methods or in sophisticated statistical techniques. Be realistic in your expectations and reasonable in your requests. Have an alternative plan in case help from other staff is unavailable. It is also worth remembering that your supervisor is likely to be the first marker for your report. If you do get advice from another member of staff, make sure that you discuss that advice with your supervisor and agree on the best course of action. Your supervisor could mark you down for failing to follow their advice, if they have not been consulted about it.

A student's experience . . .

    I had a good relationship with my supervisor, who was very helpful. I had designed a project that matched her own research interests, and she helped me to identify what my dependent and independent variables were, and what kind of design I had (I always found that hardest). However, I was getting worried that she thought that I didn't know what I was doing really, because I always had to check with her on really basic things that other students just seemed to know. We had discussed what kind of analysis to do, and I did it on my own. I was really upset when none of my results were significant and I was concerned that I had done it wrong, so I went to see the member of staff who had taught me SPSS the previous year. I had to wait in a queue to see him, there were that many students asking him for help. By the time I saw him he was tired but very kind when I explained what had happened. He then started playing with different analyses, and he used some software that I was not familiar with to do something that he tried to explain but I am still not sure what it was that he was looking for! He told me that I did not have enough participants in my study for a significant result, but then ran some extra statistics that were significant and printed out the output and gave it to me. I wasn't sure what he had done or how I should report it, but the queue was still outside his door so I left and had a go at writing it up. When my supervisor saw a draft of my results she could not understand why I had not done the analysis we had discussed. I explained, and she told me that what I had been given wasn't really analysis that tested my hypothesis (I had not told the other tutor what I was trying to test) and they did not really make any sense because I could not even report what test had been used. I was so glad she spotted it before I handed in my work, but I wish that I had spoken to my supervisor in the first place. All I had wanted was someone to check that I had done it correctly, but then I thought that he knew more about stats than my supervisor did. The problem was that he did not know my project because I had not explained it to him clearly enough, or told him what I really needed him to do for me.

Specialist expertise is just one valuable characteristic of a good supervisor, but it may not be as important as more subtle qualities. Your supervisor is not going to conduct your project for you – they are simply a resource, a source of advice to access as you drive the project forward. This is an interactive process that requires regular contact and clear communication from both parties involved. It therefore makes sense to consider how reliable your chosen supervisor will be in responding to your requests for support and advice at various stages of your study. While all university departments have minimum standards that specify what students can expect from staff, you may have your own experience with different members of staff. You may also know from experience in lectures and tutorials which members of staff you can always understand when they explain complex concepts, as well as those whose lectures you sometimes struggle to make sense of. This might be another criterion on which you base your decision about supervision.

Finally, you might like to consider how important feedback is on both your project plans and any written work that you produce. For many students, during the dissertation is the only time throughout their degree where they get a chance to have constructive feedback on their assignment before they hand it in. Most departments allow supervisors to read and give feedback on drafts of sections of the dissertation report, and some for the entire report. Find out what the norm is in your department and make sure that you use this facility to best effect. Modifying your work in response to feedback from your supervisor could make the difference between passing and failing, and can improve your eventual mark by one or more degree classes. Responding positively to constructively critical feedback is a skill in itself. We will return to this issue in more detail later on in the chapter but, for the moment, you may want to reflect on your experiences of feedback on work in the past. Which tutors gave feedback that you understood and which helped you see how your work could have been improved? Was there anyone who gave very little detail or was so cutting that you felt wounded or discouraged? Constructive criticism is one of the most important sources of support you will need from a supervisor, so this may also be a characteristic on which you base any choices you make.

2.3.1 What if I don't get any choice of supervisor?

Much of the preceding section is intended to help you weigh up different reasons for choosing a supervisor. However, as we mentioned earlier, some universities allocate students to staff with or without referring to students' preferences. This is often done for very good reasons. Sometimes students struggle to select the most appropriate supervisor because they are not aware of staff interests and expertise. Sometimes they will have only a vague idea for their topic or research question, which makes it hard to identify who best to approach. Often one or two popular members of staff are swamped with requests from students whose needs do not match the expertise that lecturer can offer, or the numbers involved would mean they would never have time to give the students the attention that they deserve. Some staff only work part-time or have particular academic duties and may only take on one or two students in any given academic year.

Being allocated a supervisor rather than choosing one for yourself should not discourage you in your supervisory relationship. On a personal level, lecturers are often different when you get to know them one-to-one as opposed to the more pressured and impersonal environment of lectures and seminars. So someone who you felt did not pay you much attention in a class of 120 may well be more enthusiastic when they have a chance to talk to you in the relaxed environment of an office. From an academic perspective, initial project ideas often evolve in the course of discussion with your supervisor, so rather than being thwarted by being allocated to a supervisor you would not have chosen for yourself, you might end up with a better topic or more interesting research question than you originally envisaged.

Finally, being allocated someone you would never have chosen might turn out to be a valuable learning experience that will work to your advantage long after your report is submitted and you have left university behind. Many careers require us to work alongside people for whom we feel no affinity, or with whom we have a mismatch of skills and experience. Being able to manage this effectively is important for both our personal well-being and our career success. Employers often value people who can work constructively to resolve any problems in their relationships with colleagues. Viewed from this perspective, being allocated a supervisor is an opportunity for personal and professional development, which might provide useful material for job applications and interviews that follow on from your studies.

2.4 FIRST MEETING WITH YOUR SUPERVISOR

Some departments recommend that students meet with prospective supervisors towards the end of the academic year before they begin their dissertations, or during the summer vacation. Even if this is not a requirement in your department, you may well like to arrange a meeting. If you plan to leave this until the summer vacation, check that the person you want to meet with is likely to be available at that time. They may be away doing research, attending conferences or on holiday over the summer period.

Whether you want to assess someone you are thinking of choosing as your supervisor, or have a preliminary meeting with someone that you have been allocated to, very similar principles will apply. This is a chance for you and the member of staff to find out about each other and identify how best to take your project idea forward. Knowing what to expect and being well prepared for this meeting give you the best opportunity for success in your project. It may well set the tone for the rest of your meetings throughout your dissertation.

We have already highlighted some issues that you may want to weigh up early on in your relationship with your supervisor, but it may also be helpful to consider what they may be hoping to get out of this first meeting. Things that your supervisor may want to find out include:

- What has motivated your choice of this topic with this methodology?
- What are your strengths and weaknesses?
- Are you capitalising on your strengths and/or compensating for/avoiding your weaknesses?
- Do your research question and your methodology match up?
- Are you genuinely enthusiastic about your project or just going through the motions?
- Might you be at risk of being too personally or emotionally involved – with effects on your objectivity/well-being?

It should be apparent from this list of questions that not only do you want to find out about your supervisor, but there is a lot they want to know about you. It follows then that this first meeting should be an exchange in which you are both asking and answering questions, in order to clarify your plans and choose best how to get you started on your project. This means that you need to be well prepared for the meeting, and ready to act on any next steps that are agreed in the course of the discussion. You may like to note your answers to the questions listed above, and bring them to the meeting. Do not worry if, at this stage, you have not absolutely decided on your topic or research question, or if you still have some uncertainty about the design of your study. Your supervisor will help you to firm up these issues in your first few meetings.

It may help to bring along with you any other materials you have produced or collected with regard to your project. This might include, for example, any relevant articles or book chapters that you have read, and any outlines, mind maps or other plans that you have sketched out. These materials may give you an idea of what to discuss in your meeting, but it might also help if you draw up an informal agenda. This is a list of the issues or questions you would like to discuss, in the order you wish to discuss them. Taking an agenda to the meeting can help you to ensure that you do not come away with only some of your queries answered and unable to proceed until you have seen your supervisor again. You might email your draft agenda to your supervisor in advance of the meeting, and ask if there is anything they would like to add. Suggested items for your agenda might include:

- review of project proposal;
- negotiation of supervisory style;
- type of contact;

- frequency of contact;
- agreed tasks for next meeting;
- date and time of next meeting.

Of course, some of you will be very familiar with agendas, from your own student and/or professional life but, if you do not have much experience of using this tool in meetings, this is a great opportunity to practice and refine this skill from the beginning of your working relationship.

2.4.1 Negotiating supervisory contact and style

You may also want to come to your first meeting with some ideas about the style of supervision you want, and how you will achieve this.

Do you want to be stretched and challenged intellectually, or do you just want a reasonable level of support to make sure you do not go horribly wrong?

Your supervisor will be better able to support you if you make it clear what your preference is. Remember, though, that supervision is a two-way process, so be prepared to hear your supervisor's point of view on how ambitious you should be. Whatever you decide should be mutually acceptable.

How often do you think you are likely to want meetings, as opposed to other forms of supervisory contact, such as email?

Your department will have its own norms for the type of supervisory contact, and individual supervisors have their own preferences. Sometimes there are no clear indications in the documentation provided to you by your department. To avoid misunderstanding and disappointment, you may like to agree several things at the outset:

- number of hours of contact overall;
- frequency of contact;
- methods of contact.

There is quite a bit of variation across universities regarding the level of contact between dissertation students and their supervisors. This is an area where it is important to check the norms and regulations in your department. For example, part-time students and those conducting the project over a period of a year or more may see their supervisors somewhat less frequently than full-time students who may be doing their research over a brief period of six months or less. You should find out what the expected number of contact hours is for your department. Does it include time spent in face-to-face meetings, telephone consultations, online or video conferencing and email contact? In some universities an overall number of hours specified may include time spent with your supervisor doing preparatory work over the summer vacation, if available, and time your supervisor spends reading drafts. It is highly unlikely that you will use up all of your allocated time very early in the process. Indeed, time spent on planning and preparation at this early stage may pay dividends later on. If you are in any doubt about how far you have 'used up' your supervisory entitlement, just ask your supervisor who will be able to reassure you.

Even within the same department, people vary in the frequency with which they expect to see students for supervision. Some supervisors may like to see you once a week, perhaps more often they will suggest once a fortnight or even once a month. This is something that needs to be negotiated between you, and which may need renegotiation as you begin to make progress with your work. If you have to complete the project in six months or less, then seeing your supervisor once a month may be a little too infrequent, unless you supplement it with email and other forms of contact in the meanwhile. If you insist on seeing your supervisor weekly or more often, they may infer that you are unable to work independently or meet agreed targets. Remember though: you should initiate contact. It is not your supervisor's job to chase you for progress reports.

Since most meetings are the basis for deciding on actions, it is generally useful to take some kind of notes. You might like to use your agenda to record the advice that your supervisor gave you, or the actions that you have each agreed to take as a result. This might be, for example, you agreeing to conduct a particular literature search before coming to the next meeting, or your supervisor agreeing to send you the contact details for a colleague who has access to a particular piece of equipment. Whatever the action is, it is important that you both agree that it is realistic and achievable, since you are committing to complete it by the time of your next meeting. If you do not feel competent to undertake the agreed action, you need to renegotiate it rather than setting yourself up to fail. As we mentioned earlier, one of the things your supervisor will assess you on is your ability to get on with tasks you have agreed to do, and your responsibility in asking for help if you need it to proceed.

As well as the actions you have each agreed to undertake, you may also wish to agree the date and time of your next meeting. This should be realistic in terms of allowing you enough time to do the work that has been advised, but not so far away that you lose the momentum or begin to drift from what has been agreed.

COMMON PITFALLS

Postponing meetings when you have not made progress

Sometimes you may not have managed to complete all the actions you agreed at your last meeting. You may be tempted to postpone or rearrange the next meeting, to give yourself more time. Before doing this, have a brief discussion with your supervisor, by telephone or email. Will it be okay to go ahead with the meeting, even though you have not managed to do everything that was agreed? Attending the meeting may help you avoid unproductive 'drifting', and your supervisor might help you to resolve any difficulties you have had with the agreed tasks.

2.5 THE LITERATURE REVIEW AND DESIGN PHASE

Once you are settled into your supervisory relationship, one of your early objectives is likely to be confirming the design of your study. It is important at this stage to remain flexible about the final shape of your research. While it is a good idea to get as far as you can with your design independently (Chapters 3 and 4 can help you with this), you need to be willing to make changes to your plans as a result of feedback from your supervisor. Remember they have valuable experience to draw upon and have your best interests at heart.

Some of the common reasons why students need to change their project plans include:

- insufficient rationale for study;
- mismatch between chosen research question and methodology;
- practical barriers, e.g. access to special participant population, materials or equipment;
- project too ambitious for the timescale available;
- ethical problems with design of the study, e.g. unwarranted deception.

In the next chapter, we will discuss in more detail the academic reasons why it is important to have a rationale for your study. We will discuss, for example, how your study should add something to the existing body of scientific knowledge, if you are to have a chance of gaining a good mark. Your supervisor may advise you to change your project plan because your study is simply repeating research that has already been done. They may worry that you are, therefore, setting yourself up for a low mark from the outset. Your supervisor might also point out a key practical barrier: that any ethics committee reviewing your proposed study is unlikely to give approval. An ethics committee will be concerned with protecting participants, not just from physical or psychological harm, but also from having their time wasted on a study that simply did not need to be conducted. For that reason, they will want to be persuaded that your study will add something new to our body of knowledge, rather than purely giving you some data for your project. The best way to do this is to make sure you have thoroughly reviewed the research literature, to find out and then summarise what is already known on your topic. Again, this is something we will discuss in more detail in a later chapter, but we mention it here because your supervisor is well placed to help you to ensure your literature search is rigorous. The rest of this section gives you some tips for getting the most effective support from your supervisor on this.

MAXIMISING MARKS

Getting supervisor's feedback on your literature search

You may find it helps if you take to a meeting, or email to your supervisor, a summary of your literature search to date, including search strategy, keywords, databases and list of the references you have identified for inclusion in your literature review. Ask your supervisor if there is anything obvious that you have missed out. Remember, though, only do this if your supervisor agrees, and allow plenty of time for your supervisor to review what you have sent.

Assuming that you have reassured yourself that your research question merits investigation, another design issue that is important to consider is whether your chosen methodology is appropriate to assess that research question. Sometimes students base their choice of methodology on their familiarity with certain methods, or the fact that they have done well in assessments that used particular techniques. As we suggested earlier, this is perfectly reasonable but, before you get stuck into serious design or data collection, you can use your supervisor's judgement to assure you that your method will really work for the research question you have chosen. Let us take an example of how this might come up in practice.

Chloe wants to investigate whether there are gender differences in the motivations of people attending slimming clubs to lose weight. She got a really good mark for her second year qualitative methods report, which was based on interpretative phenomenological analysis (IPA). She enjoyed doing that coursework and is planning to use it for her dissertation project. Chloe's supervisor suggests that she might need to rethink, as qualitative methods such as IPA are not really appropriate for testing for differences between groups.

Chloe has a number of choices:

- She could ignore her supervisor and stick to the original plan. After all, she is more comfortable doing qualitative analysis, and she knows that there is not much research already done in that specific topic area. She may enjoy conducting her planned semi-structured interviews, get lots of interesting material on people's motivations, and find the analysis pretty straightforward from what she learned in her second year. **Can you foresee any problems that she might encounter at any stage of the project?**

● She could ask her supervisor for advice on how to reconcile the mismatch between methodology and research question. This might include the next two options.

● Chloe could keep her original research question and change to a different methodology and design. In order to test for gender differences she might use a validated measure of motivation, and have male and female slimming club users complete this. She would then be able to test statistically for differences between them. **Can you foresee any problems she might encounter at any stage of the project?**

● Chloe could change her research question to one that is more appropriate for qualitative methods. This does not have to be a complete change of topic and can often be a seemingly minor alteration. If Chloe is willing to make her study an *exploration* of the motivations and experiences of slimming club users, she can realistically achieve this using IPA. Once she has the data she may well be able to identify some interesting patterns suggestive of gender difference, which might then form the basis of further research. She might enjoy the process of collecting and analysing the data, and feel just as satisfied as if she had pursued her original design. **Can you foresee any advantages that Chloe might experience as a result of making this choice?**

The following are some suggestions on using your supervisor to test the appropriateness of your design. You might like to complete your answers to the following and take them along to a meeting with your supervisor:

● Why I have chosen this research question.

● Why I have chosen this methodology.

● Why I think this methodology is the most appropriate for investigating this research question.

Remember to put this issue on your meeting agenda, if you want to make sure it is addressed before moving on. In your meeting, tell your supervisor your answers to these questions, and ask their views on your design.

You will, we hope, reach agreement with your supervisor about the best design from a purely logical, academic point of view, but it is also worth getting some feedback on the practical viability of your study. You might, for example, want access to special populations of participants, such as hospital patients, children, or people detained in criminal justice facilities. However, while it may be possible and appropriate in some cases, this is not always the case. Perhaps you have read of interesting studies conducted with such populations, and based your design on having access to them. In reality, though, it can often be difficult to recruit beyond your own university department, and some universities have regulations that discourage or forbid you from doing your research with outside groups. It is a good idea to check with your supervisor what is allowed in your department and what they think is realistically feasible for you to do for your short individual study. For example, even getting sufficient numbers of male participants or people aged over 40 years can be a problem, if you are limited to recruiting from other psychology students.

Another practical consideration, which may affect your design, is the availability of specialist materials or equipment for the study. Once again, the published literature may be replete with fascinating studies conducted with psychometric tests, brain scanners or video vignettes, which may or may not be available to you for a student project. Some tests are expensive or only available for use by specially qualified professionals. Your supervisor will be able to advise you on how realistic it is for you to obtain tests and/or whether someone in your department can supervise you to use them. Unless your department is particularly fortunate, it may not have access to brain imaging equipment and, even if it did, this might not be available for undergraduate research. On the other hand, your supervisor or colleagues may be undertaking research that already uses this facility, and you may be able to 'piggy back' on work they are already conducting. Similarly, your supervisor may be able to suggest how you might obtain copies of video or other stimulus materials, or how you might liaise with technicians to produce your own.

Your supervisor may feel that your project proposal is for a fantastically interesting and worthwhile study, but one that is simply too ambitious to be completed in the short timescale available for an undergraduate dissertation. This is not necessarily all bad news. If you cannot complete everything that you want to achieve within your dissertation, why not consider taking it forward as part of a postgraduate research programme?

A final issue on which your supervisor's advice may be invaluable at an early stage, is the practical ethics associated with your design. You may have studied ethics as part of research methods classes at an earlier stage of your degree, but making ethics work for real in the case of your own research project can be trickier than it appears at first. We have devoted a whole chapter of this book to research ethics, and outlined some practical suggestions that will be of use wherever you are undertaking your research. However, the details of applying for and gaining ethical approval vary somewhat from university to university, and your supervisor is best placed to advise you on requirements in your particular department. In some departments they will read a draft of your ethics submission to check it for any obvious issues before you submit it for formal consideration. They may also help you to figure out how to deal with any problems or amendments that the ethics committee require before your study can proceed.

The following are some suggestions for using your supervisor to test the practicality of your design:

- What restrictions are there on whom I may recruit into my study?
- Who should I contact to request access to particular groups of participants?
- How likely is it that I will be able to recruit sufficient numbers of the participants I need?
- What measures, materials or equipment do I need?
- Can my department provide access to and support for these?
- From whom do I need ethical clearance for my study?
- Are there any ethical issues with my proposed design?
- Does my ethics submission make sense, and does it look like it stands a chance of being approved?

Remember to attempt your own answers to these questions, put them on your meeting agenda, discuss them with your supervisor, and ask them for their views.

2.6 DATA COLLECTION PHASE

Once your design has been settled and you are ready to begin data collection, your supervisor will continue to be an important source of help and advice. Before they launch forth to test their data collection skills on real participants, some students like to have a practice run with the help of their supervisor. This might involve role-playing a data collection situation in which your supervisor plays the part of a would-be participant, and is treated exactly as you would treat a participant in the real study. This can be an excellent way to ensure that you iron out any potential sources of confusion in your instructions. Similarly, it can be a good way to test that interview questions and general interviewing style are appropriate and do not make you feel that you are being ridiculous or rude. Many students conducting qualitative studies find that their original interview questions feel awkward when they try to speak them out loud and for real. It is much better to discover this with your supervisor in the privacy of their office, than with a precious participant that you have taken trouble to recruit. Perhaps you intend to collect all your data at one sitting with a large group of students. A bit of practice with your supervisor may seem embarrassing, but it is bound to be less toe curling than getting your instructions wrong in front of a lecture theatre or laboratory full of students.

In some unusual circumstances, your supervisor may actually be present when you collect your data, at least at early stages of your study. This is more likely to be the case if you are using special-ist (or expensive) equipment that requires direct supervision or support. You should check with your supervisor if they expect or are prepared to do this before committing to a study of this type.

Your supervisor might also play a role in arrangements to protect your personal safety. As you will see in later chapters, ethics committees often want reassurance that students will not be exposed to unreasonable risks in the course of their study. If you intend to collect data off campus or with 'high risk' individuals, you might consider having an arrangement with your supervisor whereby they can access the details of your participant in the event of concerns. It is important that whatever arrangement you make is one that is mutually agreeable. Not all supervisors will be able to provide this level of contact, so check what is genuinely available before relying on any arrangement.

Perhaps more often, your supervisor will agree to be contactable if you need any advice in the course of your data collection. This might be a problem with your interview schedule, your mea-sures, recruitment or some other aspect of your design. If you discuss these with your supervisor before proceeding further, they may offer you some useful advice on how to solve the problem. They may also be able to help you deal with unexpected outcomes that are more subtle than pure design issues. You may find that you or your participants are personally affected by taking part in the study, perhaps in ways that neither could have anticipated. This may be especially true with qualitative and open-ended research, but it can occur in any type of design.

You might also, subject to confidentiality considerations, and their agreement, give your super-visor copies of your raw data. One reason to do this might be to check that you are collecting data in the appropriate format, or that your interview style is getting the most from participants.

You might like to give your supervisor data in batches as you collect it, because they are inter-ested in seeing it at an early stage, or purely as a backup in case your own copies become corrupted or destroyed. Bear in mind, though, that ethical and legal guidelines require you to handle data sensitively (more on this in Chapter 7), and your supervisor may not necessarily welcome large quantities of data arriving on a daily basis. Be sure to agree in advance what, if anything, you are going to send.

These are all ways in which your supervisor may be a source of support in the course of data collection, but they do require good communication and negotiation on your part. Your supervisor may have other students to supervise, not to mention numerous other duties and responsibilities, so it is not fair to assume that you will be their number one priority, whatever stage of project work you are at. If you are going to use their advice and support, you need to check the best means of contacting them, and how soon you can realistically expect a reply. It is best not to leave these arrangements until you have set off 'into the field', so following are some suggestions to discuss with your supervisor:

- Can I role-play my instructions or interview with you?
- Does anyone need to be present when I use the equipment?
- Will my supervisor be present or should it be someone else?
- Should I set up a system for checking-in during data collection?

- Will my supervisor be this contact?
- If contacted what will they do?
- What is the best way to contact my supervisor in the case of needing advice?
- How soon can I realistically expect to get a reply?
- Who else can I contact for help or advice if I cannot contact my supervisor?
- Would my supervisor like to receive raw data as I collect it, or would they prefer to wait until I have begun the analysis?

You may want to make this an agenda item for one of your supervisory meetings.

Keeping your supervisor informed of your progress means that they will be well-placed to offer you advice if you ask for it. Getting feedback early on in the data collection process may help you to avoid wasting your time and that of your participants.

COMMON CONFUSION ?

If you admit to your supervisor that your first data collection had some problems they will think you are incompetent

If your first episode of data collection does not go quite as you had hoped, it is best to get your supervisor's advice as soon as possible. Remember: your supervisor's role is not to chide you. If you discuss the problem, ask for advice and then follow it, you will be demonstrating a skill that all independent researchers need to have.

2.7 DATA ANALYSIS PHASE

Once your data have been collected, you will need to begin preliminary analysis. You may, if you are conducting a project with several different phases of data collection, or a grounded theory study, need to analyse some data before going on to collect more. Naturally you will have made some plans for data analysis when you were designing the study, and we give some more detailed advice in Chapter 9. So our focus here is on how you can best use your supervisor's support to aid your analysis.

Being confronted by a spreadsheet of raw figures or many pages of interview transcript can be daunting to even the most experienced researcher. Fortunately, your supervisor should be able to help you make sense of this process.

Most supervisors will expect you to attempt analysis of your data by yourself first, and to send or bring an overview of your analysis to them for discussion. The reason they do this is to allow you the chance to work independently, and accumulate marks for doing so. If your supervisor seems unwilling to step in and make suggestions for analysing your data, it may well be because they have your interests at heart.

2.7.1 Getting your supervisor's help with analysis

If you are really stuck and do not know where to begin (this may be especially true for inductive or qualitative analysis) ask your supervisor to help you get started. Arrange a time when you can look over some data together, but do not expect your supervisor to provide you with answers. It may be more likely that they ask you lots of questions instead. They may try to tease out of you what you think the striking features are in the data, any trends you have noticed or any hunches you have developed. They will then be able to give you feedback as to whether you are heading in the right direction. This can enhance your confidence and encourage you to get stuck in. There are three keys to using this type of meeting successfully:

- *You need to allow your supervisor enough time to look at the data.* Some people are very good at making instant sense of complex material, but many of us need time to read material carefully and formulate our own ideas about it. There may not be time for your supervisor to do this during a 15–30 minute appointment with you sitting beside them in eager anticipation. It is a good idea then to check with your supervisor if they would like to receive the data in advance.

- *You need to be prepared to have a go yourself.* Your supervisor is unlikely to have time to do analysis for you. And, if they did, you would be giving away the opportunity to score points for independent effort. So come to this meeting with some ideas of your own, however unsure you may be about them. Only if you share them can you get helpful feedback on whether you are setting about your analysis in the right general direction.

- *You need to use the feedback you receive on your ideas to take forward the rest of your analysis.* Once you have had some suggestions on how to continue analysing the data, it is important that you note them carefully and put them into practice independently. If time permits, your supervisor may be happy to have another meeting to talk about your analysis. As we will see in the next section, they may also give you feedback on a draft results section. However, they will almost certainly expect you to have done some more analysis before you contact them again.

MAXIMISING MARKS
Have a go at analysing your data by yourself

Bearing in mind that this is an independent project, you may want to take the opportunity to show how much of the analysis you can do by yourself. Many supervisors will expect this. You may find it helpful to bring some kind of analytical outcome to your meeting with the supervisor. This might be summary or descriptive statistics or a list of thoughts or ideas you have about what was particularly striking in the data. Your supervisor may then make some suggestions for additional analysis, which you should follow up on after the meeting. Remember to check how much of the analysis your supervisor expects you to attempt on your own.

2.8 REPORT WRITING PHASE

Having collected and analysed your data you may well feel you are well on the way to completing your work, and perhaps even feel that your mark is pretty well determined by this stage. It is worth remembering, though, that most of your mark is likely to derive from the report that you hand in for assessment. So by writing your work up in the best possible way you may somewhat redeem a less than perfect project. Conversely, of course, a poor write up can let down a good study and limit the marks you can be awarded. For this reason, it is essential that you make the most of your supervisor's expertise to improve your report.

2.8.1 Why get feedback on drafts?

The short answer to this question is that none of us is perfect. Even the most experienced and successfully published researchers have to take feedback on drafts that they have written. Indeed many are successful partly because they actively seek constructive criticism of their work. Many research papers submitted to academic journals come back with pages of reviewer criticisms, which the writer has to address before the paper can be published. We sought and received constructive criticism from numerous colleagues across the UK in the course of drafting and redrafting the chapters of this book. You may well have some comments of your own about how it could be improved!

The following are some examples of issues that can be identified by supervisor feedback on drafts:

- You have understood a concept in your own mind, but not demonstrated this understanding in your report.
- You have written in a way that is confusing or ambiguous.
- You have described your study in a way that is somewhat unbalanced. This might be too much discussion of the study's strengths, leaving you open to criticism from markers who may assume you are unaware of its weaknesses. On the other hand, it may be that you have undersold your project, being overly negative about its limitations, not doing justice to its clever research question or design.

2.8.2 When is the best time to submit drafts?

There are several things to consider when deciding when to pass a draft to your supervisor. You need to weigh these up to get maximum benefit from the process. There is a wide range of practices regarding how much feedback project students get and when it is given. Some departments only allow supervisory feedback on one draft of each section within the report. Some limit this further by permitting feedback on some sections such as introduction and method, but not others, e.g. results and discussion. This means that you will need to decide whether to submit work at a very sketchy stage, or wait until you have polished it to the best of your abilities. If you submit a draft that is very incomplete you may get pointers about how to develop it, e.g. content, but then miss a chance to get fine grained feedback on structure and style at a later stage. Some supervisors may ask you to hand in a draft introduction section before you submit for ethical approval or begin data collection. If you agree to do this, bear in mind that your introduction may well need to be rewritten after the study is completed. Finally, some supervisors are happy to read drafts of the report one section at a time, while others prefer to see a single draft with introduction, method, results and discussion all together.

You might like to negotiate with your supervisor so that you do not 'use up' your opportunity for feedback too soon. It might, for example, be more useful to talk through your outline plans for the introduction in an email or supervisory meeting, rather than submitting a complete draft at this stage. Getting feedback on a plan or 'verbal draft' in this way is particularly important if your department is one in which no written drafts are accepted.

As well as these academic considerations about timing, there are also more practical issues to consider. You and your supervisor need to be realistic about when drafts can be submitted and returned. Your supervisor will need enough time to read your work and provide comment. You will need sufficient time to make any changes that are recommended, and then get the work printed, bound and submitted for assessment. Individual supervisors will differ in their workloads, so it is wise to agree in advance how soon you can expect feedback on your draft. You might even like to make this part of your agreed project plan (see earlier). As a rough guide, some supervisors suggest that a week is a reasonable time to wait for comments, but remember to check what your supervisor will do. Bear in mind, too, that staff may be away on other duties or on annual leave during holiday periods such as Christmas and Easter.

MAXIMISING MARKS ✔

Talk through an outline plan

Before you begin to write your draft, you might find it helpful to discuss with your supervisor the outline you intend to write to. This can be done in a fairly brief meeting, and may boost your confidence before you start writing. So long as your supervisor is happy to do this it may mean that the one draft on which you do get feedback is much better than it might otherwise have been.

2.8.3 Asking for feedback on your work

As well as agreeing a timetable for drafts, you might like to ask your supervisor if they have any preference about the format in which you give them your work. Some staff prefer a hard copy printout on which they can write, and others an electronic copy to save on printing or enable them to add comments electronically.

You do not necessarily need to book an appointment to deliver your draft. And given what we have said earlier about staff needing time to read materials, you may not get the most constructive criticism if you expect feedback there and then. Agree with your supervisor whether a hard copy in their mail tray or an electronic copy by email would be more appropriate.

2.8.4 Making sure you get feedback in a helpful way

You can take an active role in the feedback process, by reflecting on what type of feedback you would most appreciate. Think about your typical strengths and weaknesses in academic writing. Is there something you have consistently struggled with throughout your degree? Consider your draft as objectively as possible. Which bits are you most confident about and which do you think are the weaker aspects?

You might, for example, know that you have a problem with the structure of your assignments in the past. You might like to ask your supervisor to comment specifically on this aspect of your draft. Alternatively, you may feel confident in the way you have described previous research in the introduction, but feel that your evaluation may not be as strong as it could be. Again, you might ask your supervisor for comment on this dimension.

You could also consider how the feedback will be given. Would you prefer handwritten comments on your draft, an annotated electronic copy, or even an overall summary of the type that you might get on a formal coursework assessment? It is worth agreeing this with your supervisor before you provide your draft. It is also worth reflecting on the process by which your feedback will be delivered. Some supervisors will leave an annotated draft for you to collect in person, some will mail it and others will return it by email. Email has the advantage that you may get comments quickly, leaving you time to respond to them, but you may prefer to wait and talk through your feedback in person for various reasons. Having feedback in a conversation allows you to check that you fully understand what your supervisor has suggested. It can also feel less bluntly critical than receiving a written list of criticisms. Having your supervisor explain what needs improvement may feel less of a personal dissection if it is accompanied by warm and reassuring non-verbal behaviour.

MAXIMISING MARKS

Talking through feedback

Your supervisor may already have a preference for the type of feedback they will give on drafts, but you can also make suggestions. You might like to ask for feedback on an annotated electronic copy of your draft, perhaps using the comments function of your wordprocessing program. This might be easier to read than handwritten comments. Whether your feedback comments are handwritten or electronic, ask to talk through them in a meeting wherever possible to ensure that you understand why you are being asked to amend or add something. It will help if both you and your supervisor have copies so you can both refer to the same points.

As we have mentioned earlier, feedback on drafts should be one of the key benefits of having individual supervision. However, it can be a bit of a double-edged sword. You have worked closely with this member of academic staff to develop your project, collect and analyse data, and taken on board the constructive comments they have shared in supervisory meetings. You have written your introduction, method or results discussion section up to be as good as it can, and given your supervisor a copy. What do you do if you receive many critical comments? This is one area where there is potential for students to feel disappointed or hurt in their supervisory relationship. Before you head for the hills, or turn to the troubleshooting section of this chapter, we think it may help to reflect a bit on your supervisor's motivations, and what critical comments mean for you and your writing.

● Your supervisor may have criticised your work because they feel it falls short in some way, but ultimately this may be because they want you to get the best possible mark for your project.

● Your supervisor's criticism is not necessarily a comment on *you* and your abilities. It is simply a comment on what is on the page in front of them, which may or may not reflect your abilities.

● Your supervisor is not saying that you are not good enough, rather that the draft you have produced could be made better.

● Criticism does not mean that your research is no good – remember that staff who publish their work receive this kind of criticism all the time.

Finally, it is much better to receive these critical comments now when you can do something about them, rather than seeing them set in stone on the feedback sheet after the report has been submitted and marked. So, if an aspect of your work is criticised, be sure to ask for an example of how it could be made better. Do your best to amend the final version of the report to include these suggestions. Responding positively to feedback is something the markers will be looking to award you credit for when they assess your report.

If you bear these points in mind you stand to gain a great deal from your supervisor's expertise and experience. Remember to thank them for their contribution in the acknowledgements section of your final report.

2.9 AFTER YOU HAVE SUBMITTED YOUR REPORT

Once you have submitted your dissertation report, you may feel that your supervisory relationship is over. After all, there is not really anything you can do now to affect your mark. That may well be true, but there are still benefits you can derive from retaining a good relationship with your supervisor.

As we mentioned at the beginning of this chapter, you may like to keep in contact with your supervisor for several reasons:

- You may wish to prepare a jointly authored conference presentation or journal articles based on your project research.
- You may have an opportunity to extend your work into a postgraduate research degree under their supervision.
- Your supervisor may be a useful source of careers advice, which can be personally tailored, since they know your individual skills and interests.
- At the very least, you may need to ask your supervisor to provide you with academic references when you apply for employment or further study.

If you are very confident and proactive, you may identify an academic conference to which you could submit your work, or your supervisor may suggest this. If your supervisor encourages you to submit for publication, this a good sign in the sense that your work must have some originality or relevance. Be careful, though, not to assume that this is a sign you are about to be awarded a high mark for your report. Sometimes students conduct interesting studies but produce reports that have significant short-comings. Often student projects need some rewriting, or even extra data collection or analysis, before they are ready for a wider audience. You may well get a mark with which you are happy but, even if you do not, joint working with your supervisor to achieve publication is one way to redeem a less than perfect dissertation experience. Your supervisor may admire you for having the creativity and sense of adventure to try something new. An idea that was not fully realised in your undergraduate work could form the basis for a doctoral thesis or a paid research post in the years to come.

Even if you have no plans for extending your research once the dissertation is submitted, there are still ways in which you can use your supervisory experience to your advantage. You can reinforce the good relationship you established with your supervisor by providing them with a copy of your up-to-date CV, and perhaps a summary of your future career plans. This will equip your supervisor to write more detailed and appropriate references for you before and after graduation.

You can also use the experience you gained conducting your study to provide a self-assessment of your skills and development needs. Employers are often keen to hear concrete examples of projects you have worked on, and evidence that you learn from those around you.

TOP TIP   Write a (reflective) account of your experiences

You may find it helpful to write a reflective account of your project experience, ideally while it is still fresh in your mind. This account may provide excellent material for you to discuss with prospective employers at any job interviews you attend. It may also help you prepare for any future work or research projects you take on. Some departments find these accounts of the student experience useful in planning their future curricula and support for project students. Your account might also inspire or forewarn students starting their final year projects.

2.10 TROUBLESHOOTING YOUR SUPERVISORY RELATIONSHIP

Our focus throughout this chapter has been on maintaining a positive working relationship, and getting the maximum benefit from supervision. A healthy part of this involves recognising problems and solving them by mutual agreement. This is one of the most important skills that dissertations are designed to assess. However, if it is your first experience of this kind of working relationship, there may be times when you feel confused as to what you and your supervisor should be doing, or dissatisfied with some aspect of the supervisory relationship. We encourage you to troubleshoot these problems for yourself. Here are some common problems and our suggestions for solutions you might try.

2.10.1 Mismatch between supervisor and student research interests

We discussed earlier how your initial research question and methodology might evolve in the course of discussion with your supervisor. It is possible that one or both of these will change to match your supervisor's interests and expertise. However, there are occasions when students find that they would be better off being supervised by someone else. If you think that this may be the case, it is a good idea to discuss it with your supervisor to avoid misunderstandings. They may well be happy for you to change supervisors, but a bit puzzled if you simply disappear without explanation. Most departments have a member of staff with responsibility for overall coordination of dissertations, and this person may have an overview of which staff might be able to take you on for supervision. You should never leave one supervisor without having agreed an arrangement with another, and the dissertation coordinator will need to know who your new supervisor is and why. This is because students may struggle without supervision and, without some kind of overview, some staff may end up with an unfair workload of student supervision. Constructive feedback on your experience of supervision may also help the dissertation coordinator identify any problems in the system of allocation, and take steps to prevent them recurring in future years.

2.10.2 Supervisor does all the talking in meetings

Have you ever been in a meeting when your supervisor simply gabbled at you for 30 minutes, not leaving an opportunity for you to get a word in edgeways? You may come away confused without the support or advice that you need.

A supervisor's experience . . .

66 As a supervisor I feel really enthusiastic about undergraduate dissertation projects. I am almost envious of students who have the chance to choose any topic that interests them, and develop it into a viable and worthwhile study. It was being interested in just this stuff that made me interested in becoming an academic in the first place. Unfortunately, though, so much of my life is spent frantically preparing lectures, attending meetings and marking student coursework, that months can fly by without me ever touching my own research work. So when a student comes to see me about a possible project, I can sometimes get a little over-excited . . .

After my first few years of supervising dissertations, I became aware that some students seem more forthcoming than others. After students had left meetings I occasionally found myself feeling a bit guilty. On reviewing my notes of the meeting, I felt I had made lots of suggestions to the student, but not had much back in the way of ideas or opinion. While it would have been tempting to conclude that the students concerned were just shy, or lazy, or perhaps not very bright, I knew full well that some of them were hard-working, assertive and had very good marks in their other coursework. If the explanation didn't lie with the student, I knew that I must look elsewhere. Next time one of the students (Mary) came to see me, I made a conscious effort to observe our interaction, and see what was going on . . .

Mary arrived looking very positive, if a little nervous, extremely polite as ever. I began by asking if she'd completed the tasks we'd agreed at the last meeting. It turned out that she hadn't, so I did the best I could to tell her what I thought she should do next. Mary listened attentively and noted down everything I said. We agreed that she'd do as I advised, and we arranged to meet again.

Reflecting on the meeting, rather than feel pleased that I'd been so helpful in solving Mary's problem, I realised that I had gabbled at her for the entire meeting, leaving no chance for her to ask the questions she needed answers to. She may well have needed a solution to the problems she was facing, but I'd taken away the opportunity for her to find this for herself. Rather than wait for her to contact me again, I emailed her immediately:

Hi Mary
I was just wondering, was there anything you wanted to talk about that we didn't get to cover in our meeting today? I felt that maybe I was a bit overenthusiastic in making suggestions, but I wonder if you have any thoughts about what to do next? Do you want to come and see me again? Or have a quick exchange of emails/chat on the phone – whichever's best for you.
Cheers
Harry T. 🍃

There are various reasons why your supervisor may do most of the talking in meetings. They may simply be very enthusiastic about your research, unable to contain their excitement at all the possibilities it offers. Alternatively, they may be socially awkward and feel compelled to fill any silences that are left in the interaction. More worryingly, they might have the impression that you lack initiative, and that they are going to have to make every suggestion. Perhaps you do not seem to have much to say, or seem passive in meetings, waiting for your supervisor to take the initiative.

Whatever the reason, this pattern of interaction should always be a cause for concern. You need to work out why your meetings go like this and take steps to ensure they are more productive in future. We discussed earlier the potential of plans and agendas in managing your supervisory relationship. This is a prime example of the agenda as a problem solving tool. To ensure every meeting is a balanced exchange, you may find it helps to draw up an agenda and send it to your supervisor in advance. If you are clear what you want to get out of the meeting, your supervisor is less likely to feel the need to fill the time on your behalf. If it looks as though there will not be time to cover everything that is on your mutual agenda, consider booking another appointment to deal with any remaining issues.

2.10.3 Supervisor does not give you the help that you need.

Most student supervisor relationships proceed positively and effectively, but when there is dissatisfaction, this is probably the most common complaint that is made.

A student's experience . . .

I chose my supervisor because I enjoyed the lectures he gave us in our second year. It wasn't just that the topics were interesting – it was that he always went out of his way to make sure that his lecture notes were up to date, and that we knew everything there was to know on the topic. I was always confident preparing for exams, as I knew he had covered everything on the syllabus, and short of giving us the actual questions, told us clearly what to expect in our assessment. He was one of the most popular lecturers and I was delighted when I was allocated to be supervised by him. I still think he is a great guy, even though our supervisory relationship was tested almost to destruction – by the way we behaved in our early meetings.

To begin with, I looked forward to each meeting. He was always very positive, and seemed interested in my project. We'd agree tasks for me to complete before we next met. The trouble started when I'd go back to discuss my progress …

I felt I ought to be polite and let him take the lead – he was the expert after all. Take, for example, our fourth meeting, when I mentioned that I'd not yet secured access to the equipment I needed to run my experiment. He spent the entire remainder of the meeting listing things he or his previous students had done to solve similar problems in the past. I didn't like to interrupt and tell him that I had already taken steps to solve the problem myself: I'd actually submitted an application to the technicians for the equipment, and was simply waiting for them to get back to me. Meanwhile, I didn't get a chance to discuss a more tricky matter – how to make the changes to my protocol recommended by the ethics committee that had reviewed it. Before I knew it, we'd run out of time and I'd agreed to a whole bunch of stuff I wasn't ready to do. In thinking about why I agreed to this, I guess it was because I didn't want him to think I was being dopey. I'd come with one problem to which he'd had to offer solutions – I didn't want him thinking that I couldn't come up with answers for myself.

I left that day, feeling a bit of an idiot and I was about to email to postpone our next meeting when a message from him popped up on my screen. Luckily, instead of yet more advice on what I should do next, it was actually a really sweet note asking if there was anything I wanted to discuss but had not had the chance to. I had a brief chat on the phone and updated him on where I was with accessing the equipment. We arranged another meeting where we worked through the ethics stuff I needed his help with. That meeting went really well, mainly because I emailed him an agenda the day before – just a list of the queries I wanted to deal with. I could tell he was having to make an effort not to start gabbling at me again, but he did manage to keep a lid on his enthusiasm, and I came away feeling much more satisfied. It was quite funny looking back on it, and I still think he's a brilliant lecturer. "

Let us start by considering why you might not always get the help you need from supervisory meetings:

- Do you *know* what help you need?
- Have you *asked* for it?
- Have you allowed your supervisor *time* to understand the problem and offer a solution?

Supervisors are endowed with many skills and personal qualities, but mind reading is rarely one of these. An experienced supervisor will have a pretty good idea of the sorts of things students may struggle with, but they may have no way of knowing what you are stuck on if you do not know yourself. You might find it helpful to spend some time reflecting on what exactly it is you need help with, then note this down to take to your next supervisory contact. Your supervisor may be able to provide helpful suggestions immediately, or may need some time to work out how best to advise you. However, you can only get this sort of help if you ask for it clearly and specifically.

2.10.4 When you cannot get in touch with your supervisor

One thing that your supervisory relationship relies upon, is you and your supervisor being able to get in contact with each other. This is a two-way process, so make sure that you have an accurate note of your supervisor's work email address, telephone number, etc., and that you have provided your supervisor with an email address that you actually use. Ideally this should be a university email account, as many university spam filters automatically exclude messages sent from commercial webmail sites such as Google. If you have sent your message from an address such as 'sillysausage@webmail.com', and do not receive a reply within a working week, it may be that the spam filter has prevented your supervisor receiving it.

Occasionally, though, there may be other reasons why your telephone or email queries remain unanswered. Rather than delay, it is worth checking with your departmental office in case your supervisor is absent from work due to illness or other personal circumstances. If it looks as though they will be unable to respond to your query, or attend a planned meeting, you should contact the person with overall responsibility for student projects. They will be able to advise you how to proceed with your work, whether this means seeing an alternative or temporary supervisor, or perhaps even requesting an extension to the deadline for submitting your report.

2.10.5 Personal and academic issues get muddled together

Sometimes the kind of help that you need is more personal and pastoral than academic in nature. In some universities, a student's dissertation supervisor is also their individual personal tutor. It makes sense for these roles to coincide, since your supervisor will be seeing you regularly and will get to know you well in the course of your work. However, the downside of this arrangement is that the supervision of your project can sometimes be compromised by your relying on the same person for support, with personal difficulties not directly related to your research. The best defence against this happening is to remain aware of the different roles that your supervisor is playing at different times in the relationship. If you feel you would rather keep your pastoral care and research supervision separate, you might like to suggest booking different meetings to deal with these issues separately. You might even consider whether you want to seek pastoral support elsewhere.

2.10.6 When to ask for help from other staff

Sometimes you may have a problem with your supervisor that you have been unable to resolve using any of the strategies we have suggested. Rather than giving up or losing momentum with your project, this is a good time to seek out alternative sources of support. University departments differ in their local arrangements for student support, but there is usually someone else you can talk to, in confidence, about your concerns. In many cases, this will be the dissertation coordinator, but it might also be your year tutor or head of department. These people should also be your first port of call in the event that your supervisor is off ill or otherwise absent or unavailable during the course of your project.

Going to see someone else to discuss your project worries does not necessarily signal the breakdown of your supervisory relationship. You may find that the conversation helps to clarify your problems and devise ways to make your supervision work more successfully. The spirit of these discussions should be constructive problem solving, so it is best to be sure that your criticisms are well-founded and professionally presented.

Talking things through with someone else is not necessarily the same as 'snitching'. It does not mean that you have abandoned your supervisory relationship. Talking to someone else may help give you perspective, or suggest some solutions you might try in your next supervisory contact.

Be careful to make clear to the member of staff you talk to:

- whether you are happy to for them to discuss your concerns with anyone else;
- whether you would like them to take any action.

Remember: you are only seeking this other person's advice, not handing responsibility to them for managing your supervisory relationship.

CHAPTER SUMMARY

- It is worth managing the relationship with your supervisor, for the sake of both personal comfort and academic achievement. It is your responsibility to take the lead.

- There are various reasons for choosing a supervisor, including personal affinity and topic/methodology matching. It is important that you consider all of these and weigh them up if you are choosing a supervisor. If you have to work with a supervisor who is allocated rather than chosen, this may be an opportunity to develop new skills.

- In your early meetings be prepared to receive more questions than answers. It is important that your supervisor probes you to check that your study is well conceived. They are not giving you a hard time for the sake of it; they are giving you the opportunity to show initiative – one of the things markers look for in really good dissertation students.

- Showing your supervisor the literature you have reviewed can help reassure them that your study has a sufficient rationale. Your supervisor may also be able to advise if you need to do more background research. They may also be able to advise on practical feasibility issues.

- Supervisors are a good source of advice on your data collection, both before you start and as you go along. It is better to practice on your supervisor, or admit that there are problems, than to wait until all your data are collected and may turn out to be unusable.

- Showing your supervisor some preliminary data analysis may boost your confidence before you analyse the whole dataset. It will also show your supervisor that you are capable of doing work by yourself.

- The opportunity to revise drafts following constructive feedback from your supervisor is a valuable aspect of the supervisory relationship. Give your supervisor drafts when you are genuinely ready to benefit most from their feedback. Give your supervisor plenty of time and ensure that you understand their comments before responding.

- Your supervisory relationship should be characterised by mutual respect. If you encounter problems, it is best to be proactive about addressing them. The initiative and responsibility you show in resolving your difficulties may earn you more credit than crossing your fingers and hoping for the best.

FURTHER READING

Moon, J. (2008). *Achieving Success through Academic Assertiveness:* 1. London: Routledge.
This book focuses on ways that you can act positively and communicate effectively to achieve academic success.

The UK GRAD Programme (2008). Managing Yourself. Published on The UK GRAD http://www.grad
.ac.uk/cms/ShowPage/Home_page/Resources/Just_for_Postgrads/Managing_yourself/p!ecdXagi
This site contains materials to help you evaluate your skills, set personal objectives and develop plans
to achieve these. Although it is intended for PhD students, it should also be helpful for undergraduates.

CHAPTER 3
THE LITERATURE REVIEW: IDENTIFYING YOUR RESEARCH QUESTION

This chapter will explain how to move from a general idea to the formulation of a research question. To do this, we will guide you through a structured approach to searching and reviewing the literature to arrive at a question that is rooted in past research and theory. We will explain how to search using research databases as well as other resources, and guidance will be given on how to judge the appropriateness of material found on the internet. The chapter will also explore how to structure a clear theoretical framework.

BY THE END OF THIS CHAPTER YOU WILL:

- Know how to conduct a literature search that will enable you to formulate a research question.

- Know what a research question is.

- Understand what is meant by a 'theoretical framework', and why it is important to construct one for your research project.

- Have an idea of how to approach the evaluation of research papers.

3.1 CONDUCTING A LITERATURE SEARCH

So far, you have an idea for a project topic but that is not the same as saying you have an idea of what your project is going to be. In order to develop your project idea, you first need to conduct a search of the existing literature, with a view to identifying what research has not yet been conducted. This is sometimes referred to as **identifying a gap in the literature.** In other words, you need to look at all the research that relates to your project idea and identify in a systematic way what has already been done and what has not. Only then will you have a clear sense of what kinds of project you could aim to do.

3.1.1 Building a general knowledge of work in the area

The first step in conducting a literature search is to begin to build up your general knowledge about research in the area of the topic that you are interested in. A common mistake is to start by using research databases to search for journal articles. When students do this they often complain that they cannot understand the content of the papers that they have located. This is because they have not yet developed a general knowledge of the research in that area that is necessary to understand the terminology in the papers and the issues that surround research of that kind.

The fastest way to acquire a good general knowledge of an unfamiliar area is to locate some good textbooks on the topic in question. So, if you are interested in conducting a project into 'theory of mind', for example, you might want to start off with a recent textbook on cognitive development that has a good introductory chapter to theory of mind listed in its contents pages (also check the index, in case relevant material is embedded in a chapter on a more general topic). Such chapters will provide you with definitions of key terms and accounts of classic research in the area. They will also give you a sense of who is known for conducting research into the topic, and what tasks and methods are typically used to assess it.

The next type of textbook to try to locate is a 'reader' in the area. This is a book that consists of key papers and chapters by different authors that have been edited together into a textbook that gives an overview of theories, issues and developments in the field. The advantage of looking at these types of textbook is that, not only are they useful collections of primary sources that offer a cross-section of research in an area, but also they are typically accompanied by some form of editorial commentary which highlights the significance of certain ideas, papers and unresolved debates. Moreover, some edited collections also include specific chapters that are intended to perform this function. These editorials and overview chapters are really useful in signalling what current thinking in the area looks like, which questions are under researched, as well as providing a critical commentary on some of the studies that have been conducted to date. Reading through these accounts will, therefore, not only give you a sense of what research has gone before, but it will also give you the basis for evaluating and critiquing that research, and building a rationale for your own study.

From reading around the topic in this way, making notes as you go, you should have a list of articles that look as though they are relevant and could help you to develop your ideas further. Try to get as many of these as you can as primary sources (i.e. get hold of copies so that you can read the accounts for yourself, if you have so far only read other people's summaries of them). This may mean that you will have to request some material through interlibrary loan if your library does not hold it. There will usually be a small charge for this service but, if the material looks like it could be central to your own project, it is well worth the investment.

3.1.2 Using research databases

Once you have some notes from your reading of the book-based sources indicated above and you have a sense of what research in the area more generally 'looks like', you can then begin to search using the research databases available to you. It is a good idea to limit your search at this stage to relatively recent papers. To know when to start your search from, have a look at the publication dates of the textbooks you have been using so far. If the books that you have been reading were published in, say, 2008 then it is a good idea to look for research papers that were published from 2006 onwards. This is because it can take up to two years for a textbook to come out in print and so this way you will pick up any research papers that were published between the book being written and it being published.

In terms of which databases to use, the most commonly used ones are **PsycINFO** (note the spelling) and **Web of Science** (although there are many more and you should find out what databases your subject librarian would recommend). These cover the social sciences and Psycinfo, as its name suggests, focuses on the psychological literature. Web of Science is particularly useful if you are trying to gauge the relative significance of papers, as it tells you how often a paper has been cited by other researchers (and you can see who has cited it). Obviously, papers that have only recently come out and are less than two years old will have low citation rates just because it can take several years for journal articles to be published after they have been accepted (this is called publication lag) and so it can take a while for a paper's influence to become visible through citation. However, if a paper is only a few years old but it already has other academics citing it (perhaps only three or four), then it is worth looking at (you will see some papers may be five or ten years old but have never been cited – this may be telling you something about the interest or significance of such work). However, it is also worth reading one or two of the papers that are citing a particular paper, as sometimes papers have high citation rates because they are frequently cited as examples of poor methodology!

There are other databases that may contain relevant information, so it is worth finding out which ones are available to you by contacting the psychology subject librarian at your university library (all subject areas are allocated a librarian, and they will know what databases are relevant to your area). However, other databases that you might want to consider are **ERIC**, an educational research database, which often contains research relevant to educational and developmental psychology topics, and **Medline** or **PubMed**, which cover research relevant to neuropsychological and biological psychology topics.

In terms of how to go about searching, there are many ways to approach this, but we would suggest the following:

1 Try to think of as many key psychological terms as you can that relate to the topic you are interested in. Remember to think of any alternative terms that might be used to refer to the same thing (e.g. in North America dyslexia is often referred to as 'learning disability'). Write them out as a list or, if you prefer, you could draw them as a mind map or spider diagram. It is a good idea also to include the names of researchers whose work you think may be relevant.

2 Take any two terms from your list/diagram and enter them into the database as search terms (e.g. 'dyslexia' and 'music'). We suggest you use the 'advanced search' (or equivalent) to do this. If you want to search for a particular author, use their surname along with a key term, otherwise you will be inundated with a lot of irrelevant research by people with the same surname.

3 Limit your search to papers published after the date you have identified as your cut off (i.e. papers published two years before the publication date of the main textbook you have been working from so far).

4   Look at the abstracts that result – you will find a good deal of material that may not be relevant, so be selective about making note of which papers you think are going to be most useful in terms of giving you ideas that are going to be appropriate for your own project work.

5   Print out relevant articles, if they are available via your library's e-journal collection. Otherwise, make notes of the reference details of papers of interest (you can normally compile a list of such papers by 'marking' them on the database and printing them out as a list later). See if your library has them in hard copy. If not, think about whether it is worth obtaining them via interlibrary loan.

6   Then repeat steps 2–5, using a different pair of search terms each time, until you have exhausted your list and used all the likely combinations of terms.

TOP TIP   Keep a research notebook

When you are beginning to get ideas for a project, it is a good idea to keep these together in a single research notebook. Put all your ideas, no matter how random, down into this notebook, with as much detail as you can on what gave you the idea in the first place. Use this notebook to keep track of your literature search and key terms too. When you need inspiration, or want to get back into an old train of thought, this notebook will help you, and it will help to keep you organised too. Use it to keep notes of any supervision meetings that you have and make sure that you write a 'to do' list every week to stay on top of the jobs that you need to complete. It is also a good idea to glue a copy of your project schedule (see Chapter 5) in the inside front cover of your notebook.

3.1.3 Using the internet wisely

The internet also has a role to play in helping you to develop your literature search but this has to be done in a thoughtful and appropriate way, as this resource is fraught with pitfalls. Some departments firmly dissuade students from using global search engines (e.g. Google) for conducting preliminary research, insisting that they either use a carefully managed database such as Psycinfo or at least a research-oriented search tool such as Google Scholar (http://scholar.google.co.uk/). Of course, there is a whole universe of inappropriate material to be waded through, particularly where a topic such as psychology is concerned, but there are some very simple guidelines that can make even the most all encompassing search engine very useful in the preliminary stages.

Let us start off in the forbidden territory that is Yahoo! (We have chosen Yahoo! just because it is a global search engine with no pretensions to scholarly status, but the following points apply equally to most global search engines). You can enter in key terms, just as you were doing in the research databases mentioned earlier, but with internet search engines it is sometimes more helpful to type in complete phrases. So, instead of typing in 'theory of mind' and 'play', you could type in 'theory of mind is important for pretend play'. By doing this, you can limit the amount of irrelevant websites that contain your key terms. This will provide you with a mixture of material and you now need to decide what material comes from a reliable and reputable source (in academic terms) and what does not. To do this, look at the domain name of the web address. If the first part of the web address ends with **.ac.uk**, or **.edu** you can be pretty confident that you are dealing with a *bona fide* academic source, as these endings are typical of university web addresses, or organisations that are linked to universities, such as organisations that fund research. You can be more sceptical about the content of web pages that end .com or .co.uk as these are typical of corporate websites that have commercial interests. Newpapers and other media corporations can also have this designation (e.g. www.bbc.co.uk) and they can contain useful and credible information, but do be aware that some of the content will have been produced by journalists rather than academics, so you do need to double-check any facts presented there. Web addresses that contain **.org** are often useful as they are commonly associated with charities and other public service organisations that aim to disseminate information on a particular topic to the public. Again, it is worth double-checking any facts against academic sources, but generally these can be useful sites for basic information about things such as psychological conditions. Such sites can also make you aware of how the same condition is referred to in different countries.

MAXIMISING MARKS
Using the net to find key people

As psychology students you are usually encouraged to focus on locating research papers, rather than *people*, when conducting research on a topic. Occasionally, people have given their name to theories, or an author has become so prolific on a topic, or an individual paper so well-known, that a certain amount of fame accrues, but it is the product rather than the person that drives inquiry in psychology. However, the internet has given individual researchers a bit more presence than previously: you can now find the homepages of famous psychologists who are still alive. Not only will this enable you to see what a person looks like and where they work, but academic homepages typically list projects that they have recently been involved in and details of research papers that are not yet published. Sometimes you can even download copies of these papers directly from the homepage. They often also have links to the homepages of colleagues doing similar research all over the world, and specialist websites (e.g. a research centre specialising in your chosen topic). It is always worth following up additional authors with whom your key individual has been working. They may have interesting and useful homepages too!

Also be conscious of any websites that you find that have the term **'wiki'** in their web address. Wikis are websites that allow their users to create pages and edit content. They are intended to be mechanisms for pooling collective knowledge and, in many cases, collaborative working. The best known wiki is that of Wikipedia (http://en.wikipedia.org/wiki/Wikipedia:About), which is an online encyclopaedia that invites its users to add their own entries and edit and update existing entries. Although very useful, such resources are dangerous for two reasons. Firstly, whilst they are monitored and maintained, you do need to be aware that you are using a resource that is vulnerable to incorrect information being uploaded, albeit temporarily. You have no way of knowing whether you are accessing the resource during a period when someone has changed an entry, either for fun or in the genuine (but mistaken) belief that they have the 'correct' information. As Wikipedia states:

> Because Wikipedia is an ongoing work to which, in principle, anybody can contribute, it differs from a paper-based reference source in important ways. In particular, older articles tend to be more comprehensive and balanced, while newer articles more frequently contain significant misinformation, unencyclopedic content, or vandalism. Users need to be aware of this to obtain valid information and avoid misinformation that has been recently added and not yet removed (see Researching with Wikipedia for more details).

This is where your own general knowledge about the area is vital, as it will help you to discriminate between the more well researched and better maintained sites and sites that are less stringently validated. You are advised always to find some way of verifying whether the information you have read about is correct. This usually means reading some of the primary sources or good published textbooks in the area.

The other reason why wikis (and other types of online material) are dangerous is because it is too easy to plagiarise their content by cutting and pasting material into your notes, and later forgetting that it was copied verbatim from the web source. Copying from the internet is the easiest type of copying to detect and so you *will* be caught if you do this.

COMMON PITFALLS

Accidental plagiarism

When using internet sources you are particularly vulnerable to accidental plagiarism, if you are not careful. As mentioned above, the most common mistake people make is to cut and paste directly from internet sites, because it is quicker and easier than taking summary notes. However, it is too easy to forget that the material you have in your document is a verbatim copy from the internet. Even if you have done it with the intention of 'writing through it' in your own words, it is too easy to make only superficial changes to the content, and close paraphrasing of text is still detected by plagiarism detection software. As with all material that you take notes from, you should *never* copy material verbatim unless you are planning to use it as a direct quote, in which case you should put quotation marks around the material and type up full details of where you got the quotation from (and, in the case of web sources, when you accessed it). Always make short bullet point notes in your own words from the outset, so that you will *have* to expand the material to fit it into the narrative of your literature review (to avoid paraphrasing inadvertently). Acknowledge the source of that information using the referencing style stipulated by your department. Remember that plagiarism is unacceptable, and there are often even greater penalties applied to students who plagiarise in their final year project work.

3.1.4 Finding the gap

At this point you will have a large amount of material and now your task is to work through it to identify your own gap in that literature. There are lots of ways that you could do this, but a good systematic approach is described below.

For each study you have read about, have a large index card or piece of paper that summarises the following information:

- The full reference for the study (very important!).
- What was the research question being explored?
- What populations were being sampled?
- What design was used?
- What method of analysis was applied?
- What was found?
- What theories were used (or proposed) in the discussion to make sense of the results?
- Whose research is cited as central to the study (give about three names and dates)?

Work through each study, filling in a card in the above way. When you have done this for the material you have located, sort the cards into different piles according to the design that was used in each study. So, for example, you might have a pile of observational studies, a pile of experimental studies and a pile of correlation-based studies. If you do this, and only have one pile in front of you (perhaps because all the research in the area has been experimental in nature), this is showing you a gap in the literature straight away, i.e. there has been no observational work, or any survey work, or any qualitative designs applied to the area. Consider for a moment whether you could think of a study in this area that does use a different design, and make some notes in your notebook to that effect.

Next, sift through each design-based pile you now have in front of you, and look at what population was sampled from (e.g. students or children) and what the research question was. You may well find that the same population is being sampled repeatedly within a particular type of research design, or that variations on the same research question are being asked within that specific type of study. Make some notes on any patterns that you notice. It may be that you can take an existing research question from one tradition of research studies but use a different methodological approach to address it.

Next, sort the cards within each design pile into little subgroups, based on what variables or features are being measured and, in the case of experimental work, being manipulated. Again, can you spot any patterns? Are there any variables that you are interested in that have not yet been assessed by one of the design types? Are there any variables that are always measured in experimental work but have yet to be assessed in observations, or explored in the context of interview research?

TOP TIP Sorting within a spreadsheet

If you want to be more high tech or environmentally friendly, you could do this exercise using a spreadsheet such as Excel to do the same thing. Use each row in the spreadsheet to record the information about the reference you have found (the columns will consist of the headings indicated in the list given above, such as 'reference' and 'what was found'). Use keywords to help you to summarise the content of the material. Then select all your rows and columns and use the 'sort' command to shuffle your list of references into different orders, according to the content of the 'design' column. This will group your papers into the different designs that were used. You can repeat this process for the other column headings too, to sort them into related groups of studies.

Also, look at the research that is forming the basis of the studies in each pile of cards. You may well find that very different theories are underpinning the research in each design pile. Consider whether there is scope to use the theoretical ideas from one tradition to develop the design of research in a different tradition.

COMMON CONFUSION

Originality

Coming up with an original topic idea is something that you are strongly encouraged to do in order to maximise your chance of getting a good mark for your dissertation. However, when we talk about originality, we are not necessarily talking about doing something that is radically different from what has gone before or identifying a whole new topic area that has yet to be researched. Instead we mean small changes to the design of research that has already been done in a particular area, such as sampling from a different population, or changing a task, or even using a different method of data collection (e.g. doing naturalistic observation instead of experimental work). Remember that a small change that results in an elegant and well considered design is just as impressive as the discovery of a brand new topic area.

Finally, if you think that you have located a gap in the literature, do one last check that the study you are thinking of has not already been done. Go back to the research databases that you used originally, and specifically search for evidence of a study that has the features of the one that you think you would like to do (i.e. the same sample, variables, etc.).

3.2 THE RESEARCH QUESTION

Now that you have identified a gap in the literature you are ready to articulate what your research question will be. The research question is the single most important feature of any study. As you will see, it is pivotal to the design of your study, your chosen analysis and how the success of the project and the write up of your report will be evaluated. Yet it is surprising how often students experience difficulty in articulating what their research question is. Research questions can be precise ('are people motivated to recycle because of feelings of guilt and shame?') or vague ('what kinds of personal explanations do people give to account for why they recycle or not?'), but they do have certain features that are important to bear in mind when you are trying to come up with yours. For example, it is easy to get muddled about what the difference is between a research question and a hypothesis. To add to this confusion, some authors, such as Coolican (2004), make a further distinction between 'hypotheses' and 'research predictions' (see Common Confusion box).

So, a research question is a question that we currently do not know the answer to but which can be addressed by a well-designed piece of research. In this way the question **indicates the 'gap' you found** as a result of your search of the literature. Although they can be quite general in nature, they still need to have **a clear focus.** It is also important that they **pass the 'so what' test:** that is, once you have written down your research question, imagine someone (who is clearly very rude) saying 'So what?' to you as a response. You should be able to argue why the research is important and needed – there should be important implications to asking and answering that question. In short, you need to be confident that there are strong theoretical (and perhaps practical) reasons for asking and answering the research question that you have identified. From a practical point of view, it also needs to be something that you can achieve in the time and resources that are available to you.

COMMON CONFUSION ?
Research questions, hypotheses and research predictions

Research questions, hypotheses and research predictions are all different in important ways:

- A research question is exactly that: it is a question, as in 'What factors predict exam stress?' They tend to be generally expressed.

- A hypothesis is a specific prediction about what we think we will find as an answer to that research question, as in 'It is anticipated that examination stress can be accounted for by individual differences in students' levels of extraversion, their experience of examinations and their success in coursework'.

- Research predictions are similar to hypotheses, but are specific to the study that you are conducting, as in 'It is predicted that Nonesuch University students' scores on the Bloggs' (2001) scale of examination stress will be predicted by their extraversion scores on the Eysenck Personality Inventory, the number of academic examinations that they have taken since the age of 15, and the mean of their Level 1 coursework grades'.

So, a bad research question for a psychology dissertation might be characterised by one, some or all of the following:

- It is not phrased as a question.
- It cannot be answered.
- It is overly ambitious (e.g. you need a team of people or major financial support to collect the data that you need, or it will take a long time to gain access to participants, clear ethics or complete the data collection).
- It is too superficial.
- It is not rooted in the psychological literature.
- It is based on an assumption.
- It is missing!

COMMON PITFALLS
Making assumptions

Do not make assumptions about 'how things are' in the way you phrase your research question. For example, a question such as 'Why do all students with dyslexia have low self-esteem?' is problematic because it assumes that all students with dyslexia have low self-esteem. This sort of claim should not be assumed, it needs to be demonstrated by the past empirical work in the area. If there is a consistent and large amount of research in the area that does demonstrate this, then it will make sense to have a research question of this kind, as it is not making an assumption as much as it is building on what we can already claim to know. However, sometimes it is safer to be more open minded and ask 'Does the reported self-esteem deficit in dyslexic undergraduates still exist, given the levels of support that they now experience at University, and what variables are associated with levels of self-esteem in this population?'

So, why is it so important to get the research question just right? It is because it is central to how your project and your write up of it will be evaluated. Firstly, as we have already noted, the research question should articulate the gap that you found in the literature. From your research question you will develop a general hypothesis or prediction about what you expect to find, which will in turn be articulated as a specific research prediction in the context of your research project. So, if you get the wording of your research question wrong, you may end up with predictions that do not 'match' it. Having a mismatch between your research question and your research predictions is a serious error and will result in lost marks.

For example, imagine your research question is something like 'Does use of text abbreviations detrimentally affect children's literacy development?' Your hypothesis might be something like 'It is anticipated that the extent to which children use text abbreviations in their text messages will predict their subsequent reading development'. This would be fine. However, it would be very easy to come up with a hypothesis that 'drifts' from the research question set, such as 'It is anticipated that children who do not use a mobile phone will have higher reading scores than children who do'. This hypothesis, although on a related topic (mobile phone use), does not directly address the question of children's use of text message abbreviations.

As you can see from the hypotheses above, the research question is also central to the design of the study itself. That is, the design you adopt and methods you use must enable you to answer the question you are asking. For example, sometimes students ask questions about what *causes* a particular phenomenon but then design a study that is *correlational* in design (you will recall that simple correlational designs do not allow us to assess cause and effect – although longitudinal designs do, as you will discover in Chapter 4). So you should always check that you have worded your research question in a way that matches the design of the study you eventually come up with. For the same reason, you also need to ensure that your data analysis enables you to answer the question you have asked.

Your research question will also be the focus of your discussion. That is, having designed the study and analysis around this question, by the discussion you should be in a good position to answer it. So your discussion of results should also focus on this question. Once again, you will lose marks if there is a mismatch between the focus of your discussion and the question you originally set out to answer.

3.3 BUILDING A THEORETICAL FRAMEWORK

You may find that your supervisor or other lecturers refer to something called a 'theoretical framework'. A theoretical framework is the theory and related research that underpin the hypotheses that you are making about your study. The best way of thinking about it is to return to your stacks of index cards that you were sorting through when you were looking for a gap in the literature. This time sort them into piles based on whose work they are drawing on in the discussion of their results (i.e. the last bullet point on your index cards). Each pile that you now have in front of you represents a particular theoretical 'tradition'. That is, you will have sets of research studies that all explain their results by reference to a particular theory or set of ideas. If you read the studies, you will find that, even if they are not drawing on a grand theory as such (e.g. Piaget's theory of cognitive development), there will still be a set of theoretical ideas that the authors are proposing in their discussion, in an attempt to make sense of their findings. You need to read through each pile and decide which stack of studies offers you the best theoretical framework for interpreting your results. To do this, you will need to evaluate the quality of the research evidence that is in that pile of cards. We will explain how to do this in a moment.

After your evaluation of the evidence is complete, you will have a stack of studies that you can align your research ideas with, theoretically speaking. However, the other pile(s) also represent theoretical traditions. They are important too, as they represent theoretical ideas that are either complementary to the one you have selected as your main framework (and can be referred to as such in your literature review), or they will offer competing or contradictory explanations. These competing ideas are far from problematic. You will incorporate them into your literature review as work that offers an alternative framework for understanding the results of your study. The important thing that you will need to do in your literature review is explain to the reader why you have aligned yourself with one set of ideas over the other. In other words, you have to **justify your choice of theoretical framework.** To do this you will have to offer an evaluation of it and of the alternative ideas.

All good contemporary theories are based on evidence from a set of research studies, because, just like you, theorists will have grounded their ideas in past research evidence. So, if you want to evaluate a theory, the easiest way to approach this is to evaluate the quality of the evidence that the theory is rooted in.

3.3.1 Being evaluative

You will see in your marking criteria that you get better grades for writing in a critical way. A common assumption is that, when we ask students to be critical of what they are reading, it is assumed that we always want them to find fault with what they are reading. In fact, critiquing research means scrutinising a set of ideas of a study and identifying its strengths as well as its weaknesses. For this reason we prefer to use the term 'evaluation'.

Another common misconception is that any research that has been published is 'perfect' and beyond criticism. This also is not true. Research papers do undergo 'peer review' before they are published, which means that normally at least two other academics who are familiar with that area of research have read and commented on the paper, and have been satisfied that it is good enough to warrant publication. However, sometimes a decision is made to publish something that is methodologically weak, because so little research has been done in that area at the time. Also, it is important to recognise that 'peer review' means exactly that – the reviewers are not necessarily the top experts in the field, they are just representative of other people who do research of that kind. As a result, their view of a study may differ from that of other psychologists who come from other traditions of research.

Book chapters are less stringently scrutinised. Generally, chapters are invited and, although in good books there will have been some process of review and scrutiny, this may not be as rigorous as a journal review process. After all, a book contract may have already been issued, so the author or the editors will be concerned about completing the book on time and having enough material to fill it. That is not to say that all book chapters will be weak, but it is worth being aware that they may offer more partial accounts of literature than a journal article. This is another good reason for having a sound general knowledge of your research area: so that you can spot biased accounts of the literature when you come across them.

There are two main areas to consider in your evaluation of the work you are reviewing: the quality of the argument and the quality of the evidence.

3.3.2 Analysing and evaluating arguments

If you are evaluating the introduction or discussion of a journal paper, or the content of a book chapter, there are ways in which you can check the robustness of the arguments that you are presented with. Chris Hart's (1998) chapter on argumentation analysis gives a good general introduction to this. In it he refers to a notation technique developed by Fisher (1993), which offers you a good way of marking up the different elements of an argument so that you can see at a glance whether or not a set of claims is unsupported. We describe a slightly simplified version of this technique, as follows.

Fisher's notation technique (adapted from Hart, 1998)

1 Quickly skim through the text to get a sense of what the chapter/article is about. Remember, if you are reviewing a journal paper, you only need to consider the introduction and discussion sections for assessing the quality of argumentation.

2 Now work through the text, and draw a ring around any 'inference indicators' (i.e. words such as *thus*, *hence*, *consequently* and *therefore*).

3 Look for any conclusions that are offered. Underline them.

4 Look for any reasons that are given for drawing those conclusions (such as research evidence). Put pointy brackets < > around these reasons. These are sometimes preceded by words like *because*, *since*, *it follows* and so on.

5 Now look through and see if you can identify from the underlined statements which ones are intended to be the main conclusions from the text. Write a capital C beside these. You should be able to see how the other (sub) conclusions build to produce these main conclusions.

6 Now, look back through your text. Can you spot anywhere where a conclusion is being offered without a reason (supporting evidence)? All conclusions should have associated reasons.

You should find that, with practice, this technique for notation will become second nature and it is more helpful than just highlighting sections of text, as this technique draws your attention to aspects of the text that will help you evaluate it. You will see straight away if there are some sections of text that lack evidence and are essentially employing rhetorical devices to try to persuade you that their interpretation is a plausible one. Hart (1998: 98) provides a list of the rhetorical devices that are sometimes employed to this effect, although the use of such devices should be quite rare in psychology papers.

✳ TOP TIP   Applying Fisher's notation to your own work

It is also worth applying Fisher's notation to your own introduction and discussion sections (and your own essays too), as you can also use it to check that your own work has a fully developed argument clearly stated within it, and is supported by appropriate reasons/evidence. If you find it hard to do this to your own work, swap work with a friend and mark up each other's writing in this way. It is best to know if you have made a slip in your argument before you hand your work in!

Fisher's technique is about analysing the constituents of an argument, and checking that they are complete. It is helpful, because it will enable you to spot a slip in the development of an argument through the omission of a set of evidence. What it will not signal to you is whether there has been a misinterpretation of a set of evidence or of someone's ideas that they are drawing on. The only way you can know this is if you have developed your own good understanding of work in the area through the techniques described at the beginning of this chapter.

3.3.3 Evaluating research evidence

Another thing that you should evaluate is the quality of the research studies that authors are using to justify their argument. As we have already noted, a theory is only as good as the evidence it is rooted in. The following are some pointers of things to consider in your evaluation of research studies. Remember that you have to offer a balanced account – just as you are finding weaknesses in the argument, you should also highlight any strengths of a paper.

- If a specific finding from a study is being cited by an author as evidence, is this finding a 'one off' or has it been replicated? Is it a consistent conclusion that any other authors in the area would recognise and agree with?

- Look at the method of the study being cited. Does it seem to be a good way of addressing the research question under consideration?

- Is the method too contrived? Could the same research question have been addressed through a more ecologically valid procedure? However, do be aware of the practical and ethical difficulties of using a more valid design. Often there are good reasons why the researchers adopted a given approach.

- Look at how the variables in question are being assessed. Do those measures (questionnaires, observations, reaction times) really 'capture' the construct under consideration? How have other people looked at it? Is this the standard way of assessing that construct?

- Was the study the first study to demonstrate a particular effect?

- Was it the first study to use a particular methodological technique?

- Do the results of a given study have potential 'real world' relevance and application?
- Was it the first article to propose a particular idea?
- Is the study significant because it is working with a population or type of data that is hard to access?
- Did the study come up with a sensitive or novel way of working with a challenging population? Was that approach successful?

MAXIMISING MARKS

Remember your editorial notes

At the beginning of the chapter we recommended that you read and make notes from editorials and overview chapters in textbooks, because they often have a critical commentary that evaluates particular types of research or the work of particular authors, and contextualises their work appropriately for you. Now is the time to reread those notes you made, and apply some of those criticisms and evaluations to similar papers. Some review papers will also provide you with a basis for this.

One of the worst things that students often do is fail to acknowledge the historical location and significance of research studies. We have even seen students criticise a study published in the 1970s for not acknowledging theoretical ideas that were not published until 1990! It is very easy to see the flaws in a study with hindsight, but you should also give credit for what it contributed to the literature at the time when it was published.

Another common way that students criticise research is to make comments about the nature of the sample or its size. While this can be appropriate, generally speaking students tend to be too quick to damn research because it appears to have a modest sample, without taking into consideration why the sample is so very small. Sometimes a study may be working with a group of people who are relatively hard to find (e.g. blind children). Alternatively, the nature of the study itself might mean that it is only feasible to test a small number because the study takes a full day to run, or requires participants to abstain from something or is very repetitive. The question that you should ask is not just 'how big is the sample?' but also 'what sampling method was used?', if you wish to comment on how generalisable the conclusions of the study are. A small, but truly randomly selected sample is often better than a large opportunity sample. So who is taking part and how they were recruited is just as important.

MAXIMISING MARKS

Remember research karma!

Remember that, if you plan to criticise someone's study because of methodological limitations, you need to make sure that the design of your own study does not make the same mistakes! You will be judged by your own standards. If in your introduction you make great play of why a study is limited, because it used an opportunity sample of undergraduates, it will look very bad if you adopt the same design in your own study!

So, to conclude this section, your choice of theoretical framework needs to be justified via an evaluation of available evidence. You should be able to argue that your theoretical approach is best because it has the best quality research evidence associated with it.

CHAPTER SUMMARY

- Begin your literature search by identifying good textbooks in the area that will give you an overview of the literature and current debates in the field. It is important that you use such sources to build up your general knowledge about the research area you are looking into.

- Generate a list of key terms and significant authors relevant to your project idea, and use these terms to conduct a systematic search of recent literature, using research databases.

- The internet can provide helpful material, but you need to be selective. Try to stick to web sources that contain **.ac.uk** and **.edu** in their web address. Other sources need to be treated with caution and facts verified.

- Locate a gap in the literature by systematically comparing and contrasting the characteristics of the literature you have found.

- The research question is a question that we do not know the answer to at the moment but that can be addressed by a piece of research. It should have a clear focus and have theoretical significance.

- A theoretical framework is the network of theories and related research studies that underpin the predictions that you are making in your study.

- Research studies can be evaluated by examining the coherence of individual arguments and by considering the quality of the evidence that is being presented.

FURTHER READING

If you would like a more detailed guide to searching for relevant literature, We would strongly recommend the following book, which has plenty of good, practical advice for locating relevant sources:
Hart, C. (2001). *Doing a Literature Search: A Comprehensive Guide for the Social Sciences.* London: Sage.

We are going to revisit the topic of how to approach writing up the various sections of your report in Chapter 10. If you are looking for detailed guidance on both organising and writing a review of the literature we would recommend this book, by the same author, as it also contains a lot of detailed practical advice:
Hart, C. (1998). *Doing a Literature Review: Releasing the Social Science Research Imagination.* London: Sage.

If you are more specifically concerned with developing your skills of evaluation and critique in relation to research papers, we would also suggest that you read the following, which explains and demonstrates how to critique both qualitative and quantitative research papers of different kinds.
Girden, E.R. (2001). *Evaluating Research Articles: Second Edition.* Thousand Oaks, CA: Sage.

CHAPTER 4
DESIGNING YOUR STUDY

It is vitally important that you have a clear design for your study. A well-designed study practically runs itself: you know how much data you need to collect, what data, from whom, when, and you know how you are going to analyse it. More importantly still, in a well-designed study it is clear what research question you are asking and how you are going to use the data to answer it. So the research question and the design are inextricably linked.

BY THE END OF THIS CHAPTER YOU WILL:

- Have a broad knowledge of the most common types of study design used in psychological research.
- Appreciate the advantages and disadvantages of each type of design.
- Be able to select a study design that answers your research question.
- Appreciate the importance of careful planning before data collection.

4.1 INITIAL DECISIONS ABOUT STUDY DESIGN

Once you have decided on a research question – or even a topic – you have already, perhaps unknowingly, entered the world of study design. Indeed, you cannot really finalise your research question without having an idea of the design itself, since the design of the study will dictate what *kind* of question you can actually answer with the data. It is no good coming up with a hypothesis about between-group differences and then trying to 'test' this using discourse analysis! So to some extent the research question and design will go hand in hand.

However, we plan to use this chapter to give you some help with the more fine grained details of study design once you have settled on the broad topic and you have some idea of the question you are hoping to resolve.

4.2 ISSUES IN EXPERIMENTAL DESIGN

Most psychology students acquire a sound knowledge of experimental design at an early stage of their studies, so we are confident that you will not need us to go over the basics. Instead, we have chosen to focus this section of the chapter on some of the issues faced when designing more advanced experiments, typically of the 'factorial' variety where you have more than two independent variables.

COMMON CONFUSION ?

Repeated measures

Over the years, psychologists have applied different terms to aspects of experimental design that effectively mean the same things. A common mistake is to learn each type of design separately, rather than obtaining a firm grasp of the basics. For example, what is the difference between an unrelated design and a between-groups design? Or between a related design and a within-subjects design? The answer, in both cases, is nothing, they are just different ways of labelling the same fundamental distinction between experimental designs. If you have a repeated measures design, then it means that the comparison you are making is 'within-subjects': that is, the same people are measured twice or more on the dependent variable rather than separated into different groups. If you did separate them into different groups, then the main comparison in the study is 'between' (those) groups.

4.2.1 Between or within?

One of the most important questions you need to ask yourself, before dealing with the more intricate aspects of design, is whether you want to compare two or more groups of participants on a particular measure, or compare the same individuals on more than one measure (or even the same measure at different time points). How you decide on a between-groups, a within-subjects or a mixed design (where some of your independent variables involve between-group comparisons, but others involve everyone doing the same measure twice) depends on a variety of factors.

1 *Participant recruitment.* As is often the case, even in professional research, the first consideration is a practical one. Are your participants easy to get hold of? If not, the between-groups option may be risky because you will need to collect a larger sample for a between-groups design than

you would for a within-groups design (typically no less than around 20 participants per group as a rough rule of thumb, but see Section 4.2.4). On the other hand, you need to think about how long it will take to test each participant. If recruitment is relatively easy, but each participant will have to spend a long time completing all the measures, it might be worth thinking about a between-groups design.

2 *Research question.* Is it essential for your research question that you compare different groups? Put another way, are you more interested in the reactions of different people, or the effects of different stimuli? In the former case, you may well have expressed your hypothesis in group terms (e.g. 'it is anticipated that psychology students will demonstrate more performance anxiety on a novel task than sociology students'), which means you *need* a between-groups design in order to test that prediction. On the other hand, if you are interested in performance anxiety in relation to audience size, it might not matter what discipline the participants come from. You could then test the same participants on a series of novel tasks and vary the audience size in each condition. Often you may weigh up these considerations and decide that you need a mixed design, with both between- and within-group comparisons.

3 *Potential confounds.* If you want to compare groups on a measure, make sure that there are no serious between-group differences to begin with (e.g. social class, IQ, level of education, age) that might affect the variable you are comparing them on. For example, it is often the case that individuals with dyslexia have a slightly lower vocabulary than individuals who do not, because their reading difficulties may have limited their exposure to more advanced forms of language. In this case, if you found a significant difference between these two groups, it might have been caused by your independent variable (experiencing dyslexia) **or** the confounding variable of 'vocabulary level', unless you took care to either match your participants in your two groups on their vocabulary as part of your recruitment process. Also make sure that there is no overlap: it is quite common for people to compare students to an occupational group, but check to ensure that you do not pick a sector that employs a lot of part-time students!

MAXIMISING MARKS

Spotting confounds

It is a good idea to spend some time thinking about possible confounding variables that could offer an alternative explanation for the results of your study, and thinking about whether it is possible and practical for you to include a simple measure of them in your design. For example, if you are assessing memory recall as your dependent variable, you might also like to include a simple measure of speech rate or articulation speed, because your participants' recall may be compromised by their ability to encode information subvocally (articulation speed and phonological short-term memory have been linked in the psychological literature). By controlling for articulation speed in your design you are able to present a somewhat 'purer' measure of memory recall, because it is less contaminated by individual differences in encoding ability. If you can measure possible confounds, then even if you cannot eliminate them from your design through matching participants, etc., you can control for them statistically (see Chapter 9).

4 *Measuring interventions.* Many experiments involve some kind of intervention – for example, you may like to test the effect of introducing a stimulus of some sort, such as playing a piece of music to affect mood. Such experiments will always need to have a within-subjects, or repeated

measures, component, even if you are fundamentally interested in the way this stimulus affects the behaviour of different groups of participants. Typically, intervention studies take the form of a *pretest-post-test* design. For example, if you want to study the effect of a stimulus on mood, you must have a *baseline* measure of your participants' mood before the stimulus is introduced to them, or you will not be able to draw any meaningful conclusions from the results. In most cases it is also necessary to include a control group to show how someone's mood might differ over time anyway, otherwise the apparent improvement in mood that you were able to demonstrate could simply be the result of a normal effect of someone's mood improving (or deteriorating) over the course of an hour.

Once you have decided on a basic design, your next challenge is to assign your participants to different conditions. Within-subjects designs are often constrained by the need to present the conditions in a specific order, although in studies with a group-based design (between-subjects and mixed), you will need to come up with some rationale for allocating participants to one group or other. The best way of doing this is through *random assignment,* and while you could do this simply by picking names out of a hat, it is probably best to use a computerised random sampling procedure, such as the one on SPSS which randomly allocates cases to groups on a systematic basis.

4.2.2 Factorial designs

A factorial design is one in which there is more than one independent variable. In these instances the independent variables are referred to as *factors*. These studies are usually set up with an ANOVA calculation in mind (see Chapter 9, Section 9.1.2), so you should already have a clear idea at the outset about how you will interpret your statistics. If you do not, you should discuss how your data might be analysed with your supervisor, who may be able to help you to spot potential difficulties in your design regarding making your study too complex.

The whole point of a factorial design is that you are interested in the *interaction* between two or more factors on a dependent variable. The interaction is more than just an additive effect of the factors. For example, Table 4.1 shows a hypothetical table based on a study in which people were asked to recognise faces following presentation either of still pictures or moving pictures; half of each set of pictures had a soundtrack of the individual speaking, while the other half was silent.

The data suggest that moving pictures are more accurately recognised than still ones. They also suggest that pictures with sound are more accurately recognised than silent ones. These two findings would probably emerge as significant *main effects* in an ANOVA calculation. For example, the main effect of the 'sound' on face recognition is the overall result obtained if we look at the effect of our sound manipulation on face recognition scores (regardless of whether the pictures were still or moving). Similarly, the main effect of 'movement' on face recognition is the overall result obtained if we look at the effect of our 'movement' independent variable on recognition scores, regardless of whether the faces shown were speaking or not.

TABLE 4.1 Face recognition data
(DV = mean recognition accuracy out of 100).

	Moving pictures	Still pictures
Sound	84	63
No sound	73	61

However, if we are just interested in the main effects, we may as well simply run two *t*-tests. The whole point of a factorial experiment is that you have set it up to explore an interaction – in other words, when the effect of one factor on another factor varies according to the different *levels* of that factor. In a simple 2 × 2 design such as this, each factor only has two levels, so interpretation is fairly straightforward. Adding sound to still pictures (level 1 of the movement factor) has little effect. Adding sound to moving pictures (level 2), however, boosts recognition by what could well be a significant amount.

In the ANOVA calculation, this contrast between the effects of sound at the two levels of movement would probably constitute *a significant interaction* between the factors of movement and sound. While interpretation is easy with a simple design, for more complex designs (where you have more than two factor levels), you would need to carry out post-hoc tests, such as Scheffé, or Bonferroni corrected *t*-tests at each of the factor levels, in order to fully interpret the significant interaction.

MAXIMISING MARKS

Keeping it simple

Students often get carried away at the design stage, wanting to add a lot of independent variables in the mistaken belief that complex designs automatically ensure higher grades. In reality, this is seldom the case, usually because not enough thought has been put into the analysis of that design, which means that the student is unable either fully to analyse or interpret the data. A good piece of advice when it comes to factorial designs is to minimise the number of within-subject factors (independent variables) in your design and, where you do have them, try to keep the number of levels in those factors to a minimum (ideally just two conditions). This is because, if you have too many levels and/ or too many within-subject factors, post-hoc analyses become very difficult indeed. Elegant designs, well-justified and explained, are more likely to attract higher marks than overly complex and poorly explained designs. Think about the studies that you consider to be 'classics': usually these have very basic designs that are simple and test a key idea (not ten!).

4.2.3 Balancing and checking

There are a number of important checks that you will need to carry out when designing an experiment. First of all, if you are presenting your participants with more than one single task or measure, you will need to consider some form of *counterbalancing* the order of presentation in order to eliminate potential order or practice effects.

Let us return to the performance anxiety example from Section 4.2.1. You are interested in the effect of audience size on task performance and so you need to collect a number of measures of anxiety. You could use a self-report measure but you also want some physiological data, so you fit your participants with a BioPac and measure heart rate and galvanic skin response.

You also want to assess performers on a variety of tasks. Suppose you have three different manual tasks: one involving balance; another involving hand/eye coordination; and a target-hitting exercise. It is possible that these tasks differ with respect to difficulty. It is also possible that a good performance on one task facilitates performance on the next (through elevated self-confidence or whatever). Therefore, the order participants carry them out may accidentally interfere with the main variable (audience size).

In order to minimise any of these potential confounding factors, it is good practice to randomise the order that participants carry out the tasks, so that task difficulty, practice or any other cumulative advantage cannot be held accountable for your eventual results. One way of doing this is to use a *latin square*. A latin square is an array of symbols in which each symbol occurs once in each row and once in each column. You start by drawing up a list of your participants, and then work out the total set of possible combinations of tasks or measures. Table 4.2 shows a latin square for the first three participants in our performance anxiety experiment.

TABLE 4.2 Latin square for performance anxiety task.

Participant	Order of task		
1	Balance	Coordination	Target
2	Coordination	Target	Balance
3	Target	Balance	Coordination

This latin square has not exhausted all possibilities of order. How about target-coordination-balance? In fact there are 12 different possible latin squares that you could have come up with for this particular (3×3) array. You could create a new latin square for each set of three participants and wait until participant number 37 before starting all over again. Or you could, if you prefer, simply repeat this latin square *ad nauseam*, so that participant 4 follows participant 1's order, and 5 follows 2, and so on.

Another important experimental check is known as a *manipulation check*. This is a way of finding out if your manipulation has been successful; in other words, it has produced the effect that you were after. In studies where you want to manipulate mood it is essential. Imagine you wanted to induce sadness by playing a sentimental piece of music. You could not simply assume that the participants in the 'sad' condition would be feeling sad because the piece of music you have chosen to play them makes *you* feel sad! Here, the manipulation check might be nothing more than a self-report mood inventory that participants fill in after the task or measure is completed. Ideally this is the sort of thing that you would check during the pilot study – it will be too late to change the music, if you leave it till the main data collection phase!

4.2.4 How many participants?

In recent years, psychologists and, perhaps more importantly, sources of research funding have become increasingly concerned about the **statistical power** of their studies. Jacob Cohen and other figures (see Cohen, 1994) have claimed that many (typically experimental) psychology studies are 'underpowered' – in other words, they do not involve enough participants to be confident of detecting significant differences. (Incidentally, low power does not mean that a study will always be non-significant, but it means that you might overlook a real difference.) There is now some very good software available that you can download (for free!) in order to carry out an *a priori* power analysis. This means that the program will calculate how many participants you need in each group in your study for it to be sufficiently powerful to detect a significant result. It is called G*Power (version 3.0) and can be downloaded from the University of Dusseldorf's website (Heinrich Heine Universität Düsseldorf, 2008). All you need to specify are the following criteria:

- type of statistical test you hope to run (ANOVA, regression, etc.);
- number of different groups or variables;
- alpha (typically p < .05);
- anticipated effect size (unless you are very confident, always choose medium, which is around d = .5).

You will usually find that G*Power is somewhat harsh on experimental sample sizes, and rather generous on correlational designs. That has got more to do with the nature of the statistics involved than any deep-seated bias. However, although advocates of power calculation are quite vociferous, one thing that needs to be borne in mind is that, for some studies, you have to accept low statistical power – when studying hard-to-recruit populations, for instance, such as unusual clinical groups. After all, just because a study of 20 very interesting people is low powered, that does not mean it is not worth carrying out!

4.2.5 Hypothesis testing

Of course, one of the major considerations in research design is that your study will enable you to answer your research question. When doing experimental research, this should be a straightforward business if you have designed your study carefully, because you will ask very precise questions indeed: hypotheses that relate your independent variables (or factors) and dependent variables to one another.

Whatever your research question, you will find it helpful if your hypotheses are as explicit as you can make them (so long as you have provided sufficient evidence to support those predictions in your literature review). Unless you are doing genuinely exploratory research, and taking a leap into the unknown, it is best to avoid *two-tailed hypotheses*, as it is very unlikely that someone would go to the trouble of designing an experiment of which they genuinely have *no idea* what the outcome is likely to be.

It is not enough even to say 'there will be an interaction between X and Y'. You should really have set up your experiment to test a specific effect, and be able to articulate what that effect is likely to be. Ultimately, two-tailed hypotheses are for speculators – people who are so determined to obtain a significant result that they refuse to make any clear prediction.

One potential hazard you may have already come across, during research methods or statistics classes, is *Type 1 error inflation*. Type 1 errors are referred to as 'false positives' – in other words, you claim evidence of an effect when there actually is not one. These kinds of errors can be made when reading significance values from large tables of correlations (for example) and pouncing on any spurious association because it has an asterisk next to it. They are always a possibility when you are making multiple comparisons – for example an independent variable with five levels.

There are two methods for dealing with Type 1 error inflation. The first is the *Bonferroni correction* that you apply when carrying out post-hoc significance tests between pairs of means. In a one-way ANOVA with five conditions, your chance of finding a significant pair of means is several times greater than in a *t*-test; not because your design is more powerful, but simply through the laws of probability. Bonferroni's correction states that you divide your alpha (usually .05) by the number of comparisons you want to make in order to obtain a new, more stringent, alpha. In other words, if you want to compare three pairs of variables, you would convert alpha to .0167 (.05 divided by three), so that you would have to consider a *p* value of .02 as non-significant.

This correction might be seen as unnecessarily harsh in some eyes. Indeed it *is* harsh, because there is a second, preferable way of dealing with multiple comparisons: the *planned comparison*, where you set up your design with the comparisons already predicted in advance, so you do not have to make all those extra comparisons that incur the wrath of Mr Bonferroni. You do this by setting up your SPSS program so that you weight each of the variables according to your hypothesis. So, if you predict that of your three variables one will be highest, one in the middle and the other lowest, you accord those variables the values +1, 0 and −1. SPSS then calculates a formula based on the expectation of this emergent pattern. It is much more powerful, and much more sensitive to actual means differences, than Bonferroni's correction.

4.2.6 Single-case experiments

These are far less common than group-based experiments, but occasionally undergraduates get the opportunity to have access to clinical populations, particularly in an area such as neuropsychology. A single-case experiment is much harder to design than a group experiment because of the restrictions on control – you certainly cannot have a control *group* if you only have one participant!

The classic single-case design incorporates two experimental phases – a *baseline* phase and a *treatment* phase. This is referred to as an *A-B design*. At its simplest, you would take a series of measurements during the baseline phase to establish the pre-treatment level of functioning, and then a longer series of measurements to observe the effect of the treatment.

You can mix up baseline and treatment phases in order to observe the effects of withdrawal (bear in mind that this type of design has serious ethical implications), thereby creating A-B-A-B designs. You could also introduce a second treatment (A-B-A-C). Any combination is possible. Alternatively, you might wish to create a more complicated design in which you observe the effects of treatment on several different behaviours, known as a *multiple baseline* design.

Of course, single-case designs are not restricted to neuropsychological cases. You could construct a similar design to observe the effectiveness of a teaching intervention or relaxation technique. However, these types of study are reliant on you delivering the intervention, so be careful if it is something that requires a degree of training. Your supervisor should be able to recommend the best practice in this instance.

MAXIMISING MARKS ✔

Reporting single-case experiments

To get a sense of how single experiment designs are written up and the data presented, have a look at single participant or small N studies in the *Journal of Applied Behavioral Analysis*. This area of psychology very commonly uses A-B type designs with small numbers of human participants, and you can get a sense of how to present such data effectively.

4.3 CORRELATIONAL DESIGN

In this section, we consider the types of study that rely on correlational data for their analysis – not just correlations but also regressions and other complex designs where you are essentially asking about associations between variables, or the ability of one or more variables to predict performance on another variable.

4.3.1 Basic types of correlational study

In psychology, the vast majority of correlational designs are put together with some form of multiple regression in mind. That is, you begin with a variable of interest (say, physical well-being), and then identify a set of variables that you believe has a collective impact on that variable (typically, a set of psychological constructs or possibly social phenomena). The former is referred to as a *criterion* variable; the latter as a set of *predictor* variables.

In theory, you can have as many criterion variables and predictor variables as you like, but there are some restraints imposed in relation to statistical power: for each predictor you add to a multiple regression equation, you need to find more participants in order to achieve satisfactory power (20 participants per predictor variable is a good rule of thumb). Also, it is potentially an analytical nightmare to have more than a couple of criterion variables, since you will need to find some way of presenting a whole series of regression equations. For undergraduate project work, it is probably best just to identify *one* criterion and stick with it.

COMMON CONFUSION

Terminology in regression designs

If you are conducting a study that is aiming to predict scores on a measure, you will have a predictor variable (or several) and a criterion variable (i.e. the variable that you are trying to predict). However, some statistical packages will ask you to identify your 'independent' variable and your 'dependent' variable when performing a regression. When this happens, you can think of your predictors as independent variables and your criterion variable as your dependent variable.

There are two basic formats for correlational research. The first is the *cross-sectional* study, which is sometimes referred to as a 'snapshot' approach because it captures your sample at a particular moment in time. The second is a *longitudinal* study, or sometimes a *panel* design, where the same sample is contacted at a later date and then re-tested. *Time* then becomes a key predictor variable in your study.

MAXIMISING MARKS

Pilot studies

Do I need to carry out a pilot study? The answer to this question very much depends on how confident you are in your study design and materials. The rule of thumb is that, the more original the study the greater the need to pilot. If you are doing a study in which all the materials have been used before in published research (e.g. a set of psychometric instruments), then a pilot is not really that necessary. If, on the other hand, you are creating a unique set of stimuli or a new scale, or are interviewing someone on a specific topic or observing a particular behaviour for which there are no standard checklists, you will need to incorporate a pilot phase into the first part of your study. Pilot studies can be used simply to fine tune: to see if questions make sense in an interview schedule, to see if participants can see the visual stimuli on the screen, etc. Or they can be more exploratory: to see if a particular topic generates stimulating interview data, to see if participants can actually perform the task that you want to use to measure your dependent variable (DV). In this latter case, you need to be prepared to scrap the whole idea and start again (as far as the materials are concerned, that is). On the other hand, you may find that the pilot goes swimmingly (if that is not too much of a mixed metaphor!) and that you can use all your pilot data in the final analysis. That is the risk you need to take. An original study without a pilot phase, appropriately reported (see Chapter 10), will probably lose marks. Above all, never say, in your Discussion, something such as 'the failure of the experiment to find significant differences resulted from participant boredom due to the length of the trials', if a good pilot study could have eradicated this potential confound.

Of course, whether you choose a cross-sectional or panel design depends on your research question – if you are examining changes over time (perhaps in response to some kind of intervention, such as an educational initiative or a treatment of some type) then a pretest-post-test design will be your absolute minimum, and you will need at least one follow up study at some later time point. However, few final year undergraduates have sufficient time to prepare such long-term studies and so, for practical reasons above all else, the cross-sectional study is by far the more common at this level.

4.3.2 Other multivariate designs

There is a vast array of multivariate statistical procedures now available to psychology researchers, and it may be that your supervisor has enough confidence in your ability to allow you to design a study that can be analysed by advanced techniques such as structural equation modelling or multidimensional scaling. Such designs are beyond the scope of this chapter, so we recommend that you seek out a specialist text such as Tabachnick and Fidell (2007).

However, you may wish to use correlational analyses to deal with the data collected by a humble questionnaire, where, rather than identifying discrete measures such as self-esteem or anxiety that have their own psychometric scales, you have simply asked a series of isolated questions on a particular topic. Typically, such questionnaires are used alongside more established psychometric measures, in order to collect demographic data, or to explore a particular behaviour that you would like to relate to psychological variables, such as alcohol consumption or media use.

In these situations the challenge is to create meaningful measures out of your individual items. Tips on how to do this well can be found in Chapter 8 (Section 8.4.2).

4.4 OBSERVATIONS

Observational studies fall neatly into two types: **non-participant** (or **remote**) and **participant**. We will begin by discussing the advantages and disadvantages of each in turn.

A *remote observation* is one where the researcher is physically removed from the location where the observed behaviour is taking place. Some research questions demand remote techniques, such as the observation of animals or infant humans, where the presence of the researcher cannot be explained to the observees, and where interference in the behaviour of the group would contaminate the study findings. Another reason for remote observation is the need for large numbers – for instance the study of shopping behaviour in a busy mall might be more efficiently undertaken without any direct contact with shoppers themselves.

Naturally, the limitations of such a study are obvious: you run the risk of collecting superficial data that tell you little about the private cognitions, cultural influences or social motivations that are driving the behaviour. Nevertheless, you are left with the feeling of having captured a 'slice of real life' as it happens in a natural environment.

Participant observation differs in that the observer actually becomes part of the natural environment, in either an *open* or *covert* fashion. Participation is said to be open when the observees are fully aware of the observer's status as a researcher; in a covert study, the observer takes care to conceal their identity, often by 'infiltrating' a group in order to gain an insider's perspective while not apparently interfering with the group's behaviour.

The disadvantages of participant observation appear obvious, particularly in the open type of design, while covert designs contain a multitude of ethical problems for both observers and observees. In practice, participant observations are not nearly as common in psychology as in other social sciences, particularly at postgraduate and postdoctoral levels, where they can be carried out over long periods up to a year or more and tend to be referred to as *ethnography*, but there are many research questions for which they might still be useful even within the short timeframe of an undergraduate project.

In addition to the participant/non-participant distinction, another way in which observation studies differ is in relation to the type of data collection. Methods for collecting data will be discussed in more detail in Chapter 8, but, in short, observations may be based around a schedule – where you decide in advance what behaviour you wish to observe and draw up a checklist to record it – or may take the form of a narrative, based on the observer's notes that they have collected during the course of the observation (usually referred to as *fieldnotes*).

To illustrate the distinction with reference to a psychological project, imagine that you wish to study the interaction between stand-up comedians and their audience. What determines whether a comic is successful or not? Is there a kind of pattern you can identify that is common to all comedy performances? A structured observation would necessitate drawing up a list of predictable behaviours for both audience and performers – laughter, applause, derision, catcalls and interruptions as audience responses, with person characteristics, types of material, timing of material, asides to the audience and so on, as performer behaviours.

A narrative might simply record the chronological sequence of events surrounding the arrival on stage of the performer and the audience reaction. It might even take a spatial form as you observe the patterns of reaction in different sectors of the audience. And in both types of design you would anticipate visiting several performances in different settings to try and generalise from one particular audience to another.

A final consideration for observation research is the use of electronic recording devices. It might seem rather old-fashioned to rely solely on fieldnotes and tick lists when you could use a video recorder to capture the behaviour you are coding or describing. However, these are more of interest for remote studies than for participant observation, where the experience of participation (actually 'being there') is all part of the study design.

4.5 DESIGNS BASED ON INTERVIEWS, FOCUS GROUPS AND OTHER INTERACTIONS

Perhaps the most common method of data collection is some form of *conversation*, often recorded on audio and transcribed for analysis. One way to do this is for the researcher to conduct a number of interviews with participants. These interviews might be structured, unstructured or semi-structured, conducted on a one-to-one basis, face-to-face or remotely, or they might involve more than two people at a time. Alternatively, you might organise one or more focus group discussions. It is worth considering the differences between these alternatives when designing your study. *How much structure do you want to impose on your interview?* Too much and you may elicit very short and superficial responses, or deny participants the opportunity to talk freely. Too little and you may end up with data that seem irrelevant to your study. *How might the data generated in a one-to-one interview differ from that produced in an interview where there are more than two people present? How might participants talk in a remote (and possibly anonymous) interview situation, as opposed to one where they meet the researcher in person? What makes a focus group distinctive? Why is it not simply a 'big interview'?* We discuss these issues in more detail in Chapter 8 but, before you attempt to collect any data, it is critical to consider these questions as part of your design.

Perhaps one of the primary questions, which will concern you when designing your study, is *how much data you need to collect*. This will be closely linked to questions about sample size, and you may need to decide this in order to finalise the protocol you submit for ethical approval. As with many things in qualitative research, there is no definitive answer to this question, and it very much depends on the exact nature of your study. However, a few years ago a team of qualitative psychologists in the UK put together a set of recommendations for sample sizes in qualitative projects. This was done to introduce some degree of parity across students and departments, and to address concerns that some students were collecting large quantities of data, and doing lots of analytical work, while others were obtaining similar credit for smaller datasets and much less analytical effort. We have reproduced a table, summarising the conclusions that a group of UK psychologists came to (see Table 4.3). As this is guidance rather than regulation, and as it is not universally accepted, you should discuss with your supervisor how much data you require for your particular study.

4.6 ANALYSING ARCHIVAL DATA

Much of the discussion above is based on the assumption that you will be collecting your own primary data for your study. Do not assume, though, that this is the only way to design a qualitative study. Psychological research, using some form of archival data, has become increasingly popular in recent years, partly because of increased interest in the influence of cultural material (particularly the media), but also because of the increased popularity of qualitative methods such as conversation and discourse analysis. With the arrival of the internet, in particular, there is now so much archival data available for study that it is frequently seen as an easy option for students looking for a short cut that does not involve hours of running experimental trials or handing out questionnaires. However, because this sort of research may be seen by some staff and students as a soft option, it is all the more important to design your study carefully. You will need to make a convincing case that analysing archival data has something more to offer than analysing data you have elicited from participants yourself. You should also check that your department permits archival data to be used for dissertation projects. In the UK, for example, some university departments interpret course accreditation criteria from the British Psychological Society as requiring students to collect their own primary data for dissertation research.

4.7 DESIGN DECISIONS RELATING TO THE ANALYSIS OF QUALITATIVE DATA

Qualitative researchers often have large quantities of talk or text as their data, and transform this detailed and complex material into a smaller number of more manageable 'analytical units'. These units might capture key concepts or processes identified within the data, for example themes, narratives, subject positions or discourses. You may well be keen to get hold of some data of your own, as soon as possible, in order to make a start on your analysis. Before you get to that stage, though, it is essential to consider the *design* of your qualitative study.

In order to obtain a good mark, it is very important that there is a sense of *coherence* between the broad approach you take in the introduction to your project report, the research questions or aims you set for your study, the type of data you collect and the technique you use to analyse the data. If, for example, you adopt a phenomenological approach in your introduction, and set out to 'explore the lived experience' of your participants, you need to make sure that you collect data that *captures* individuals' lived experience, and use an analytical technique in which experience is the *central focus*. To take another example, if you adopt a social constructionist approach, and set out to investigate how racism is constructed in the media, you need to collect data that capture media constructions, and analyse that data using discursive techniques.

TABLE 4.3 Recommended sample sizes for qualitative undergraduate projects.

Method of analysis	Inductive		Discursive				Structured		
	Interpretative phenomenological analysis	Grounded theory	Discourse analysis	Narrative analysis	Free association narrative	Conversation analysis	Repertory grids	Attributional analysis	Q methodology
Minimum amount of interview data	5 hours	5 hours	3–4 hours	3–4 hours	3–4 hours	1–2 hours	5 grids and elaborations	6–8 hours	5 sessions (sort task and interviews)
Demanding of supervisor		Yes	Yes	Yes	Yes	Yes	Yes	Yes	Yes
Strong theoretical background needed			Yes	Yes	Yes	Yes	Yes	Yes	Yes
Demanding of student time	Yes	Yes	Yes	Yes	Yes	Yes			Yes

Source: Madill *et al*, 2005, reproduced with permission from *The Psychologist*, © The British Psychological Society

MAXIMISING MARKS

Coherence of approach

A good project is one in which there is a *logical coherence* between the broad approach adopted, the research questions/aims, the design/data collection and data analysis. This means that your choice of design and data collection method should be logically compatible with the theoretical position you have established in your introduction. If you already have in mind a particular technique you plan to use to analyse the data, be sure to check that your design will *produce* appropriate data.

The field of qualitative research in psychology is extremely diverse. We are not going to attempt to explain every possible qualitative design, as that is beyond the scope of this book. What we will do is the following:

● Discuss the distinction between an inductive or 'data driven' design, which is typically exploratory, and a 'deductive' or more theory driven design, in which answers to specific questions (or hypotheses) are expected.

● Highlight what is distinctive about each broad approach, so that you can clarify which is the most appropriate for your study.

● Direct you to some further reading that will explain each approach in more depth.

4.7.1 'Hypothetico-deductive' versus inductive qualitative designs

One fundamental aspect of a qualitative design, is the extent to which your study is:

● driven by a set of questions, or predictions you already have in mind;

or

● exploratory/'open-minded', with you prepared to see what turns up in the data.

You will be familiar with quantitative designs in which the logical purpose of collecting and analysing data is to test one or more *hypotheses*. Typically, in this kind of 'hypothetico-deductive' study, the researcher reviews what is already known about the topic in hand, usually by examining the existing research literature. They then make a well-informed prediction about the relationship between variables. They will choose a design that measures the variables in question, and allows the hypothesis to be tested. This type of design is less common in qualitative research but is not unknown. One technique that is sometimes used for hypothesis testing in qualitative research is *deductive content analysis*.

4.7.2 Deductive content analysis designs

Content analyses may be carried out on any type of data that can be organised into meaningful categories, from visual material such as photographs to complex verbal data such as interviews or magazine articles.

If you have a hypothesis to test you will need to ensure that the data can be coded numerically. For example, you might wish to compare modern day children's literature with children's literature from a previous historical period to see if there is an increase in certain types of content (one possibility is that, for cultural and social reasons, the number of 'mental state' references, or inferences, has increased). In order to test your hypothesis, it would make sense to adopt a coding system to be used, before you begin to analyse the data. You might decide to pick out and count all instances in the data that refer to or infer a 'mental state'. So long as the coding category is well-defined at the outset, you should be able to count how many instances there are in your sample of historical literature, and how many in your modern day sample. By comparing the numbers in each sample you should be able to test your hypothesis and draw a conclusion.

The chief consideration, with this sort of study, is that your sampling technique is systematic and convincing. How do you go about sampling children's literature? What sort of texts would you include? How many texts would it be necessary to analyse? (Oh dear, an as-long-as-a-piece-of-string question so frequently asked by students, and so frequently disliked by supervisors!) Then you have to decide how plausible it is to match your texts in the two samples. At the most extreme you could aim to create a *matched pairs* design, where each modern text is matched to an old one. This is a more powerful design from a statistical analytic point of view, but would, in practice, be extremely difficult with this sort of data.

One advantage of this deductive/hypothesis driven approach, is that you can be fairly confident in advance that analysing the data will make it possible to test your predictions. The logic of the study is highly structured, and the scope for confusion in the analysis is minimised. Can you think of any disadvantages though?

You may well notice, in the course of coding the data, that there are interesting issues or processes within it, that do not fit into the coding categories you had prepared in advance. Perhaps, on reading samples of modern day and historical children's literature, you find that there is some very interesting material that is about models of cognition, but not quite about 'mental state' *per se*. You might feel that this material will add something to your analysis, but there is no place for it in the design that you had originally set out. You may end up feeling that using your preplanned coding scheme misses out on, or glosses over, what is really going on. Because of this concern, some researchers prefer to use a more *inductive* approach to content analysis, that is more sensitive to issues the researcher may not have known about in advance.

4.7.3 Inductive content analysis designs

Given the same set of systematically sampled qualitative data, an alternative approach to using predetermined coding categories is to *develop* categories in the course of reading the data. Let us take a specific example. One of the authors does research on the psychosocial impact of a particular health condition (polycystic ovary syndrome, PCOS). She was supervising a dissertation student whose study was a content analysis of messages posted by women with the condition on an online health discussion forum. The assumption was that the messages would reflect women's concerns about having the condition. Previous research done in hospital settings had measured the impact of different *symptoms*, such as infertility and weight gain, on women's quality of life. The original design for the student's study was going to be a deductive content analysis, counting how many of the messages on the discussion forum referred to each of the different symptoms of the condition, for example infertility or weight gain. This seemed an appealingly straightforward approach, well grounded in what was already known about PCOS. However, early on in the pilot stages of the study, it became apparent that many of the messages posted had little to do with symptoms as such. Many of the messages were to do with problems dealing with the healthcare system. Some women seemed bothered not so much by the symptoms of their medical condition but by the way their doctors spoke to them, or the difficulty they had in obtaining treatment. After discussing this in a supervisory meeting, the student and supervisor decided to develop a coding system that included both the symptom categories derived from a review of previous research, and new categories that were added *as needed*, as new concepts emerged in the data. The analysis took much longer than originally anticipated. Once the list of categories was completed, both student and supervisor had to recode the data, using the complete list of categories. The number of messages referring to each of the categories was counted, and a picture emerged of forum users' concerns. Because the student in question was genuinely interested in the data, and willing to be flexible in amending her design after some pilot work, the findings produced were both sensitive and original. Rather than repeating or replicating the findings of previous research, the study added something new, which ultimately merited presentation at a national conference (Percy & Murray, 2007).

If you allow your analysis to be driven by the data in this way, you are less likely to skim over interesting issues that you had not considered in advance. However, you should be aware that this type of inductive design may require a lot of thought on your part, and take longer to complete than a more structured or predetermined analysis. Ultimately, you and your supervisor need to discuss and agree which approach will be better for your particular study.

In both the inductive and deductive examples of content analysis referred to above, the researcher ultimately *quantifies* the data. The student comparing modern day and historical literature counts the numbers of mental state references in each, in order to see if modern day literature contains more. The student coding messages on a discussion forum may not be testing a hypothesis *per se*, but she is counting how many are about symptoms of the condition, and how many about problems using the healthcare system. She may then be able to infer which aspects of the condition are most troubling to the women using the forum. In both cases, data that are originally qualitative are transformed to produce *numbers* from which relationships can be inferred. This is a widely accepted approach to qualitative research, but can you think of any problems or limitations? It might be argued that some of the complexity and meaning within the data is lost when it is coded into categories and counted in this way. For that reason, many qualitative designs have been developed that keep the data in *non-numerical* or textual form throughout the analysis. We turn to these next.

4.8 PHENOMENOLOGICAL DESIGNS

Phenomenological researchers attempt to capture the nature of *experience*, with an emphasis on the unique perspective of the individual. They pay close attention to the personal experiences described by individual participants, and hope that their analysis will transform the implicit, particular and commonsensical material of 'raw data' into something more explicit, generalisable and psychological (Giorgi & Giorgi, 2003).

Phenomenological researchers are often seeking answers to questions such as 'What is it like to be ...?', or 'What does it mean to ...?'. By analysing data from one or more individuals, they hope to capture something of psychological *significance* about the experience in question.

As the phenomenological approach assumes that experience is best understood from the perspective of the individual, researchers typically use data 'straight from the horse's mouth'. If they want to understand what it is like to suffer a stroke, then a stroke survivor is the best person to ask, rather than, perhaps, their carer or another family member.

The type of data considered appropriate for phenomenological research is typically one or more first-person accounts of experience. Ideally this data would be produced spontaneously, and contemporaneous with the experience in question. Examples of this type of material might include personal diaries, letters, emails, telephone calls, conversations, weblogs, video or audio diaries recorded by the individual at the time they were having the experience in question. If you think about the example we used above, though, it will become apparent that projects using such 'ideal' phenomenological materials are quite rare. A researcher, wanting to use this type of data to explore the experience of a stroke, would need to locate and gain permission to use a personal account produced by someone who had suffered a stroke, perhaps at the time of the event or soon after. Producing data records of this type may not be the first priority of the individual concerned. In the case of stroke, they may not have the capacity to produce it. Even were such data to exist, a researcher would face huge challenges in locating it and gaining permission to use it for research.

In practice, phenomenological researchers often use data that are more readily accessible, and even material that has been produced specifically for the purposes of research. Participants might, for example, be asked to keep a diary or weblog for the purposes of research. They might be asked to take part in an unstructured or semi-structured interview. It is worth bearing in mind, though, that this type of data is less than ideal, as it may be subject to various forms of distortion. The participant may not be able to give an accurate account of their experience because time has passed and they have forgotten. Their account might also be shaped by the fact that it is being told to a researcher rather than produced for personal use. As with most aspects of qualitative research, there is considerable debate as to how critical these issues are. Some academic journals do not accept for publication projects that are ostensibly phenomenological but use data from semi-structured interviews. Others will happily publish such research. Your decision may be based on both theoretical and pragmatic grounds. If we return to our example of stroke survivor experience, it might be better for a researcher to do phenomenological research on interview material collected some time after the stroke event, than to leave the research question unaddressed altogether.

4.9 DESIGNS USING INTERPRETATIVE PHENOMENOLOGICAL ANALYSIS

Interpretative phenomenological analysis (IPA) is similar to phenomenological approaches, in that it emphasises the key role of personal experience. However, as its name suggests, it places additional emphasis on the role of the *researcher* in *interpreting* participants' experiences. The originators of IPA acknowledge that it is impossible to access another person's experience directly, and that data analysis inevitably draws on the researcher's subjectivity (Smith *et al.*, 1999). In common with phenomenological approaches in general, the analysis done in IPA often involves identifying the psychological significance of experiences, or psychological processes that may be represented in participants' accounts.

IPA studies typically address similar questions to phenomenological research in general, for example 'What is it like to be …?', or 'What does it mean to. …?'

If you are not sure how to chose between phenomenology and IPA when designing your study, you may find it helps to read a bit more about how the analysis is performed. In IPA the procedural steps you must follow tend to be more clearly defined than in phenomenology. You may prefer having an explicit set of instructions to fall back on when attempting data analysis. We say a bit more about this in Chapter 9, and you might want to read through the relevant section before making your decision.

COMMON CONFUSION ?

Language as description or *construction*

Both phenomenological and IPA approaches assume that people have *experiences,* and that they are, to some extent, able to report these to the researcher. Or, put another way, it is assumed that the data collected from interviews, web forums, diaries, etc., are more or less accurate descriptions of what the person has *really* experienced. In the case of IPA, researchers do make a point of acknowledging that the researcher has a role in interpreting participants' experience, but it still generally assumed that the participants' words describe the lived reality of their lives.

You may well be familiar, though, with an alternative approach to talk (and text), which argues that participants' words do not just describe reality, but actually shape or construct it. Researchers who adopt this alternative perspective, that of *social constructionism,* often use designs that incorporate *discursive* techniques.

It is very important that you are clear in your own assumptions about language. Is your design one that assumes participants' talk is an accurate description of experience?

4.10 DESIGNS USING DISCOURSE ANALYSIS

Discourse analysis (DA) is distinctive for its emphasis on the socially constructive nature of talk (Willig, 2003). Discourse analytic researchers' key assumption is that when people talk, they are not simply communicating or transmitting information, they are engaging in *social action.* Discourse analysts study talk (and text) because they believe that realities and identities are constructed, threatened and defended within it.

Discourse analytic research often asks a complex combination of questions such as: *'What is being said?', 'How is it being said?', 'What is being left unspoken?', 'Why might some things be said and others unmentioned?', 'Why might the speaker be using that vocabulary or turn of phrase and not others?',* and *'What is being achieved by the speaker saying that particular thing and in that way?'* All of these questions relate to the identities or versions of reality being constructed in a particular piece of talk or text, and the social or political implications of these. To take some more substantive examples, discourse analytic research might ask: 'How is racism perpetuated in discourse about asylum and immigration?' (Capdevila & Callaghan, 2008), or 'How do women who drink and fight account for their behaviour?' (Day, Gough & McFadden, 2003).

Discourse analysis can be conducted on any talk or text. This might include any of the first person accounts used in phenomenological research, but the potential pool of data sources is much wider. It might also include spontaneous conversation, interviews of any kind, focus group discussions and formal speeches. Any textual material can be subjected to discourse analysis, and this might include published materials such as books, magazines, newspapers, websites, transcripts of television programmes or information leaflets. Because discourse analysts often conduct very fine grained analysis, talk is typically transcribed with more paralinguistic detail (pause lengths, overlaps between speakers, etc.) than in other forms of qualitative research.

A student's experience . . .

" *I wanted to do my dissertation on the experiences of students studying away from home for the first time. I knew I wanted to do some interviews with first year psychology students, and I thought it would be easy to do my analysis, once I got through ethics, and I'd got the slow bit of transcription out of the way. We did discourse analysis for our second year mini-project, and I got quite a good mark for it. Our workshop tutor had given us really clear instructions and I felt it was much easier to do than the IPA report we did first on the module.*

My supervisor kept asking me why I thought discourse analysis was the most appropriate design for my study. I thought it was obvious: it's a qualitative method, so it's good for finding out about people's real experiences, and there was no point picking IPA as I'd done much better on my discourse report. She kept harping on about it though, saying she was worried I might not get a good mark for my report if the method didn't fit my 'theoretical assumptions'.

To be honest I was getting a bit fed up with her hassling me, and I did think about seeing if I could change my supervisor. She sent me away to read a chapter each on discourse analysis and IPA from a research methods textbook. I found them hard going, but I could actually see what she meant about discourse analysis. She said if I wanted to use DA, I'd need to write my introduction in a 'social constructionist' style, to set up the case for using discourse analysis. I never 'got' social constructionism when we did it in the second year – and there's no way I could write my whole introduction on it. The book chapter I read said that IPA is a way to really get at what people are telling you about their lives and their experiences. It also had some easy steps I could follow to do the analysis. My supervisor had to hold my hand a bit, but I got my analysis done and I got a good mark for my report. My supervisor said that if I'd tried to use discourse analysis without really understanding why I was doing it, I might have gotten quite a low mark. Strictly between you and me, I think she was probably right! [Andy, just graduated, looking for a job in market research.] 🙶

A supervisor's experience

🙸 *I was worried that Andy wanted to use discourse analysis for the wrong reasons. I don't think it was unreasonable to want to pick a method that you've had some success with in the past, but given that he'd only had one go at both IPA and discourse analysis, I didn't think this was sufficient basis to plump for DA. Everything Andy told me about his research questions and aims suggested that he was interested in exploring students' lived experience. If he'd said he wanted to examine how new students constructed their experiences, or the discourses they used to make sense of them, I might have encouraged him to use discourse analysis. When I asked him how a social constructionist approach would be useful in understanding his participants, he looked a bit shifty as if I'd asked him something really embarrassing. It can be hard to explain social constructionist ideas – especially when someone's put you on the spot – so I thought a bit of reading might help him to clarify. Once he had some reassurance that IPA is quite a structured method of analysis, he was more willing to give it a go. He did a really good job with his interview data, and his report held together in terms of the 'story' it told. I think he's pleased that he followed my advice, but you never know . . .* 🙶

4.11 NARRATIVE DESIGNS

Researchers who take a narrative approach to qualitative analysis give specific attention to the 'storied' nature of human experience. They argue that people use stories (narratives) to make sense of the world and their place in it (Murray, 2003). Their research typically collects and examines these stories, on the assumption that they can shed light on psychologically and socially significant phenomena. Stories are often structured in a particular sequence, for example beginning, middle and end. The way a participant uses this sequence, and the description they give of the transition from one stage to another may offer an insight into their experience or perspective on the world. Let us return to the example of the stroke survivor study we mentioned earlier. A narrative analysis of an interview with a stroke survivor might explore the shape they give to the experience of stroke. The story might be organised into several phases: life before stroke; life 'when it hit me'; recovery in hospital; and adjustment at home. Closer examination might reveal that the participant described themself in different ways at different times in their story. Moving from one phase to another might be characterised by a shift from 'carefree' to 'mindful', sometimes active, sometimes passive. A narrative analysis attempts to transform the specific details of the individual participant's case into an explicit account of the psychological significance of stroke. The types of questions asked in a narrative study might include: 'What is it like to ...?', or 'How do people experience ...?'. Published examples have addressed questions such as 'What is the experience like for parents of people who cannot speak?' (Hemsley, Balandin & Togher, 2007) and 'How do people combine "orthodox" and complementary therapies?' (Prussing, Sobo, Walker & Kurtin, 2005). In our specific example, a research question might be 'What is the illness journey like for a person experiencing a stroke?'

A wide range of data sources is used for narrative research. Some researchers design their data collection specifically to produce material with a narrative sequence. They might, for example, conduct semi-structured interviews which ask participants to describe their experience in chronological order. Other researchers look for narrative features in data from a wider range of sources. This may include any of the data sources already mentioned as being appropriate for phenomenological or discourse analytic research. The precise choice of data source will depend on both *pragmatic* factors (e.g. what data you can legitimately use for your project) and *theoretical* issues. The latter merit a bit more discussion:

MAXIMISING MARKS

Being clear about the theoretical significance of narrative features

- Some researchers would argue that stories are such a fundamental part of human consciousness, that participants will produce narratives *spontaneously* when describing their experiences. If this is the case, then one might expect to find narrative features in any participant's account of experiences or events. Alternatively, it might be that participants' stories take on the shape of a story, because an interviewer has specifically asked to talk in that format. It is worth being aware then that the method of data collection may *shape* the data collected. This is particularly the case for semi-structured and structured interview data.

- Narrative approaches can be used by researchers with subtly different *assumptions* about their data. If you adopt a phenomenological perspective, you might seek to analyse first person narratives, on the assumption that they tell us something significant about individual experience. Alternatively, if you adopt a more social constructionist approach, you might treat narratives not as a window into 'real lived experience', but as a linguistic form that participants use to construct particular versions of reality.

To maximise your mark, you need to think about these issues and be clear how they apply to *your* study.

4.12 DESIGNS USING CONVERSATION ANALYSIS

Researchers doing conversation analysis share discourse analysts' assumption that talk is a form of social action. Where they typically differ is in their specific interest in *conversation* (Drew, 2003). Conversation analysts regard conversation as a special form of discourse because it involves so much interaction. When two or more parties engage in conversation, however apparently mundane, they are engaging in a highly organised social practice, with rules that are more or less explicit. Conversation analysts argue that close study of the features of conversation, such as turn taking, adjacency pairs and so on, can shed light on significant social processes.

Conversation analysts' research may ask such questions as: 'What social process is occurring when women talk to their beautician?' (Toerien & Kitzinger, 2007), or 'How is racism maintained in everyday conversation?' (Stokoe & Edwards, 2007).

Because of its specific emphasis on *conversational interaction,* and the key role of fine details such as pauses, overlaps between speakers and so on, conversation analysis typically requires a very particular type of data. This should be a conversation, ideally transcribed verbatim, with a great deal of paralinguistic detail.

4.13 DESIGNS USING THEMATIC ANALYSIS

The appeal of thematic analysis to some researchers may be that it is quite flexible (Braun & Clarke, 2006). It can be used by researchers with a wide range of theoretical standpoints (or indeed those with *no* explicitly stated standpoint).

The focus of thematic analysis could be personal experience (as in phenomenological or IPA research) but it might equally be discursive. It may be very broad indeed to include not just personal experience, conversation and other forms of discourse, but also a whole range of conceptual processes or units, not all of them necessarily psychological. For this reason, thematic analysis has been popular in other disciplines, including, for example, nursing and sociology. Researchers using thematic analysis are often inductive in their orientation to data. As a consequence, they may not wish to prescribe in advance the type of phenomena on which the analysis will focus. Alternatively, they may be guided in their analysis by a particular theoretical orientation, or by some theory that is specific to the phenomenon under investigation.

The kinds of research questions that a thematic analysis might ask include a very broad inductive question such as 'What concepts best capture the phenomena being described in the data?', or a more specific, deductive or theory-led question such as 'What themes in the data relate to (say) social support?'

Because thematic analysis is so flexible, it can be used on a wide range of data. In psychology projects this might typically include any transcribed talk or text. The process by which themes are extracted from the data is also rarely prescriptive. Different researchers may employ different techniques to move from raw data to themes. In 'theory-led' thematic analysis, the researcher might specifically select those portions of a transcript that relate directly to the theoretical concept being studied, and code or label it accordingly. Researchers doing more inductive thematic analysis are likely to generate themes from the data themselves. We will discuss how you might do a thematic analysis in more detail in Chapter 9.

4.14 GROUNDED THEORY DESIGNS

Researchers who use grounded theory (GT) are often interested in developing a comprehensive description of a phenomenon, including the constituent parts, concepts and the relationships between them. They may also seek to develop a working model or 'middle range' theory that accounts for the phenomenon in question. In psychology research, this phenomenon might be a psychological process, but, as grounded theory was developed for use in the wider social sciences, the focus might be on something broader.

The distinctive feature of grounded theory research is its commitment to *inductive* analysis (Charmaz, 2003). Researchers attempt to suspend any preconceptions they may have about the subject under investigation, and to work from the data upwards. Strictly speaking, grounded theory research includes *cycles* of data collection and analysis. A researcher may collect some data, analyse it and then base their next episode of data collection on the outcome of the first analysis. This might mean changing the nature of the sample, or the questions asked in the interview, or perhaps conducting a focus group, or observation rather than an interview. There are some practical constraints in doing this for a psychology project, especially if you have a very limited time in which to complete your work. If you have been given ethical approval for a study with a specified sample and data collection technique, it may be difficult practically to go back and have a revised design approved once you have analysed your first set of data. Perhaps because of these difficulties, many projects that appear to use grounded theory actually only employ grounded theory procedures to *analyse* their data, once the whole dataset has been collected. This is considered legitimate in many published research papers but, if you decide to use grounded theory in your project, you will need to make clear whether you have used GT principles for both data collection and analysis, or data analysis alone.

COMMON CONFUSION   **?**

Grounded theory research versus grounded theory analytical techniques

Grounded theory was originally developed as a broad approach to research. It involved researchers in a *cycle of data collection and analysis*. Strictly speaking, a grounded theory *study* is one in which analysis of one set of data guides the collection of more.

It is possible to use the principles of grounded theory to analyse a *single body of data*, without going on to collect a further set. This is not strictly speaking a grounded theory study, but is a grounded theory *analysis*.

As grounded theory has such a broad, inductive focus, it can be applied to a huge range of data. This might include talk, text or observations, e.g. in the form of fieldnotes. There are differing opinions as to the exact process for moving from raw data to analytical outcomes. This typically involves assigning descriptive *codes* to conceptual chunks of data, and refining these descriptive labels. Researchers often look for relationships between descriptive codes and use them to develop a more abstract analytical framework. The precise means of doing this are described in a number of grounded theory methods texts. We do not have space to discuss them here, but two points are worth emphasising:

- *Grounded theory research is cyclical.*
  Even if you are not collecting your data in cycles, the process of doing the analysis is still expected to be cyclical. Each time you add to your analytical framework, you need to go back to the raw data and check that the framework and data fit well with each other.

- *There are two broad schools of thought in grounded theory research.*
  One of these is very prescriptive about exactly how the data should be processed. Researchers in this school tend to favour methodology texts that give a lot of detail on how data must be treated, and studies which follow these instructions very closely. The other school of thought is less concerned with prescribing the exact set of procedures to be followed. Researchers in this school tend to use those GT procedures that they feel are most appropriate to their particular dataset. They are more concerned with the inductive spirit of grounded theory than with the precise procedural details.

CHAPTER SUMMARY

- The most important thing to bear in mind, when designing a study, is that your data will enable you to answer your research question.

- If your study is an experiment, one of the most important considerations for design is whether your participants form separate groups (between-subjects), or whether you are comparing the same group's responses across different conditions (within-subjects or repeated measures), or whether it is a mixed design – in each case, the design will determine what statistical test you use.

- Are you more concerned with type 1 error (declaring statistical significance where none exists in reality) or type 2 error (failing to detect a genuine significant effect)? The latter can be avoided by using a power analysis to inform your sample size.

- Designs using qualitative data may quantify them for analysis, or leave them in qualitative format. Qualitative analysis may be *deductive* (i.e.) driven largely by theory or *inductive* (driven largely by the data).

- Qualitative designs vary according to the *assumptions* they make about the nature of talk and text. Approaches that treat talk as *description* of lived experience tend to require first person data for analysis. Approaches that treat data as *social construction* may be used on a wider range of material.

FURTHER READING

Smith, J. (Ed.) (2003). *Qualitative Psychology: A Practical Guide to Research Methods.* Thousand Oaks, CA: Sage.
This book is a good practical guide to a range of qualitative techniques, and is one that students tend to find accessible.

Tabachnik, B.T. & Fidell, L.S. (2007). *Using Multivariate Statistics: Fifth Edition.* Boston, MA: Pearson Education.
As mentioned in the chapter, this book is an excellent advanced text for tackling designs which involve multiple independent variables.

CHAPTER 5 PROJECT PLANNING AND MANAGEMENT

You may think that managing your research project is relatively straightforward, and it is just a matter of starting in good time and 'being organised'. Of course, in many ways this is perfectly true. However, there are good reasons why so many project students, despite early starts and their best intentions, find themselves in the middle of difficult situations, often because they have fallen behind schedule. Is this situation avoidable? Yes, but you will need a more detailed and considered approach to your planning, and you also need a sense of what kinds of things can and do go wrong, how to prevent them, and how to plan for them so that if they do occur you are able to recover from them without falling behind. This chapter will cover these issues, as well as introduce you to some principles of good project management. We will show you how to break your project down into its constituent tasks, and plan a timeline for your project that you can use to schedule the components of your project work and use your time to best effect.

BY THE END OF THIS CHAPTER YOU WILL:

- Know what stakeholders are and why you need to look at your research from their perspective at the planning stage.
- Be aware of the need for effective communication.
- Understand the need for planning your access to resources as well as people.
- Know what a Gantt chart is and how to prepare one.
- Know how to identify risks to the successful completion of your project at the planning stage, and have an idea of some typical ones.
- Consider how to disseminate your results to stakeholders.

5.1 OWNERSHIP AND STAKEHOLDERS

Your final year research project is your responsibility. You have to design, prepare, manage and report on every aspect of your project work. However, there are other people who have an interest in the conduct and outcomes of your project. These people are known in the project management literature as 'stakeholders':

> ... [people or organisations who are] actively involved in the project, or whose interests may be positively or negatively affected by execution or completion of the project (Project Management Body of Knowledge, cited in Burke & Barron, 2007: 39).

Stakeholders are therefore, by definition, a group of people who have the potential to impact on the successful completion of your project, if their involvement is not managed appropriately. So, according to the above definition, although you may not have thought about them in this way, the following people are stakeholders in your research:

- your supervisor;
- any organisation or person who controls access to the population from which you wish to sample (gatekeepers);
- any other students with whom you are working (if you are working as part of a team project);
- the module leader;
- your university;
- your participants;
- the ethics committee;
- any groups or individuals who share characteristics with your participants (for example, if you are working with people with reading difficulties, individuals with dyslexia, or societies who represent them, could be interested in the implications of your results for them);
- anyone who may be affected by the results of your research, if you are in a position to publish them (this may include other researchers in the area and other people who have related interests, such as families or certain professionals).

Stakeholders will vary in the extent to which they are supportive of your research. Although some stakeholders are only indirectly involved in what you are proposing to do, their influence is likely to be felt because their concerns will be recognised and passed on by other concerned parties, such as your supervisor or the ethics committee.

The extent to which good relationships with stakeholders, who are directly involved in your study, are established and maintained is something that you have responsibility for from the outset. Chapter 2 discusses how to establish a good working relationship with your supervisor and manage that relationship effectively, but you also need to manage all the other stakeholder relationships well. The key to good relationships is good communication.

5.1.1 Communication

It is very easy to assume that aspects of your project work do not require explicit communication (because they are obvious in some way or have 'nothing to do with them') or to take some relationships for granted (such as your relationship with your supervisor or an outside organisation to which you already have a connection). It is also very easy to come across as self-interested or arrogant in the way that you interact with others. Because of these concerns, it is important that you take time to see your research from other people's point of view and be respectful of any concerns or constraints they might have to take into account to protect their interests. This may seem like an obvious point, but it is very common to see students neglect this aspect of their project work in their attempt to work efficiently, especially when deadlines are looming.

A student's experience . . .

"I was collecting data in an organisation and I had received a written letter from the manager giving permission for me to come in on a specific day to distribute the questionnaires. I had believed that time would be made available for the employees to complete the questionnaires while I waited, as I was only available for about an hour that day. However, when I got there the head of department had no idea I was coming and was not best pleased. With hindsight I should have offered to go home and come back another day (or better still, thought to ring ahead to make sure it was still okay and that everyone knew I was coming). However, at the time I was quite cross that the head of department had not been told, and he seemed very hostile to the topic of my project when I let him read the briefing and look through the questionnaire. He made it clear that he was not going to allow his department to complete the questionnaire in company time and told me to leave the questionnaires on one side for people to do at the end of the day. I was not even allowed to introduce myself to the department. When I came back a few days later to collect them, only a few had been completed. One of the participants commented to me that they had been dissuaded from completing them because the head of department felt that it was a covert way of the company management getting information on their working practices and he was worried about how the data would be used. If I had realised that he might perceive the study in this way I would have definitely made a separate trip before the study started to brief him more fully about the context of the work and ensure that he understood that it was just for my use. There were even ways that I could have involved him so that he felt part of the project and could have used the overall results of my project to benefit his department and send a positive message to his manager."

Some good general rules are

- **Be deferential and respectful** in all your interactions with stakeholders, both face-to-face and in your written communication with them. If you approach stakeholders with an air of entitlement, or even if you are too casual in your attitude to them, you may well find that they will refuse to work with you.

- **Don't assume, ask.** Be very explicit about *exactly* what is involved and any special requirements that you may have. These may be resources, space, time or people. Do not rely on being able to turn up on the arranged day and stay for as long as you like, or assume that you will have access to a quiet place or a private room, if you have not requested this in advance.

- Explain to gatekeepers **what is in it for them** and give them the chance to discuss your project idea at the planning stage, so that they can have some input into how you plan to conduct your project.

- **Acknowledge and address any concerns** that they may have about your project or its potential findings.

- With respect to organisations, find out who you will be working with day-to-day and contact them to **make sure they know what you are doing and when you will be working with them.** You may think that if you have been talking to someone's colleague or line manager that the message about your project will be passed on, but it is very common to discover that this has not happened. Be proactive and ask to be provided with names and contact details for the people you will be working most closely with.

- **Remember that you are an inconvenience** (in the nicest possible way). You are not doing them a favour by conducting your project, you are creating more work for them.
- **Visit any relevant locations** that you plan to work in, so that you know how appropriate the environment will be and have a sense of how you will be received.
- **Get to know the admin staff** that you will be in frequent contact with. Be aware that, in reality, these are the people who will be able to exercise the most control over your project!
- **Always be ultra polite and grateful** for their time, no matter the circumstances and how badly you might think you are being treated by them.
- **Apply the above rules to** *all* **stakeholders,** not just outside organisations. Remember that participants, in particular, are entitled to be treated with respect, and people who represent your target population may well have some useful feedback on the design and nature of your project.

5.1.2 A special word about schools, clubs and similar organisations

Because schools, clubs, special units and many other organisations follow a structured weekly routine of lessons that are essential to your participants achieving their own personal goals or having their particular needs addressed, you need to be very respectful of the organisation's daily timetable and aware of any sessions that are essential for your participants to attend in full. If this means that you have to wait in the foyer or cafeteria for an hour until they are ready for you, then so be it. Always take some work with you to do in case you are kept waiting, as it is highly likely that this will occur. Similarly, do not assume that you will be allowed to join staff in the staffroom at break times – this can and does vary from place to place and you should always ask if it is okay. But the bottom line is that many organisations are very sensitive to 'psychologists' coming into their environment, and they may well believe that you have the ability to assess how well (or how badly) they are functioning as professionals. It is down to you to make extra efforts to ensure that the organisation fully understands what you are doing and, importantly, that they buy into the idea and do not feel anxious about it.

5.1.3 Assessing availability

Students frequently get frustrated by difficulties getting appointments with their supervisor, or why they cannot get to speak to a gatekeeper, or cannot understand why no one is signing up to participate in their study. Often this is because they had not been proactive in assessing the availability of these stakeholders at the planning stage of the project. Some questions to consider at an early stage are:

- How many other project students does your supervisor have responsibility for? For example, they may also have Masters and Doctoral students who have deadlines at other times of the year.
- Are there particular days and times during the week (and during the year) when your supervisor cannot attend university for meetings?
- If you plan to recruit undergraduates, look at their weekly timetable on the notice boards to know when they are likely to be free to participate. There is no benefit to advertising your availability for research at a time when they are in compulsory lectures or workshops.

- If your university teaches in the evenings, think about offering part-time evening students the chance to take part by running an evening session on a day when they have to come in for a lecture, but before or after that class is scheduled to start.

- If you plan to recruit from an outside organisation, ask when would be the most convenient time for you to come along to recruit participants. Find out if there are any times when you would definitely not be welcome. Take the time to think about the scheduling of your study from the organisation's point of view in terms of time of day, week and year. Not all organisations are open all year around. Do your research and find out what their schedule is, and design your study around that.

✳ TOP TIP   Don't forget that you have other commitments too!

The focus of this book is clearly your dissertation work, but when you are planning your project it is important to remember that you will have other pieces of coursework to prepare for and complete, family and/or work commitments, and other demands on your time that you will need to build into your project plan and take into account when you are deciding when and where you can collect data or analyse it. You cannot use problems in your dissertation work as an excuse for an extension on your other coursework or *vice versa*. So do not just plan your project activities, plan them alongside all of your other final year commitments as well.

5.2 RESOURCES

Another important, but neglected aspect of project management centres on the management of resources that you will need for your project, where to get them from and how to go about obtaining them. Students sometimes assume that everything that they will need for their project will be readily available from either the internet or their department. Alternatively, you may assume that you will need to obtain all the resources for your project for yourself, when your department may be able to support you with some or all of the things that you need. It is worth checking what is routinely available from your department and what restrictions, if any, are in place. For example, some types of equipment may need to be booked and you may not be able to take them off campus. Some resources may be very popular, so booking them as soon as possible is advisable. A chat with your supervisor and/or your departmental technician should help you get a sense of these issues. Careful thought at the planning stage should mean that you are first in the queue, rather than realising at the eleventh hour that you have taken something for granted.

So what kinds of resource do we mean? Following are some examples:

- rooms (for private testing);
- laptop computers (for running simple experiments);
- access to networked computers (for using internet-based resources during testing);
- copies of copyrighted personality tests or questionnaires;
- specific technical apparatus (e.g. blood pressure monitors, etc.);
- extension leads (electrical cables are never quite long enough!);
- databases of stimuli (e.g. faces, images, word lists, etc.);

- technician time (for producing programmes or equipment for you);
- essential oils, caffeine, etc.;
- video recorders;
- audio recorders;
- microphones;
- transcription equipment;
- headphones.

At this stage, think about the kinds of resource that you will need for your project, and where you think you will be able to get them from. You can tick off the things that you may already own or have ready access to. For more specialist resources, find out how to access them as early as possible in your project and, if you can reserve them for a particular set of dates, do so as soon as you know when you will need them.

5.3 PLANNING YOUR PROJECT SCHEDULE: GANTT CHARTS

A Gantt chart (named after its inventor, Henry Gantt) is a way of visually representing every task and phase of project work, and scheduling them so that you can see when you might usefully be doing two things at once, when one set of activities is dependent upon the successful completion of another, and also when you can build in contingency periods, in case something goes wrong. An example of one is shown in Figure 5.1.

You may have seen similar charts before but, as you can see, in a Gantt chart all the tasks to be done as part of the project are listed on the left, and the timeline for the project runs from left to right across the top of the page. You simply block out the time that you think you will need to complete each task, thinking about what jobs need to be completed first, and what ones have to be

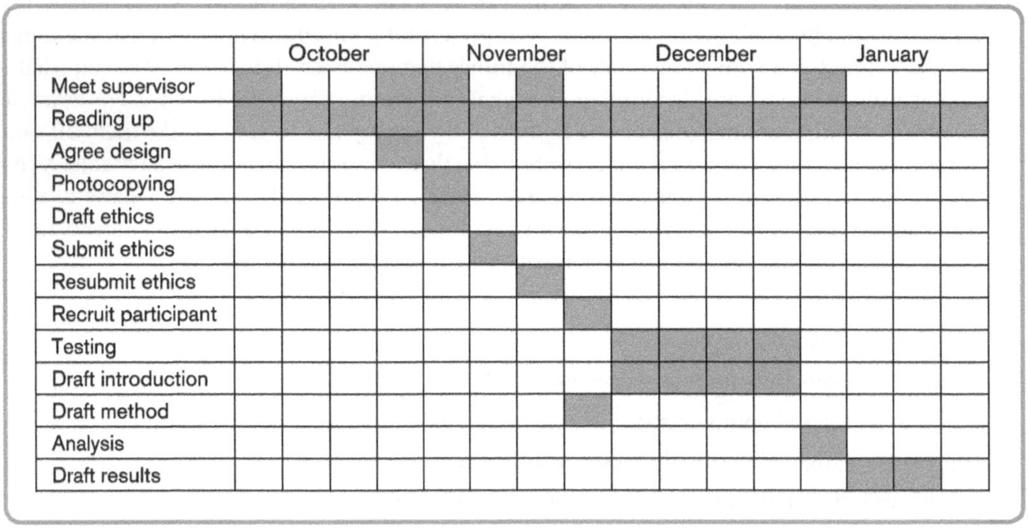

FIGURE 5.1 An example of a Gantt chart.

completed afterwards (and are therefore dependent on the successful completion of key tasks). You should use your past experience of each activity to judge how long you will need for each one (it is a very personal thing). If you are unsure about some aspect of a task, you should take advice from your supervisor. If your project is dependent on a key activity, such as getting access to a particular type of participant, you should also have a contingency plan that details what you will do if for some reason you cannot get access. This should be built into the timeline of your project so that you have time to spare if all goes well.

The key to a really successful Gantt chart is the level of detail that you put into your task list – this needs to be as exhaustive as possible and include every little job that is going to take you some time to complete. Some examples are given below, but you may well be able to think of others that relate to your own project.

- conducting your literature search;
- planning your literature review;
- designing your study;
- discussing the proposed design with supervisor;
- writing your ethics application;
- submitting your ethics application;
- waiting for ethical approval;
- making amendments to study/paperwork;
- resubmitting your ethics application (if necessary);
- contacting gatekeepers;
- waiting for gatekeepers to get in touch;
- purchasing stationery;
- photocopying questionnaires;
- accessing testing equipment/materials from technical staff;
- producing a computer program (for Superlab, etc.);
- producing your own stimuli;
- pilot testing;
- revising materials following a pilot;
- organising paperwork for participants into 'packs';
- constructing equipment;
- recruiting participants;
- collecting data;
- transcribing data;
- scoring questionnaires/tests;
- inputting data into SPSS;
- conducting data analysis;
- writing up specific sections of the report;
- giving a draft to someone to read;

- typing up and labelling appendices;
- redrafting the report;
- getting the thesis typed and bound.

Thinking about your project this way should enable you to see what jobs could be completed very early on, what jobs will continue throughout the project, and what jobs are critical for the success of the project. Do not forget also to schedule in any final year assignments, as these will also impact on your project work (as will any personal events that will take you away from your dissertation work, such as holidays, birthdays, etc.).

Each activity will have a planned **start date** (the earliest point at which that activity may begin) and a planned **completion date** (the date by which you must have finished that activity) and, of course, an anticipated **duration** for the activity itself. Once you have generated a list of all your activities for your project (and other competing pressures on your time) you should write beside each activity the start date, end date and duration. If there are any tasks that cannot start until another one has finished, you should note this too. Once you have this information, you can start to draw your Gantt chart. You can do this on graph paper or on a spreadsheet (such as Excel), or you could use a piece of project management software that will generate a Gantt chart for you (there are some simple ones available to use at no cost, as trial versions via the internet, as you will see in Chapter 6, as well as programs such as Microsoft Project). You will see that, at this stage, there should be some flexibility about exactly when certain short tasks are scheduled (e.g. you may only need one day to draft your gatekeeper letters, but you could have a two week period within which it needs to be done). Where there is flexibility like this, you should schedule tasks as early as possible, so that you have time in hand in case something goes wrong (see Section 5.4).

Activity	Earliest Start Date	Deadline	Duration
Photocopy Questionnaires	After Ethics Cleared	10th November	One Hour
Draft Gatekeeper Letter	1st October	1st November	One Day
Prep. Ethics Application	1st October	1st November	One Week
Buy Stamps	1st October	10th November	One Hour
Draft Literature Review	1st October	1st January	Three Months

In terms of the overall timeframe, for a quantitative project that starts in October and ends the following March we would normally advise you to ensure that you have finished collecting all your data no later than the end of January, but to aim to have it finished before the end of December if at all possible (this will give you a month of contingency time to allow for poor recruitment, technical glitches and other practical difficulties). If you are conducting a standard qualitative study, it is advisable that you finish your data collection even sooner (and no later than the end of December) to give you enough time for transcription and a full and thoughtful analysis (remember that the analysis phase for a qualitative project is likely to be much longer than for a quantitative project). If you are running a mixed methods or grounded theory project, you may need to think carefully about the timing of your data collection and analysis points, as these points are characterised by more than one data collection period. The bottom line is that you should allow yourself at least four to six weeks of time to draft and revise your final project. Remember that your write up will form the bulk of what is going to be assessed.

5.4 RISKS

Once you have an initial draft of your Gantt chart, look at the activities there and think about what could possibly go wrong in a way that could cost you time. Here are some typical examples:

- not passing ethics first time;
- the photocopier breaking down;
- your supervisor being ill;
- you being ill (this is almost guaranteed at some point in the year);
- recruitment of participants being slow, or problematic.
- there being a problem with the materials that you produced that you have failed to spot until after you started (or even finished) data collection;
- a gatekeeper refusing permission for your study to take place in their organisation;
- running out of ink for your printer;
- your computer crashing or leaving your data key in the library.

You need to think about how you can try to prevent these problems occurring in the first place, as well as have a plan in place for what you will do about these problems should they occur. Crucially, you need to think about how long each one of these difficulties could delay your project for, and try to build in contingency time so that your project is not thrown off schedule by a few small issues. No project goes smoothly but, if you have planned your time effectively and allowed for some mistakes and delays, you will still achieve a successful outcome.

A student's experience . . .

> ❝ I was planning to collect data from children via a school that a member of my family was working at. They had verbally agreed to take part, but at the last minute they had to pull out because of the results of an inspection visit that happened a few weeks before I was due to come in. I had allowed for something to go wrong with the data collection phase, so I had about two weeks in hand to find an alternative school. The original school was kind enough to put me in touch with another school in the area. The headteacher was very supportive, but the school governors decided that they did not want the children's time being taken up with a student project, and so that also fell through. I then realised that the school had an after-school club, and I asked if it would be acceptable to run the study there. They were very happy with this arrangement and I was quickly able to get the project back on track. ❞

5.5 MONITORING AND MAINTAINING PROGRESS

Another much neglected area in project management is the monitoring of progress towards your key milestones in the project (such as clearing ethics, finishing data collection, finishing analysis, completing the first draft of the report). Once your final year has started to get into full swing it is easy for the dissertation to slip down your list of priorities, simply because, in terms of final deadlines, it will be one of the last pieces of work that you will complete. This is why it is important that you set yourself intermediate deadlines for key tasks.

It is also important that you are disciplined with your time. In your final year you will have 'free time' in your timetable which recognises that your dissertation is going to be self-managed. This usually results in a couple of half days or a full day that is free from lessons. You should set this time aside and explicitly timetable your free day as a day when you will be exclusively working on your dissertation activities, to ensure that you have the time to progress things each week. Do not be tempted to let work for other assignments drift into your 'dissertation day'.

✳ TOP TIP   Keeping your eye on the ball

Put your Gantt chart on the wall by your desk, as well as in the front of your project note-book. Refer to it regularly to make sure that you are on track. Never schedule work over a weekend. You should be able to complete your work during the working week. The advantage of keeping weekends clear is that, if something does go wrong, you can always use your weekends as contingency time to help you get back on track quickly.

During the project make sure that your progress is not starting to slow in any area. A key area to monitor is recruitment. It is very easy to become complacent about recruitment and assume that slow recruitment will 'pick up' by itself without having to do anything extra. If, after the first few days, recruitment is slow, consider different ways of promoting your project (within the bounds of ethics, of course). Look at how you have advertised it and what other ways are available to you (always leave scope for a range of recruitment methods when you are completing this part of your ethics form – see Chapter 7). Remember not to apply pressure to potential participants to take part, but do raise awareness of the project by chatting to students and asking participants to mention the project to their friends. Often the major issue is the scheduling of the data collection itself. Consider changing or adding timeslots to make yourself more available. If you are running a questionnaire study, consider using an e-questionnaire that can be completed both anonymously and remotely, at the participant's convenience (see Chapter 8). The key thing is not to ignore poor recruitment – seek advice from your supervisor and see what you can do to improve it.

5.6 PLANNING A LOCAL DISSEMINATION STRATEGY

It is worth considering early on how you will feed back to your stakeholders the outcomes of your project. Clearly, your supervisor and university will have access to your final project report, so we are talking more about your participants and external organisations. You will give participants a general debriefing (see Chapter 7) straight after the study, but this will not indicate what the overall results of the project are. If you have been working with external organisations, consider putting your findings together in a 'corporate' way, and offer to present your work orally to a small group, or produce a folder or smart looking document that summarises the key outcomes and features of the project. Organisations often like to have something to show to visitors, so consider producing a folder that presents your project in an accessible way and celebrates the contribution of the organisation to the project.

CHAPTER SUMMARY

- Stakeholders are people who have an interest in the conduct or outcomes of your research project. You should, as good practice, involve them as much as possible at the planning stage and be very respectful of their perspective on your work.
- You should assess the availability of people that you plan to work with during your project at an early stage to minimise difficulties in obtaining access to participants.
- You should remember to incorporate other demands on your time into any project planning.
- A Gantt chart is a useful way of summarising the tasks that you have to do during your project, and planning when to do them and how to schedule your time for maximum efficiency.
- Consider the risks that your project is vulnerable to at the planning stage, and allow contingency time to deal with each one if they do occur.
- Remember to monitor your progress on the project regularly.
- Plan a dissemination strategy to feed back to participants or key stakeholders in a way that is appropriate to them.

CHAPTER 6
ONLINE
RESOURCES

This chapter will encourage you to think about the different ways in which information, software and other resources that can be found on the internet can be used to support many aspects of your project work. We will begin by recapping some key points raised in the earlier chapters of the book to do with using the internet to help you to locate relevant material for your literature review and rationale. We will then move on to discuss the ways in which you can use the internet to help you to recruit participants, manage your project, produce experimental tasks, administer surveys, conduct interviews, edit audio and video content, analyse your data and help you to produce the final written draft.

BY THE END OF THIS CHAPTER YOU WILL:

- Understand how internet resources can support your project work.
- Understand what is meant by 'open source' resources.
- Be familiar with a range of open source materials.
- Know how to use social networking sites appropriately in the context of project work.

6.1 INTRODUCTION

Although most of us use and even rely on the internet and its associated resources as part of our daily academic work, you may not have thought about the many ways in which it can be used to improve the practical aspects of designing, conducting and writing up your project work. It is worth exploring all the resources that are available at no real cost. The examples we will discuss here in this chapter are intended to illustrate the different ways in which your work can be supported, and they are current at the time of going to press, but it is important to note that technology develops so rapidly that these may already be in the process of being superseded by newer, better alternatives.

6.2 THE LITERATURE REVIEW

We have already mentioned use of online resources in detail in relation to conducting your literature search (see Chapter 3). As discussed, the obvious way to start your literature search is by using online databases such as PsycINFO or Web of Science, which your institutional library will subscribe to. However, the emphasis in this chapter is on free resources that do not require a subscription to use. To this end **Google Scholar** is an excellent way of locating relevant scholarly articles: you can search by topic or for the work by a particular author, and you can limit your search by a date range too. It is worth noting, however, that you may not be able to view the full text version of the papers or sources to which it directs you, if your institution does not subscribe to that journal. This raises the practical question of how to access that content. The solution to this problem is actually very simple. Many of the academic papers that you are interested in are likely to have been published by an academic who is still active. You can try googling for the first or corresponding author on the paper. Be aware that the author may have changed their university affiliation since writing the paper you are interested in. Look at that person's personal webpage, as sometimes they will have links to downloadable versions of their papers on their websites. If not, then you can try sending a polite and friendly email to them, to ask if they could send you a copy of their paper. Most academics are flattered by interest in their research and are happy to email you a PDF of their paper, or pop a paper copy in the post to you.

COMMON PITFALL !

We are going to reiterate here the same point that we made in Chapter 3: that you need to be selective about what sort of content you plan to use as an authoritative source, if you plan to search using a general search engine rather than something like Google Scholar, which will direct you to academic content. Look at the URL of the page that you are on. Web addresses that use university domain names (e.g. ending in 'ac.uk', or '.edu') or are familiar authoritative sources (e.g. .'gov.uk', bbc.co.uk) are likely to be trustworthy. However, pages of companies or other interested parties may not be presenting a balanced account of the topic you are interested in, and so you need to make sure you treat these sources with caution, and/or conduct a balanced search for the alternative perspective.

6.3 RECRUITMENT AND PROJECT MANAGEMENT

Recruiting participants is a significant challenge and one that can put your project at risk, so it is worth taking advantage of online resources that can enable you to maximise recruitment to your study and minimise the associated difficulties. Many psychology departments subscribe to online recruitment systems such as **Sona**, which enable you to enter details of your study onto an internal website, which can only be viewed by individuals who are part of a departmental or university-wide research participation scheme. However, not all departments use these and, even if they do, they do not offer a guaranteed method of recruitment. In fact, one of the issues around their use is that students often assume that use of online recruitment software will result in guaranteed recruitment, whereas in reality students are quite choosy about which studies they want to take part in and what time of year they want to participate. Moreover, if you are seeking to recruit from a specific population, it is likely that you will want to recruit participants from outside the university setting as well.

6.3.1 Discussion forums

Online discussion forums, especially those run by, or for, special interest groups such as charities and support groups, offer the opportunity for advertising your study to potential research participants. However, recruitment from such sites needs careful thought and management. To start with, you will need to discuss with your supervisor the wording of any potential posting for the site, and you would need this method of recruitment to be approved by your ethics committee and by the individual who monitors or maintains the webpage. Potential participants may react with hostility if you post a poorly worded or thought through request for support, as they (rightly) see the forums as a safe space in which to discuss their situation with other individuals who share their experiences. Your posting may violate a sense of privacy that has been cultivated within the forum, and so it is important that you are sensitive to such concerns and have the support of the forum manager.

6.3.2 Social networking sites

Another popular way to advertise research and recruit participants is to use social networking sites (SNS) such as Facebook and Twitter. These sites differ from the web-based discussion forums mentioned above, as advertising your study through a posting on your own webpage or by a tweet to your followers will result in 'viral' advertising of your study (the online equivalent of snowball sampling), as your friends re-post or re-tweet your request or link to your study. You need to bear in mind a couple of things here. Firstly, you need to make sure that you have ethical clearance to advertise your study via SNS as, depending on the topic area of your study, there may be some ethical issues raised by this method. Secondly, you need to be comfortable with the idea of your research being advertised by this, somewhat uncontrolled, method, bearing in mind that you will not have control over who will see the details of your study. In many cases this will not be a cause for concern, as a viral approach works well for the distribution of links to online questionnaires, for example, and will result in a broader sample. However, as with a forum posting, details of your study may be seen by individuals who have strong personal views about the topic you are investigating and so you will need to take extra care over the explanation of the background to what you are doing and the reasons why you are conducting your study. Individuals who are several steps removed from you and who have received the link to your study in a viral way may also be suspicious of your 'real' motives for the study, or may even view it as part of a scam or covert attempt at promoting a particular set of ideas. It is also possible that you will receive some unsolicited negative comments that are either directed at your study, or even you personally, because of the anonymity that Twitter, in particular, affords its users.

A supervisor's experience

❝ One of my students designed an online questionnaire on attitudes to capital punishment and distributed it widely using a viral approach to recruitment, as he was interested in comparing the views of people from different backgrounds and cultures as part of the study. We were quite cautious about how we did this: rather than use social networking sites, we distributed the questionnaires via email contacts and then asked them to pass the link on to friends and colleagues. One respondent contacted me as the supervisor to clarify the student's motivation behind the research, as he was concerned about what would 'actually' happen to the data: in other words, who would receive copies of the student's report. I think it is certainly the case that there is more suspicion about completing online forms, and participants are more likely to generate a conspiracy theory about your research if the data are collected in this way than if they were completing paper questionnaires in a context where they can meet and speak to you. ❞

6.3.3 Project management tools

Aside from recruitment issues, the next biggest threat to the success of your project is your own time and project management skills. Once again, the internet can help you here, as there are project management tools on the internet that you can download free of charge. These enable you to think through all the different aspects of your project work, when they need to be started and completed by, and how long they will take. The tools will then organise this information into a Gantt chart (see Chapter 5) for you, which shows critical dates and demonstrates very clearly just how long your project will take you to complete and how much 'slippage' you can tolerate. Some of these packages are free trials of commercial software, but there are also 'open source' tools that are designed to be free to use and freely available, such as 'ganttproject' (http://www.ganttproject.biz/). Open source software refers to programmes that are freely accessible, and users are able to (and encouraged to) modify and adapt the software so that it suits their needs if they wish to (the source code is freely available to users to enable them to do this, unlike commercial programmes). So, if you are trying to locate free resources, you can search for 'open source' as well as 'free' resources to find what you need.

6.4 EXPERIMENTAL WORK

Project management tools are not the only open source programmes available. You may be surprised to discover that you can even download fully functional psychology experiment software as part of open source projects. A good example of this is FLX Lab (http://sourceforge.net/projects/flxlab/). If you are a little more technically minded, you could also use PEBL, which is a 'Psychology Experiment Building Language' (http://pebl.sourceforge.net/). In both cases you will need to spend some time to familiarise yourself with the software and how to interpret the data that it produces, just as you would with the commercially available software packages, but these do enable you to run your own experimental projects if your psychology department either does not have a licence for the standard commercial packages such as Superlab, or does not have enough licences.

6.4.1 Locating stimuli

Once you have your programming software installed and are familiar with how to use it, you may also need some stimuli. Again, the internet comes into play here. One of the things that students often do (and we wish that they did not) is that they locate material from the internet without checking whether they are allowed to use it (because of copyright restrictions, for example). So they will use Google Images to find pictures that will act as stimuli, without realising that many of the images they are using are actually subject to copyright. For this reason, you should search for 'free images' or 'free image bank' to locate suitable resources of this nature, such as Free Digital Photos.net (http://www.freedigitalphotos.net/). Always take care to read the terms of use on such sites before downloading, to be on the safe side. Similarly, there are either downloadable or searchable word lists that you can use in the context of your project work, such as the British National Corpus (BNC) (http://www.natcorp.ox.ac.uk/) or the Children's Printed Word Database (http://www.essex.ac.uk/psychology/cpwd/).

6.4.2 Audio, video and image editing software

Something else that you may need to use in the context of your experimental project work is software for editing audio files, images or digital video recordings that you have made. There are many free software packages for editing images that are easily located and which have good functionality, such as **paint.net** (http://www.getpaint.net/). Similarly, audio editing software is also freely available, and it is possible that you already have something like **Audacity** (http://audacity.sourceforge.net/) or **Goldwave** (http://www.goldwave.com/) on your computer. These tools enable you to manipulate and edit sound files in a very easy to use way and are either free or have a free trial period. If you need to do something more specialist to do with examining specific aspects of speech recordings, then **Praat** (Dutch for 'talk') is probably the best free tool to use (http://www.fon.hum.uva.nl/praat/). For editing video, many new computers come with some sort of free video editing software installed, so it is worth checking your machine for any free software like this that you may already have (also note that many digital video recorders come with free editing software, and so it is worth asking the owner of the camera about this). If you do need video editing software, then something like **Wax** will enable some editing and special effects to be applied to your footage (http://www.debugmode.com/wax/).

> ## ✳ TOP TIP   Apps
>
> If you have a smart phone or similar device we would encourage you to conduct a thorough search of free or low cost 'apps', which you can install onto your device to increase its functions or potential uses. For example, they may include stopwatches, decibel meters and other tools, which you may otherwise need to borrow, hire or purchase.

6.5 SURVEYS AND INTERVIEWS

One of the most popular methods of data collection is to collect self-report data from either a large number of people via a survey or from a small number of detailed interviews. Online survey tools are an excellent way of collecting a large amount of data with limited effort, and commercial tools such as **Survey Monkey** and **Survey Share** are widely used by researchers, so it is worth checking to see if you can access an account via your department. However, there are also free online survey tools, such as **kwik survey** (http://www.kwiksurveys.com/). Make sure that you read the terms and conditions and frequently asked questions in relation to the tool that you are considering down-loading, as some have quite a lot of restrictions in terms of numbers of questions you can use and how long you can use it for.

Some types of psychometric test are also increasingly found online, and there are too many to really mention here, but it is worth looking for collections of such resources, such as the **International Personality Item Pool** (IPIP; http://ipip.ori.org/). When looking for psychometric tests, please be aware that there are an increasing number of websites, such as 'All the Tests.com', where many tests are of the 'just for fun' kind (such as 'What animal are you?' and 'How fluffy is your pillow?'). Sometimes they can look a lot like 'real' psychometric tests, however, and so you need to remember that a genuine psychometrics website will include things like normative data and administration instructions, as well as scoring details.

You may feel that interviews are the one type of data collection method that cannot be enhanced through the use of free internet resources, but you may be surprised. Rather than conducting interviews face-to-face, you could consider conducting your interviews via **Skype** (http://www.skype.com/), which is free to download, and free to make calls on as long as you are calling Skype-to-Skype (rather than Skype to phone). This could have a number of advantages:

- It enables you to interview people regardless of their geographical location, as long as you both have access to the internet and (and an alarm clock if you are calling across international time zones!)

- You can discuss whether you want to use a webcam (to help to build rapport) or keep it turned off and treat it as a telephone interview, to enable anonymity and frankness. (However, you will both need to find a time and place when you can talk undisturbed.)

- You can record the Skype conversation for later transcription using free call recording software produced by Skype (http://voipcallrecording.com/), which means you do not need a separate audio recorder.

6.6 DATA ANALYSIS

Most of you will have access to quantitative data analysis tools, such as SPSS, via your university. However, there are a number of sites where you can find SPSS tutorials and support, as well as general sites to support your understanding of statistical concepts and selection of the appropriate statistical tests. It is always worth remembering that such resources should be used in conjunction with support from your project supervisor, rather than instead of it, as your supervisor knows what you are seeking to achieve with your analysis.

If you are conducting qualitative data analysis, you may be interested in looking at free data analysis tools too. For example, Weft QDA (http://www.pressure.to/qda/), and the QDAP Coding Analysis Toolkit (http://www.qdap.pitt.edu/cat.htm), are designed to assist with the coding and analysis of textual data. As with any software, it is worth viewing the overviews and tutorials to see if this is something that you can work with. Not all qualitative researchers like to use software to assist with data analysis, as many like to do this process themselves by hand.

6.7 DATA STORAGE, BACKUP AND SHARING

During the course of your project, you are going to end up with quite a lot of files: drafts of your report, your ethics documentation, your data files or transcripts, any programme or stimuli, and very soon you will have a substantial amount of very precious information. Most students keep these files on their personal computer, and use USB drives to back them up. However, laptops are easily damaged (especially after several years at University), or are stolen, and USB drives are often accidentally left in university machines, or are tucked into a pocket or purse and then forgotten about. Worse still, cheap USB pen drives are easily damaged and can literally fall to pieces.

An alternative method for backing up your data is to save them to a remote 'cloud' server using a service such as **Dropbox** (http://www.dropbox.com/). The advantage of using such systems include:

- being able to access the files from any computer with an internet connection;
- having plenty of space for storage;
- being less likely to lose access to the files than if they were on a USB stick;
- enabling you to share selected folders with other people, such as your dissertation tutor.

6.8 WRITING UP

Finally, it is worth mentioning that there are online resources to support you with the final stage of writing your project up. You almost certainly already have a word processor at this point in your studies, but you may be interested to know that there are free voice recognition resources available that will enable you to dictate your work to your computer without the need for typing. These tend to be free trial versions of applications that give you access for a temporary period and then stop working without a licence key, which you can purchase from the publisher, but they are a good way of seeing if this sort of software can work for you, and whether it is worth the further investment.

The final type of resource that you may wish to consider is referencing software, which will enable you to compile a reference list in the correct format. One example is BiblioExpress, which enables you to keep track of your sources as you work on your project, and will format references into APA style for you (http://www.biblioscape.com/biblioexpress.htm).

CHAPTER SUMMARY

- Google Scholar is a good way of locating relevant research papers and associated researchers, if you are unable to access research databases or wish to supplement searches conducted via those sources.
- Online forums, social networking sites and micro-blogging sites can be useful ways of advertising your study to potential participants; but some degree of care and caution is needed if such approaches are to be used, to protect your participants, stakeholders and you as the researcher.
- It is possible to access free trial versions of project management software, as well as open source versions, which are intended to be freely used.
- There a numerous sites that offer copyright free resources, which can be used as stimuli in experimental work, and experimental software for presenting these stimuli is also available as open source resources. Similarly, video, audio and visual stimuli can be edited via free software packages.

- Online survey software is available as free to use or free trial versions, if you are unable to use such software through an institutional licence held by your department.

- There are collections of psychometric tests that you can access and use, but beware of surveys which look 'psychological' but are not properly designed or standardised.

- Skype can be a useful resource for conducting and recording interviews.

- Data analysis can be supported by both websites designed to offer tutorial support and free resources for the analysis of qualitative data.

- We recommend that dissertation data and drafts are stored and shared via free to use 'cloud' servers.

- There are some tools that will support voice-to-text conversion, and will format references consistently for you.

CHAPTER 7 RESEARCH ETHICS

This chapter will take you through the different kinds of ethical issues that you need to consider in an application for ethical clearance. Psychology departments differ in the way in which they handle the ethical review process, but we will show you how to prepare the information that you will need for most review panels, and this chapter will cover the preparation of documentation that you will need for your study in any case, such as the briefing, consent form and debriefing. This chapter also gives advice on how to draft a letter to an external organisation to ask for permission to conduct research with its employees or members, and will cover issues relating to working with vulnerable groups and data protection in the context of research.

BY THE END OF THIS CHAPTER YOU WILL:

- Understand why ethics is important in relation to research with human participants.
- Know what an ethics committee is looking for in relation to your application.
- Know how to prepare a briefing document, a consent form and a debriefing document.
- Know how to write to a 'gatekeeper' to request permission to conduct your project.
- Know what a vulnerable group is and be aware of some of the issues around working with them in a research context.
- Know what data protection is and how to apply those principles to your work in practice.

7.1 THE PRINCIPLE OF 'NO HARM'

As you should be aware of by this point in your studies, psychologists adhere to an ethical code of practice, which aims to protect participants, organisations and researchers from harm, distress or legal consequences. This code of practice is constantly under review and it is certainly true that some research studies that were conducted in the past would not be deemed ethical by contemporary standards.

The British Psychological Society's *Code of Ethics and Conduct* (2009: 19) states that psychologists should:

> Consider all research from the standpoint of research participants, for the purpose of eliminating potential risks to psychological well-being, physical health, personal values, or dignity.

The overriding principle behind research ethics is that of 'no harm'. In other words, all parties involved in the research, including you as the researcher, should be no worse off at the end of the project than you were at the beginning. You may think that this is relatively straightforward, as, in their applications to ethics committees, students often state that there are 'no hazards' in their research. Unfortunately, this is seldom the case, as 'harm' can present itself in a variety of forms and some are more obvious than others. That is not to say that you cannot conduct research that has hazards attached to it – most everyday activities may be considered 'risky' in one sense or another – it is just that it is your job to anticipate as many of the obvious ones as possible, put plans in place to minimise them, and also put plans in place regarding what you should do if one of the risks is realised.

Before you begin collecting any data for your dissertation you will be required to prepare and submit an application for ethical approval that gives details of your study, recruitment procedures and materials. This will be reviewed by a panel that will either: approve your project; approve it subject to some conditions; or ask for a resubmission, which must address any points of concern raised by the panel. You *must* wait for approval before you begin collecting data, as even pilot work needs ethical clearance before you can begin it. The following sections discuss the kinds of issue that you will be expected to cover in your consideration of ethics in relation to your proposed project.

7.1.1 Physical harm

Firstly, and perhaps most obviously, there is the issue of physical harm. You may be putting participants at risk of hurting themselves either through accident (tripping over cables), stimulation (e.g. flashing lights or rapidly changing displays triggering migraines or epileptic fits) or through activity (e.g. fatigue). If you are looking at the psychological effects of different substances (e.g. caffeine, nicotine, alcohol or food additives) these may have the potential immediate effect of causing nausea, over-arousal or intoxication. In these cases, you should think about what you can do before, during and after the study to limit the harmful impact of these substances and to take into account what the participants may need to do later in the day (e.g. drive or listen to lectures). Similarly, studies that require participants to abstain from something (e.g. smoking or food) or engage in physical exercise during the study also expose participants to potential physical harm, and the briefing, debriefing and conduct of the study each require careful consideration as a result.

- The recruitment materials and briefing need to explain clearly what is involved and indicate any exclusion criteria (so that you are not wasting the time of anyone who is not going to be eligible to take part).
- The briefing also needs to indicate clearly what the potential risks involved are and how you, as the researcher, intend to minimise them, as well as anything that the participants can do to further reduce the risk. So, for example, if your study is going to involve giving participants

alcohol, you could limit the risk by keeping the amount as small as possible, and even giving participants a breath test to determine that they are under the legal limit before you let them leave the room. You could also advise participants not to drive to the appointment that day and not to make the appointment on a day when they have lectures or have to go to work, in case they feel drowsy.

● During the study, you should have the telephone number of someone trained to give first aid on your mobile phone, just in case, along with the number of your supervisor. Consider any other assistance or contacts that you may need in case something goes wrong.

● The debriefing should include details of any important symptoms that participants should keep an eye out for following their participation, if there is a chance that there may be some delayed effects. You should also include contact numbers of people who can help, if they do experience some after effects.

A student's experience . . .

    I was interested in the effect of skipping breakfast on cognitive performance. I discussed with my supervisor what kinds of things I would need to do to minimise the risk of harm to participants. We decided that I should forewarn all potential participants that this was what they would be required to do, and I made a decision to exclude all participants who were diabetic, hypoglycaemic, dieting or pregnant, or who had to drive into campus in the morning. I made sure that they had something to eat immediately after the conclusion of the study (I provided them with breakfast bars and asked participants to bring with them something that they could eat as a late breakfast). I set the start time of the study to 9.00am so that they were not having to wait too long before they could eat again. I also had my supervisor's telephone number and that of the departmental first aid contact in case anyone felt faint or I needed assistance.

7.1.2 Psychological harm

Potential psychological harm is harder to anticipate than physical effects, but it is just as serious, if not more so, as the effects can be more long term. The most common form is that of embarrassment. This can arise as a result of being asked to disclose personal information or reveal poor performance on an experimental task. Sometimes stimulus materials may invoke disgust or possibly resonate with the personal experiences of a particular participant, which can result in intrusive thoughts occurring after the study has concluded (e.g. dwelling on a failed relationship). Another area of psychological harm is that experienced by participants as a result of the real or imagined reactions of other research participants in the context of group work or focus group interviews, in which people may reveal views or behaviours that they will later regret.

These kinds of effects can be hard to avoid, as it is difficult to anticipate people's backgrounds and personal histories and how participating in your study may affect them. However, the critical thing is to imagine the 'worst case scenario' and think through how you can go about minimising the negative impact, if something does go awry. Also, consider how you can limit the possibility of this happening in the first place. To help you think this through, following are some examples:

● What will you do if someone begins to cry during or after the study?

● What will you do if someone gets angry or aggressive (either towards you or towards other participants or confederates)?

- What will you do if someone discloses sensitive information during your study?
- What will you do to minimise the chance of sensitive information or research data becoming public knowledge?

While it is impossible to eliminate risk of both physical and psychological harm during research, the chances of experiencing them can be kept to a minimum through careful thought and planning, and the provision of support material at the debriefing stage. You should also explain in your application to the ethics committee how you have minimised such risks and what your plan is, if something does go wrong. You should be able to plan appropriate action by discussing the options with your supervisor. A basic principle of good practice is to be as explicit as you can about what your study will require participants to do or what they will experience during the study. If you tell them as much as possible at the point of recruitment then individuals who may be anxious can decide not to participate. You should never ask why someone does not want to take part – it is their decision and you must respect that, no matter how inconvenient it is for you at the time.

Psychological harm can occur (and arguably is more likely to occur) if you pressurise someone to take part in a piece of research. Pressurising participants is completely unacceptable – when you are recruiting people, they must always be aware that there will be no negative consequences to deciding that they do not wish to take part and that it is entirely up to them. If you find yourself trying to persuade (or beg!) someone to participate in your study, you are coercing them. Similarly, if you are contacting an outside organisation and mention in your contact letter that you used to work for them, or that you used to attend that school, this could be construed as coercion, as they may only agree 'as a favour' to you.

Another subtle form of pressure can arise if you offer participants sweets, money or other rewards if they agree to participate in your study. There is an important distinction to be made between compensating someone for the time or inconvenience of taking part (especially if the study involves a lot of commitment or some form of abstinence on the part of the participant) and trying to attract people to your research over that of other people's by offering 'goodies' as an inducement to participate from the outset.

COMMON CONFUSION ?

Inducement or reward?

You may have noticed that some staff research studies offer participants money in return for research participation (although this is not very common and is usually only the case for studies where participants are likely to be seriously inconvenienced). As a result, some students offer research participants chocolate bars or similar 'rewards' for taking part in their study. In addition, many departments offer research participation credits in return for research participation. However, it is important to distinguish between what is intended as compensation for, or recognition of, a person's time or discomfort and 'treats' that may be perceived as inducements to participate in a project (e.g. chocolates). An inducement is something that may result in a person taking part in your study when they would otherwise not wish to (i.e. they are doing it for the treat rather than because they are interested in the study), and which cannot be justified as a compensatory award. The distinction between compensation and inducement is a subtle one and you need to be clear why you are offering what you are offering. Generally, if participants are getting research participation credits by taking part you should not need to offer additional rewards to attract participants to your project over and above that of other people's. You may even be breaching departmental guidelines by doing so.

7.1.3 Deception

Outright deception – where a participant is led to believe something that is not true – is frowned on in psychological research and is only acceptable if it is essential to achieving the aims of a study that is methodologically sound and theoretically valuable. The British Psychological Society's *Code of Ethics and Conduct* (2009: 14) states that psychologists should avoid intentional deception unless: 'deception is necessary in exceptional circumstances to preserve the integrity of research ... [and] the nature of the deception is disclosed to clients at the earliest feasible opportunity'.

When you are engaged with conducting your final year research project it is easy to lose a sense of perspective and to believe that you 'need' to use deception in your study. This should always be discussed with your supervisor, as 'need' is a strong word to use if we remember that your study is essentially a piece of university coursework. Do you really 'need' to deceive people in a research project in order to do a good piece of work?

Of course, some areas of research do require a form of deception (e.g. some aspects of placebo research), so the important thing to remember is to indicate to participants at the briefing stage that they may or may not receive a given substance, and then to debrief them about what they did receive at the earliest available opportunity.

COMMON CONFUSION

Deception versus withholding information

Sometimes students equate deception with withholding information about the study until the end (such as not revealing the hypothesis or all the various conditions in a study until the end). Withholding information about the study is not as serious as deceiving participants (which involves actively lying to them about the nature and purpose of the study). However, if you do need to withhold information you should always signal to your participant in the briefing that they have not been told everything about the study, but that you will explain why this is necessary at the debriefing.

7.1.4 Harm through carelessness

Practical considerations also come into play. In this sense, harm includes feeling that one's time is being wasted by taking part in what seems to be a pointless or badly designed piece of research. Similarly, it is important to communicate to participants what the purpose of the research is in terms that they understand. Another type of harm that can arise as a result of carelessness is the disclosure (either accidental or intentional) of sensitive information about an individual as a result of your own thoughtlessness. An example of this follows.

A student's experience . . .

> *I was collecting questionnaires in a public space, where people had the chance to drop by and take ten minutes to complete the questionnaire between lectures. I had planned everything carefully so that the place was quiet and comfortable, but during the data collection itself I got a little bit bored, as I had to sit there while people filled the questionnaires in. I started to read through the completed questionnaires as they were handed back to me. One of the participants had written something very funny and I started to giggle. The person sitting next to me asked me what was funny, so I showed her. I didn't think any more of it. Later*

that day I discovered that one of the other participants who had been there had complained that I was being disrespectful to participants' data and disclosing it to other students (who knew who each other were because they were in the same classes together). When it was put to me like that I could immediately see why the complaint had been made. I improved my procedure by asking all participants to seal their completed questionnaires into plain envelopes and post them in a sealed box with a slot cut in the top. I brought some work with me to the session to keep me occupied and I did not open the box and envelopes until I got home and was on my own. It really made me realise how easy it can be to cause offence without meaning to. 🙶

7.1.5 Protecting yourself

You should also consider risks to you as the researcher. This is a particular concern if you are collecting data off campus or if you are working on your own with individuals. Use your common sense to identify potential risks to you personally and have an action plan prepared regarding how you will cope with the situation-if something does go wrong. If you are working off campus, always tell your supervisor or friends where you are going, when you will be there, when you expect to finish, and contact them to let them know you are home again. Leave a contact number with someone, just in case. Make sure you have emergency telephone numbers to hand in case you need them and take a mobile phone with you.

If you are working one-to-one with someone, especially someone of the opposite sex, think carefully not only about your personal safety but also about your own vulnerability in case someone you are working with accuses you of harassment or inappropriate conduct. Think about simple measures that you can put in place to limit these risks (e.g. working somewhere that is private but where your behaviour is visible to a third party, or having someone who can assist you in the context of the research, collecting data in a group setting, etc.).

7.2 HOW TO PREPARE YOUR ESSENTIAL DOCUMENTATION

University departments can vary in how much detail they require you to produce for ethical clearance of your project. However, whether it is required for your ethics application or not, you will at some point need to prepare a briefing, consent form and debriefing for your study. The following sections describe the type of information that you need to include in these documents and you are advised to prepare these at the same time as thinking about the ethical aspects of your study so that all your documentation fits together.

7.2.1 The briefing sheet

Briefing your participants properly is crucial for a well conducted and ethical study. To this end, the British Psychological Society *Code of Ethics and Conduct* (2009: 12) states that you should:

> Ensure that clients, particularly children and vulnerable adults, are given ample opportunity to understand the nature, purpose and anticipated consequences of any professional services or research participation, so that they may give informed consent to the extent that their capabilities allow.

A briefing should therefore always include the following basic information about the study:

- Information about who you are.
- Contact information for you and/or your supervisor.
- Information about the nature of the research about to be undertaken.
- The nature of the participants' experience – what will they be expected to do?
- Acknowledgement of any sensitive issues relating to participating in the study.
- How long the study will take.
- Data protection issues: who will have access to the raw data and who will not? How long will the raw data be stored for and how will it be stored?
- Assurances regarding confidentiality or anonymity.
- Confirmation that participation is voluntary.
- An explanation of the method by which participants can withdraw their data after the conclusion of the data collection session, including a deadline for doing this. They should be asked to make a note of their participation number on the briefing sheet, in case they wish to withdraw their data.

We recommend that this information is organised under the following subheadings, which are very clear and straightforward questions that you should answer for your participants before they agree to take part (and will ensure you include the right level of detail in your briefing).

1 Study title.
2 What is the purpose of the study?
3 Why have you been approached?
4 Do you have to take part?
5 What will happen to you if you take part?
6 What are the possible disadvantages and risks of taking part?
7 What are the possible benefits of taking part?
8 What if something goes wrong?
9 Will my taking part in this study be kept confidential?
10 What will happen to the results of the research study?
11 Who is organising and funding the research?
12 Who has reviewed the study?
13 Contact for further information.

The briefing should always be written in a way that an 11-year-old child would understand. This means explaining any technical terms and avoiding complex language. Make sure that you check your briefing for spelling errors and typos before you copy and distribute it to your participants. We have included a copy of a briefing – also known as a participant information sheet – here, so you can see how we would organise the necessary information under each subheading.

However, please note that there are particular issues when recruiting children and other vulnerable groups. These are covered in detail in Section 7.6 and you would need to modify the 'Participant information sheet' below, and other forms and advice given within this section, accordingly.

Participant Information Sheet

Study title:
Sensitivity to sounds in speech and its relationship to spelling ability in adults.

What is the purpose of the study?
The aim of this study is to consider whether or not people's awareness of sounds in spoken words is related to their ability to spell correctly.

Why have you been approached?
For the purposes of the study I need to recruit a large number of adult participants who can read and write. This is the only criteria that I have for recruiting people to the study, although I will also be interested to know if you experience dyslexia or if English is not your first language. However, these factors will not prevent you from taking part in the study.

Do you have to take part?
No. Participation is entirely voluntary. If you change your mind about taking part in the study you can withdraw at any point during the sessions and at any time in the two weeks following that session. You can withdraw by contacting me on email and providing me with your participant code. If you decide to withdraw, all your data will be destroyed and will not be used in the study. There are no consequences to deciding that you no longer wish to participate in the study.

What will happen to you if you take part?
You will be asked to come along once a week for three weeks to take part in short (20 minute) sessions during which you will be assessed on your verbal intelligence, your sensitivity to sounds in spoken words and your spelling ability. You will be asked to complete no more than three tasks in any given session, and each task is quite short. You will be allowed to take a break between each task and refreshments will be available. You will complete all the assessments in a private room on a one-to-one basis with the researcher running that session.

What are the possible disadvantages and risks of taking part?
Some of the tasks that you will be asked to perform are quite challenging. This is deliberate, as I am interested in the kinds of mistakes that people make. However, you may feel uncomfortable if you tend to become self-conscious when you make a mistake or are unsure of an answer. You can refuse to complete any of the tasks if you wish.

Another possible disadvantage of participating in the study is that you may feel a little tired at the end of the session. I would recommend that you do not arrange sessions on a day when you have a lot of lectures or appointments to attend. One final disadvantage is that you will need to attend on three separate occasions, which may be difficult if you have to make special childcare or travel arrangements.

What are the possible benefits of taking part?
As an undergraduate student, by taking part in this study you will gain an insight into how a psychology research project is conducted and what it is like to be a participant in such a

study. If you are a psychology student this information could be used to shape and inform how you choose to design and conduct your own final year dissertation.

If you are a psychology student, you will receive one research participation credit for each session you attend.

What if something goes wrong?

If we have to cancel a testing session I will attempt to contact you as soon as possible, using the method indicated by you on the consent form. You will receive research participation credits for any session that has to be cancelled.

If you change your mind about taking part in the study you can withdraw at any point during a session, and at any time in the two weeks following the last session, by contacting me using the email address stated below. If you decide to withdraw, all your data will be destroyed and will not be used in the study.

If you feel unhappy about the conduct of the study, please let me know straightaway. Alternatively, you may wish to contact my supervisor, whose details are given at the end of this briefing.

Will your taking part in this study be kept confidential?

Yes. Only I will have access to the raw data. All the consent forms will be stored in a separate, secure (locked) location from the raw data itself. You will only be identified on the score sheet by your participant code number. I will only retain the raw data from the project until my final mark for my dissertation has been given. They will then be destroyed. When the data have been entered into a computer file, your scores will only be associated with your code number and access to the file will be password protected.

What will happen to the results of the research study?

The results will be written up and presented as part of my final year undergraduate dissertation. If the results are novel, it may also be presented at academic conferences and/or written up for publication in peer reviewed academic journals.

Who is organising and funding the research?

The research is organised by [YOUR NAME], who is a final year undergraduate student at the [YOUR UNIVERSITY] Psychology Department. This project is not externally funded.

Who has reviewed the study?

The Psychology Department's Undergraduate Ethics Committee has reviewed and approved this study.

Contact for further information

[YOUR NAME]

[YOUR UNIVERSITY EMAIL ADDRESS]

[YOUR SUPERVISOR'S NAME]

[YOUR SUPERVISOR'S EMAIL ADDRESS AND TELEPHONE NUMBER]

7.2.2 Obtaining consent

In most types of research study you will be required to obtain the signed consent of your research participants. As the British Psychological Society *Code of Ethics and Conduct* (2009: 12) states, it is your responsibility to 'keep adequate records of when, how and from whom consent was obtained', so you should be able to do more than produce just a signature, but a signed statement about what that person understands they are participating in.

We suggest that a consent form should, as a minimum, follow the following format.

The Title of Your Study

Participant reference code:_____

- I am over the age of 18.
- I have read and understand the attached briefing and, by signing below, I consent to participate in this study.
- I understand that I have the right to withdraw from the study without giving a reason at any time during the study itself.
- I understand that I also have the right to change my mind about participating in the study for a short period after the study has concluded [insert deadline here].

Signed:_____

Print name:_____

Witnessed by:_____

Print name:_____

You can be the signature witness, but you should give all participants their own copy of the consent form with the participant information sheet. However, the consent form and information sheet must be on separate pages. Rather than photocopying consent forms, you could produce two consent statements on one page, ask participants to sign both parts, and give you the bottom half of the page back. Make sure that their copy has their participant code on it.

You could add further bullet points to the list (e.g. 'I understand that I will be audio recorded during the interview and I give my permission for this'), and even give each statement a tick box to indicate clearly that each point has been read and agreed.

The exception to this occurs if you are conducting research that consists solely of participants completing questionnaires. Clearly, if a person takes the time to complete a detailed questionnaire and hand it back to you, it can be inferred that the participant is happy for you to have and use their data. Moreover, by asking someone to sign a consent form in this situation, you are asking them to disclose their identity in a situation where this is unnecessary and avoidable. So, in the case of questionnaires, we suggest that you still provide a detailed briefing for your participants, but that you put the following on the cover of the questionnaire, instead of using a consent form:

I am over the age of 18.	☐
I have read and I understand the participant information sheet for this study.	☐
By handing this questionnaire back to you, completed, I am giving my consent for you to use my questionnaire answers in this research study.	☐
I understand that I have the right to withdraw my questionnaire at any point until the stated deadline, by contacting the researcher using the details on the participant information sheet and quoting the participant reference code written at the top of this questionnaire.	☐
I have made a note of my participant reference code.	☐

7.2.3 The debriefing

The British Psychological Society *Code of Ethics and Conduct* (2009: 20) states that you have a responsibility as a psychologist to:

Debrief research participants at the conclusion of their participation, in order to inform them of the outcomes and nature of the research, to identify any unforeseen harm, discomfort or misconceptions, and in order to arrange for assistance as needed.

A debriefing form should, therefore, include:

● a 'thank you' for participating in the study;

● a statement of the aim of the study;

● a short rationale for your study;

● a statement of what you expect/hope to find in your results;

● your contact details (an email address is fine for this purpose);

● a reminder of the withdrawal mechanism and deadline for withdrawing;

● sources of further information/support, where relevant.

This last point is important for two ethics related reasons. The first is that, in some cases, discussion of a particular topic or participation in a certain type of study may reignite some personal issues for a participant that are totally unanticipated by the researcher. Even the most innocent task or questionnaire can evoke memories or feelings of anxiety in some individuals. For this reason it is important to ensure that participants have access to additional information and/or support groups relevant to the topic, so that they can be reassured. The other reason for including this information is because it is now considered ethical good practice to 'give something back' to participants in recognition of their cooperation. Participation in the study may have triggered their interest in the topic (especially if they are first year students), and so provision of some starter references or a URL would be a nice additional way of thanking them.

Another aspect of the British Psychological Society (2009: 20) *Code of Ethics and Conduct* that you should be aware of is that it also states that you should:

Take particular care when discussing outcomes with research participants, as seemingly evaluative statements may carry unintended weight.

In other words, take particular care over the phrasing of debriefings, as sentences may be mis-construed by participants who may be more sensitive to certain terms and phrases than you are, because you are used to using them in a very academic sense. Give particular thought to explaining sensitively how participants were allocated to conditions, if this was based on some criterion such as performance on a personality scale or intelligence assessment.

An example of a debriefing is as follows.

Debriefing Sheet

Dear Participant

Many thanks for participating in this study. The aim of this study is to consider whether or not people's awareness of stress in spoken words is related to their ability to spell correctly. You com-pleted a real word spelling test, a pseudoword spelling test, a verbal intelligence test and tasks that assessed how well you were able to both detect and produce the accepted pronunciation of some real and pseudowords. The reason for asking you to complete these tasks is because this project is examining the idea that reading and writing are processes that are rooted in how well we are able to attend to certain features of speech.

Research has suggested that there is a strong association between awareness of sounds in speech and successful reading and spelling development in children. However, there remains an unanswered question: why do some people fail to develop this awareness and go on to experi-ence reading difficulties? Wood and Terrell (1998) argued that this special awareness of speech, known as 'phonological awareness' may be a by-product of the skills that infants acquire in order to segment fluent speech into individual words: sensitivity to speech rhythm. In support of this idea, Wood and Terrell (1998) found that children with reading difficulties were also significantly worse than children of the same age on a test of speech rhythm sensitivity which looked at pat-terns of stress in spoken words.

While there has been much research exploring this idea in children, less attention has been paid to the potential association between being sensitive to stress placement in spoken word and reading/spelling ability in adults. I will take the data from this study and see if I can 'predict' people's spelling scores based on how well you did on the stress sensitivity tasks.

If you would like to know what I discover, you can email me on: joe.bloggs@myuniversity. ac.uk. If you are interested in this area, you can read more about it in a Special Issue of the *Journal of Research in Reading* (Volume 29, Issue 3).

If you would like to know more about reading development and reading difficulties, the fol-lowing websites may be of interest to you:

The National Literacy Trust
http://www.literacytrust.org.uk/

The British Dyslexia Association
http://www.bdadyslexia.org.uk/

Best wishes
[YOUR NAME]

7.3 PRESERVING ANONYMITY AND CONFIDENTIALITY

It is important to recognise and take seriously your responsibilities to your research participants with respect to preserving either anonymity or confidentiality.

COMMON CONFUSION

Confidentiality and anonymity

It is easy to get a little muddled about the difference between anonymity and confidentiality. Data collection can be described as anonymous if you do not know who has taken part in your study (for example, many questionnaire studies have truly anonymous data collection). Confidentiality, in contrast, is promised in circumstances when you know who has taken part in your study but you do not divulge this information, or information about their data, to other people. You can ask research participants who have taken part in group-based studies to keep the identities of other participants confidential too.

To preserve the anonymity/confidentiality of participants, each participant should be allocated a unique reference code – this could be a number or a random word. This code should be written, instead of their name, on every response sheet/questionnaire that is given to them in the course of the study, and should be noted on the briefing and debriefing documentation so that participants have a copy of it for their own records, in case they wish to withdraw from the research study.

If you are planning to conduct a piece of focus group-based research, you must add an extra point to your briefing, consent form and debriefing, which emphasises that each participant must agree to keep the identities of the other focus group members confidential and they cannot disclose the nature or content of what was discussed to any third parties. If you are planning to either video record or audio record participants during a task or during an interview/focus group, this must be made clear in the recruitment, briefing and consent materials. Make sure that you clearly state whether it will be video or audio recording (e.g. do not just say that you will 'record' or 'tape record' participants).

7.4 RECRUITMENT

You should think carefully about your choice of participants, your sample size and your method of recruitment.

7.4.1 How many?

You should not collect more data than you need, because if you do you could be accused of wasting the time of participants unnecessarily. Often it is a misconception to believe that a larger sample will give you better marks, or will give you a more representative sample (as that will also depend on the sampling method that you have chosen). However, you also need to collect enough data to enable you to test your hypothesis or conduct the qualitative analysis you have planned. So, how do you determine how much is enough?

As noted in Chapter 4, for qualitative projects it is suggested by Madill *et al.* (2005) that you aim to obtain about five hours of data for inductive forms of analysis (e.g. grounded theory and interpretative phenomenological analysis), three to four hours of raw data if you are planning to use discourse or narrative analysis, and one to two hours if you plan to use conversation analysis (which is highly detailed and time consuming). If you are considering using repertory grids or Q methodology, five sessions worth of data should be sufficient.

For group-based quantitative projects, a good rule of thumb is to recruit 20 participants per condition of your design. If you are planning to conduct a regression or correlation based study, then 20 participants per (predictor) variable in your study is a good guide. But this is a rule of thumb, so do not worry too much if you are slightly under. Similarly, if you are recruiting from specialist populations that are hard to find, it may well be the case that such numbers are very ambitious. In these instances be guided by the kinds of sample that you can see being used in published studies. For example, studies that recruit from dyslexic populations sometimes only have 12 participants per group, but they may be carefully matched to control participants in some way (see Chapter 4).

If you are comfortable with statistics and are confident about the realistic chances of recruiting a large sample, you can conduct something called a 'power analysis', which can tell you how many participants you will need, depending on the design of your study and how strong an effect you think you are planning to detect. As noted in Chapter 4, there are simple, freely available software packages on the internet, such as G*Power that will calculate power for you and tell you how many participants you will need to detect a reasonably large effect (a power value of 0.8 is appropriate) to a $p < .05$ significance level given the type of design you plan to use. Your supervisor can guide you through the use of such packages. However, if your design is very complex, you may find that you are directed to recruit a sample that is unrealistically large, in which case revert to using the rule of thumb given above. Remember, this is a piece of coursework, not a PhD project!

7.4.2 Whom should I recruit?

As already noted, many psychology departments have a research participation scheme where first and second level undergraduates are encouraged to participate in final year research projects. We would encourage you to use these schemes wherever this is suitable, as not only will you provide other undergraduates with valuable research experience, but you will also be able to find large numbers of willing volunteers relatively easily; and you will not need to approach 'gatekeepers' for permission to conduct your research.

You may be considering recruiting from friends and family as another way of finding relatively willing volunteers. However, we would suggest that you avoid this, as you may find yourself in a difficult situation if you have knowledge of their scores on personality measures or other tests. The use of people you know well in the context of interview-based research is even more fraught, as it is in these situations that people may disclose views or experiences that you were not previously aware of, and that might colour your relationships with them.

The bottom line is that you should consider what population you need in order to test your hypothesis most effectively, but bear in mind practical considerations about how easy various types of participant may be to recruit, and the amount of time it may take to obtain access to them. You may also need to consider whether you are going to be allowed to have access to your target group. For example, if you wish to work with young children you will be required to obtain an enhanced Criminal Records Bureau disclosure or equivalent (depending on what country you are from). This may reveal information that you may not wish to disclose, and which may also prevent you from working with them. Similarly, in most cases, undergraduate students are not permitted to conduct research in prisons or in hospital contexts, because of the levels of additional external ethical clearance and background checks that you would need to undergo, which would make your project difficult (if not impossible) to achieve in the timeframe that is available to you as an undergraduate.

7.4.3 Recruitment posters and flyers

You will need to give details of how you plan to approach and recruit participants to your study. Any materials that you plan to use for this purpose, such as posters and flyers intended to advertise the study, must be appended to your project and, in most cases, are required as part of the ethics submission too. Think carefully about the wording of these. You should give enough detail on these materials so that participants know the type of person you are looking to recruit, what the study is about (in general terms), what they might be asked to do, how long it will take and how they should get in touch with you. Do not use sign-up sheets on posters, as these tell the world who has volunteered for your study! Also, remember not to advertise inducements to participate. If you plan to recruit by word of mouth (snowballing), produce a small card or flyer that contains accurate details of your study and how to contact you, which can be passed on to interested parties, rather than relying on verbal messages alone, otherwise you may run the risk of participants approaching you to participate in your project based on misinformation.

7.4.4 Use of email in research

The use of email in research is a very tricky area that needs careful handling. On the one hand, if done appropriately, email-based data collection can save you a good deal of time and effort. On the other, you can make some serious ethical blunders when using this medium. We will return to the issue of using email for data collection in the next chapter but, with respect to ethics, the following are some words of advice:

- Do not 'spam' potential research participants with unsolicited emails.
- We strongly recommend that you do not distribute questionnaires via email, as there is too great a risk that participants will complete them electronically and email them back to you. This is risky, as it is too easy to send email to the wrong person and most email addresses contain people's names or other identifying information.
- It is much better to use e-survey software, if you are interested in distributing questionnaires via email, as these systems enable true anonymity and prevent the accidental emailing of personal data.
- If you are emailing gatekeepers about research, please use your official university email address. Personal email accounts are acceptable only if they have a suitably sober name (i.e. NOT sexy-legs@biteme.com). Remember that you are representing your university, and yourself, and you do limit your chances of success if you come across as unprofessional.

7.4.5 Contacting gatekeepers

If you need to recruit participants from an outside organisation (and that can include departments other than psychology at your university), you must obtain written permission to do so from relevant gatekeepers (e.g. managers, employers, club leaders, students' union, headteachers, etc.). In some cases your supervisor will wish to be the person who negotiates access for you but, in many cases, this will be another task you are expected to undertake.

In your letter to a gatekeeper, you should make reference to the same kind of information that you would normally include in your briefing sheet (e.g. who you are, what the project is about, what it will involve, what the gatekeeper is being asked to provide, etc.). If you are planning to distribute questionnaires, these should be shown to the gatekeeper before they are asked to agree to support the project. We have provided an example of a gatekeeper letter here, to give you a sense of the tone and style, as well as content.

Dear Sir/Madam **[USE THEIR ACTUAL NAME IF YOU KNOW IT]**

I am a final year Psychology student at [YOUR UNIVERSITY] and as part of my studies I am required to conduct a piece of research. I have identified a need for research into [INSERT THE TITLE OF YOUR PROJECT HERE]. I am writing to ask if it would be possible to recruit participants for this study from your **organisation/school/company. [It is helpful here to explain why you have approached that organisation, if relevant.]**

I have prepared a description of the study and what is involved in it for potential participants, and I have attached a copy for you to read. **[If you are doing a questionnaire study, it is also advisable to append a copy of your questionnaire.]** Ideally, I would like to begin data collection on **[INSERT DATE]** but I am very happy to be guided by you on this.

[THEN EITHER]
I would anticipate that participants would contact me to complete the study in their own time and, therefore, there should be no disruption to your organisation.

[OR]
I would anticipate that the project would take no more than **[XX]** minutes, and I would need a quiet place on your premises to conduct the study. **[Here you can specify any other requirements that you may have or facilities that you would need, or even identify where in or near their building you plan to collect the data.]** I will endeavour to keep the disruption to your working day to an absolute minimum.

I hope that you find the attached project of interest and will be interested in working with me on it. Please feel free to contact me if you have any queries. Alternatively, you may wish to contact my supervisor, **[INSERT NAME OF SUPERVISOR AND TELEPHONE NUMBER HERE]** if you would like a reference or other information.

Many thanks for taking the time to read this and I hope to hear from you soon.

Yours faithfully **[Remember, if you address the letter to a specific person using their name, you should end the letter 'Yours sincerely' instead.]**

[YOUR NAME]

[YOUR UNIVERSITY EMAIL ADDRESS]

7.5 YOUR MATERIALS

If you are compiling a detailed ethics application you will normally also be required to show the committee copies of the materials that you plan to use with your participants. This is so that they can check them for wording, appropriateness and any possible risk of offence.

7.5.1 Using psychometric tests

Some psychometric tests are widely available and can be found in the appendices of published papers or on websites. Others are copyright free, if an original has been purchased in the appropriate manner. In these instances, it is fine for you to access and use these materials for your dissertation as long as you fulfil any conditions on their use (e.g. citing the relevant website, etc.). However, you are advised always to check the wording of the stimulus material or questions, especially if the tests are rather old or have been used in a highly specific context before. Some terms that are used in the USA, for example, have a different meaning in the UK (e.g. 'learning disability'), and some phrases that were acceptable terminology at some points in time are now seen as offensive.

Other tests are subject to strict conditions. Standardised psychometric tests (e.g. IQ measures, some personality tests, educational tests, etc.) should only be used by people who are qualified to do so and/or who are trained in their use, or who are supervised by a qualified person. You should always check that your supervisor is aware of the tests that you wish to use, and ensure that you are allowed to use them or that they are qualified to supervise your use of them. You should also be aware that you should resist the temptation to give participants detailed feedback on their personal performance on such measures, as these tests need careful interpretation when applied to individuals, and simple test scores can be misleading and distressing.

7.5.2 Generating stimulus materials

You may wish to overcome some of the difficulties noted above by generating your own questionnaire or stimulus materials. However, if your materials are based on those used by others or are adapted from an existing questionnaire, etc., this should be clearly stated, and reference made to the original source. If you plan to take photographs or make videos, you will need to obtain informed consent from those who take part. Generally speaking, we would encourage you not to use images of friends or family in your stimulus materials – see if you can find copyright free images wherever possible. This is because often people are asked to make judgements about those in the photograph/video, and this may cause embarrassment at a later point in time.

7.5.3 Copyright issues

- Do not photocopy questionnaires unless it is clear that it is okay to do so. Normally, copyright protected questionnaires state that photocopying them is illegal somewhere on the form and/or are printed in colours other than black to hinder the process.
- Do not assume everything on the internet is copyright free. Many resources are, some are but require you to write something in your report about where you got the material from or otherwise publicise the website. Check that it is okay to use the images/clips outside of their original context.
- If you need to make copies of, and/or edit extracts from, films or TV programmes for use as stimulus material, check with your library for how long you would be permitted to use an extract

without seeking copyright clearance. Please be aware that copying videos and DVDs, etc. without clearance is illegal – consider whether you need to copy them or whether you could instead play an extract from a legitimate first generation source instead.

7.6 RESEARCH WITH CHILDREN AND OTHER VULNERABLE GROUPS

7.6.1 What is a vulnerable group?

Children, disabled people, older people, prisoners, and people with learning difficulties are examples of 'vulnerable groups' that you may be considering working with in the context of your research project. There are three main reasons why a group of people is labelled as vulnerable: firstly, there will almost inevitably be a perceived, and usually real, **power imbalance** between participant and researcher. Secondly, their **ability to comprehend research** and the reasons why it is done may be different from those of the researcher. Thirdly, negative experiences during **research participation may have a disproportionately large effect on them,** with the risk of long-term psychological harm.

These three aspects of vulnerability each have different implications for the design of research and how it is conducted. Perhaps the most obvious of these is a concern that researchers working with vulnerable groups should not have any previous history of offending in areas that would cause concern in relation to these groups. This is achieved in the UK by applying to the Criminal Records Bureau (CRB) for a 'disclosure'. Disclosure can be requested at three levels: basic, standard or enhanced. Standard and enhanced disclosures reveal not only criminal convictions, but can include other information such as complaints made against you and failed prosecutions. If you wish to conduct research in a school that requires you to work one-to-one with a child, you will need to obtain enhanced clearance from the CRB. Also, it is good practice for anyone engaged in direct contact with children in the course of research to have a recent CRB disclosure. These can take a couple of months to come through, and are only valid for three months, so you should think carefully about exactly when you will need to make your application. More generally, we advise that you should never be left to work entirely alone with a child – a member of school staff or a parent should always be within earshot or visible through a door or window, at the very least.

7.6.2 Practicalities of working in schools

Another point to bear in mind regarding ethics is the amount of time you would need either to withdraw a child from their normal lessons or the general amount of disruption your study may cause to the school and the class. These issues should be discussed with the school when headteachers are being approached for approval. Generally, try to minimise the amount of time you plan to keep children away from their normal lessons, and find out the best times to visit the school for data collection. Think about planning several short visits to each child, rather than one long session. Talk to the school about how to distribute your consent letters to parents (do not expect the school to photocopy these on your behalf) and make sure that these are returned to you. Make sure that the school knows in advance exactly the type of environment you will need to work in, and always make sure you know (and stick to) any school procedures regarding signing in and signing out as a visitor. If you are asked to wear a visitor's badge, make sure that you do so. Also respect any dress code that may be in operation at the school and, if necessary, ask about this when you speak to the headteacher or secretary before you visit the school for the first time.

Schools often tire of being asked to participate in research and can receive little in return for their cooperation. Consider what you could do to thank the school for its support in your research. This could be the offer of voluntary work, help with playground duty or at dinner times, help with children's reading or after school clubs, or even presenting information about psychology or your project to the students and linking it to their own lessons in a meaningful way. But you should always formally write to thank the school for their support and to let them know what you found.

7.6.3 Consent when working with children

When you are working with children you **must** get parental consent if the child is under 18, as legally they are classed as 'minors'. This means that you should prepare an additional briefing and consent statement for this purpose.

When seeking consent from parents of children, you should ask them to sign a form to indicate that they are willing for you to approach their child to participate in the project. This is known as an 'opt in' procedure. This is different from an 'opt out' procedure, where you notify all parents, but rely on parents who do not wish you to include their child in your study to contact you to let you know. Generally, this is not an acceptable way of getting consent from a parent, because you cannot be confident that parents who have not contacted you have received the information about the study. An example of a letter to a parent asking for consent is provided here.

Dear Parent

I am a final year student at [YOUR UNIVERSITY] and I am conducting my final year project into **[TITLE]. [HEADTEACHER'S NAME]** has given **his/her** permission for me to conduct my research at **[SCHOOL NAME]** and I am now looking to recruit children to take part in the project.

I have described the project in detail on the attached Information Sheet, and I would be very grateful if you could read it and decide whether or not you would be happy for me to approach your child to see if they would like to take part.

All the children will be fully briefed about the purpose and nature of the research in language they will understand, and they can change their mind about taking part at any point during the study. You can also decide to withdraw your child's work from the study retrospectively if you wish (see the deadline for doing this on the attached Information Sheet and is shown on the slip below). The research will be conducted on school premises and I have Enhanced Criminal Records Bureau clearance.

If you are happy for your child to be approached to take part in the project, please sign and return the response slip at the bottom of this letter to the child's class teacher as soon as possible. If you do not return this slip your child will not be asked to participate. I have attached a copy of this letter at the back for you to retain, along with the Information Sheet, for your records.

Many thanks for taking the time to read this and I hope to hear from you soon.

Yours faithfully

[YOUR NAME]

I have read the Information Sheet attached to this letter and I am happy for [YOUR NAME] to approach my child to participate in their study on [TITLE].

I understand that I can change my mind about participating in this study at any point until [STATE DATE] by contacting [YOUR NAME] and giving the name of my child.

Name of child: _____

Name of parent/guardian: _____

Signature of parent/guardian:_____

Date:_____

You should always get verbal agreement from a child for their participation (except for babies). It is also recommended that you seek written consent from any child who is 12 years old or older. You could decide to get written consent from younger children than this if you wish, but consider how to design the consent form to make it meaningful and visual, as not all children will be able to read well enough to cope with a standard consent form. Use images to help to convey the meaning of each statement.

MAXIMISING MARKS

Vulnerable groups other than children

We are spending quite a while talking through the practicalities of working with children but, as we have already noted, other groups are also vulnerable too. Think about how some of the ideas and principles that we are presenting you with, regarding working with children, could be adapted and applied to other vulnerable groups that you might work with, such as the elderly, offenders or individuals with disabilities.

7.6.4 Briefing and debriefing when working with children

If you are planning to recruit children as research participants you need to take extra care to communicate the nature and purpose of the research to them in a manner that they can understand. You should also work with them in a way that respects their rights in the same way that you would do for an adult participant (e.g. do not assume children 'will not understand' and use this as an excuse to deal exclusively with a schoolteacher or parent instead). Always talk to children about what you are interested in, what you are proposing that they do with you, how that will help you in your work and what you will do with that information when you have finished. Even very young children will be interested in what you are doing and will be very pleased to be able to help you with your work.

What this means in practice is that the briefing sheet (Participant Information Sheet) and your debriefing may need to be expressed even more carefully and simply than you would normally do. Think carefully about layout and use pictures. Take time to explain the information to the child verbally (if you are working in schools, you could brief the class as a whole about your project, even if not all of them will take part). Examples of how to simplify parts of the briefing are as follow:

- You can decide if you want to work with me.
- You do not have to say 'yes'.
- If you do say 'yes', you do not have to do everything that I ask you to.
- We can stop whenever you want to.
- Before you decide whether you want to help me with my work, you can talk to your teacher about it.
- I keep all your work in a safe, locked cupboard.
- When I write about what we have been talking about, I will make sure that I never use your real name so that no one but you and I know the things you told me.
- I am not going to tell anyone what we have talked about today, unless you tell me that someone has hurt you.

7.6.5 Watching children's behaviour

You should always monitor the behaviour of children during your study. You must be sensitive to the fact that often children do not feel able to refuse to cooperate with an adult. This is especially true if you are working with children in a school context. So, you should be aware of any behaviour that could be indicative of a child's actual desire not to complete a specific activity, or to work with you on the project as a whole. Such behaviours might include fidgeting, being easily distracted, giving monosyllabic answers to questions, staring away from the task at hand, etc. If this behaviour occurs once, you should assume that the child does not want to complete that activity on that occasion. If this behaviour is maintained over more than one activity with you, you should assume that they do not wish to participate in the study, and destroy the data accordingly.

7.7 DATA PROTECTION ISSUES

'Data' refers to any information that you collect and store during the course of a piece of research, be it numerical, textual, verbal or observational. This can include specific information about individuals, such as their names, ages, where they live, their occupations, their scores on a test or a task, and their responses to a questionnaire or during an interview. It also includes any video material you might have collected, fieldnotes (however informal), photographic evidence, audio recordings or transcripts. All these forms of data need to be handled with appropriate care and sensitivity. Of particular significance in legal terms is 'personal data', which refers to any data 'which relate to a living person who can be identified'. Most research data would be considered 'personal data' in this sense.

Below, we have presented some principles of good practice in relation to your research project.

7.7.1 'Fair' collection of data

You should always obtain your data from your participants directly, following a full briefing and after they have given their informed consent. For example, you might wish to use students' examination scores as a dependent variable in your study. It would be unacceptable for you to ask a member of staff to let you have a list of module marks, as you would be asking them to disclose personal information and this would be in breach of the Data Protection Act. Instead, you should approach your participants directly, and ask them to give you their module marks, after explaining to them why you need them and what you will use them for. You will need to anonymise the data and promise to keep that information confidential.

7.7.2 Only collect the data that you need and explain what you plan to do with it

Resist the temptation to collect more data than you actually need in order adequately to address your research question. That is, you might think that it would be 'interesting' also to ask participants about something else or assess them on another variable out of curiosity. This is considered bad practice and bad design. Good projects justify the collection of all variables and keep data collection to a minimum as a result. If you do this, your data collection will be fast and efficient. When contacting potential participants you must properly brief participants (see Section 7.2.1 for guidance on compiling a briefing sheet) and explain what you will do with the data. Once you have explained the aim of the research you should not change the study to address a substantially different set of research questions.

7.7.3 Do not keep any personal information (e.g. consent forms that identify individuals) any longer than is strictly necessary

Your raw data and consent forms should not be held for any longer than is strictly necessary. With respect to student work, you should retain all your raw data until such time that a mark for your project has been finalised. At that point you should destroy raw data in an appropriate manner (i.e. shred paper, wipe videos and audio recordings, etc.).

7.7.4 Never give information about specific participants to anyone else

Any information about a specific individual that can identify them should never be disclosed to another person, either intentionally or accidentally. To avoid this you should anonymise each participant with a code number, and use only this on spreadsheets, transcripts, questionnaires, and video and audio labels. Consent forms should always be stored securely in a locked drawer or similar, and in a separate location from the coded data.

7.7.5 Do not make unnecessary copies of information, or leave it lying about

It is recommended that you do make backups of any data you are working with, but do not photocopy personal data or duplicate tapes. Tapes must be transcribed with code numbers only as soon as possible, and the transcripts stored securely. Do not leave consent forms or tapes left lying around on desks or visible on monitors when you are not there. Be tidy!

7.7.6 If you are working as part of a team on a project, you should not share information about specific participants via the telephone, email or other unsecure method

If you cannot be sure whether your intended recipient will be the actual person who receives the information, or if you are not sure whether other people may be able to eavesdrop on the information, you should not share personal information about participants with other people on your team. This may occur during correspondence with a participant about their data, for example.

7.7.7 Never assume that it will be okay to discuss the results of a specific research participant with another person. You must always ask the participant's permission first if you think this will be necessary

This means that you should not 'assume' that it will be okay to discuss data with a third party or give copies of data to a third party without first explicitly gaining consent from the participants concerned.

7.7.8 Information about individuals must be stored securely (i.e. locked away somewhere or be password protected)

This is an obvious point, but you should always lock your research data away in a safe place and, if it is possible to set passwords for computer files, you should do so. You should also change these passwords regularly. If you do not have access to somewhere secure to store data, talk to your supervisor about storing them in a filing cabinet in the department.

7.8 THE RIGHT TO WITHDRAW

One situation that can occur is when an individual withdraws their participation in a programme of research halfway through, or even after the project has been completed. Although happily this is quite rare, a participant is entirely within their rights to do so. As the British Psychological Society *Code of Ethics and Conduct* (2009: 14) states, you must:

> Ensure from first contact that clients are aware of their right to withdraw at any time from the receipt of personal services or research participation and. ... Comply with requests by clients who are withdrawing from research participation that any data by which they might be personally identified, including recordings, be destroyed.

We further suggest that, if someone does withdraw from your study, any data that you have obtained from this person should be destroyed with immediate effect and should not be used in any analysis or report, whether they explicitly request this or not.

The participants should always be thought of as 'owning' their data, which they have consented for you to 'use' in a particular, prescribed way. They are, in this sense, not 'your' data to do with as you wish. Your use of them is limited by their consent. Once consent is withdrawn, you no longer have the right to keep them or use them. In some cases a person will leave a study halfway through for reasons other than withdrawal of consent, and will therefore be happy for you to continue to use the data you have already collected. If you are in any doubt you should explicitly discuss this with the person concerned. Following this, if you are still unsure, you should err on the side of caution and not use the data.

Participants should be entitled to a 'cooling off' period after they have completed a study. This is because sometimes participants reflect on their responses or their performance after a study and feel uncomfortable as a result. You should set a realistic deadline for this to limit disruption to your data analysis. Make participants aware of this deadline at the briefing and debriefing, and ask them to make a note of their participant number, as this will be needed if you are to locate their data and destroy them. Any decision not to offer participants a means of withdrawing their data after the data has been collected should be fully justified in your ethics proposal and should be made clear to participants in the participant briefing materials.

7.9 A CHECKLIST FOR SCRUTINISING YOUR PROPOSAL

Once you have drafted your ethics proposal and associated documentation, it is advisable that you double-check that you have covered all the points discussed in this chapter. To help you to do this, we have produced a checklist of questions for you to work through.

1 Does this study involve deception?

(a) If yes, is the deception essential to achieve the aims of the study?

(b) Has the deception been handled appropriately in the briefing/debriefing documentation?

2 Is the method of recruitment ethically acceptable?

(a) Are reasons given for using participants recruited from outside the Psychology Department?

(b) Does this study intend recruiting from a vulnerable population?

(c) Is a CRB check required?

(d) Have recruitment materials been provided?

(e) Do the recruitment materials give an accurate and appropriate indication of the nature of the research?

(f) Is the method by which participants can withdraw their data clearly described?

3 Are data protection issues addressed satisfactorily regarding:

(a) When the data will be destroyed?

(b) How data will be stored?

(c) Whether anonymity or confidentiality is ensured throughout the study?

4 Are all the obvious risks to participants and researcher acknowledged and have they been discussed appropriately?

5 Is gatekeeper permission required? If so, does the letter to the gatekeeper include accurate details of:

(a) The purpose of the research?

(b) Who will be approached to participate?

(c) What participants will be required to do?

(d) When the study will take place?

(e) Where the study will take place?

(f) How confidentiality or anonymity will be ensured?

(g) What will happen to the results of the research?

(h) Is the letter to the gatekeeper correctly spelled and appropriately phrased?

6 Is there a letter of permission for the study from the gatekeeper? If yes, does it:

(a) Appear genuine/authentic?

(b) Make reference to the letter sent by you *or* the nature of the study itself?

7 Has a participant information sheet (briefing) been included?

(a) Does the information sheet give accurate information about the nature of the study?

(b) Does the information sheet give enough detail regarding what the participants will be asked to do?

(c) Does the information sheet indicate what will happen to the data?

(d) Does the information sheet explain about when and how to withdraw from the study?

8 Does this study need to collect signed consent statements?

9 Does the consent form/statement meet minimum requirements?

10 Are the instructions to be given to participants included?

(a) Are there any ethical issues regarding the instructions that will be used?

11 Has a debriefing sheet been produced?

(a) Does the debriefing sheet describe the expected results and the rationale for the study?

(b) Does the debriefing indicate sources of further information where appropriate?

(c) If this study is working with children, is the briefing and debriefing appropriate?

12 Have copies of any questionnaires been appended and/or have details of any tasks or activities been given?

(a) Are there any unaddressed ethical issues with the nature of the questions/tasks/activities planned?

(b) Does the student need training/supervision from the supervisor in the administration of the study?

7.10 SOME ETHICAL SCENARIOS

To conclude the chapter, we have provided some hypothetical situations in which ethical issues may arise that may not be immediately obvious to the researcher. Read each one and see if you can spot the issues of concern. These are designed to highlight issues you need to consider and will help you to see how well you have understood some of the issues raised by this chapter. Some of the possible ethical issues are discussed in the Appendix.

1 **Adhya** wants to interview first year students about their beliefs on safe sex. She puts up a poster on a notice board in the psychology corridor, which has spaces for people who are interested to sign up with their email addresses.

2 **Benny** interviews some first year students about their transition to university, to find out how they adapted to living away from home. He is interested in homesickness.

3 **Cathy** decides to recruit and interview parents of children with terminal illness by logging on to an internet discussion group on the topic. She is interested in the way that parents cope with the anticipated loss of their children.

4 **Dennis** plans to interview senior managers about their views on depression in the workplace. He is interested in discrimination towards people with mental health problems.

5 **Ellie** decides to interview her flatmates about their views on intensive farming practices. She believes passionately that battery chicken farms should be banned.

6 **Frank** decides to approach people on Friday nights in the guild for their views on men's and women's drinking. He thinks that people will express more extreme views once they have had a few alcoholic drinks.

7 **Gillian** arranges interviews about animal rights. She arranges for the participants to come to the psychology labs and have them wait there while individual interviews are conducted in the

cubicles. The people who are opposed to vivisection are to be interviewed first, and those who are not sure or in favour in the latter part of the day.

8   **Hussein** is going to interview men at a gym about their participation in sport. He is interested in the extent to which cheating, such as use of performance enhancing drugs, is seen as acceptable.

CHAPTER SUMMARY

- Any research that you conduct should minimise the risk of harm to research participants, organisations and yourself.
- You must fully brief and debrief all research participants.
- Informed consent must be obtained from research participants or their representatives where it is not appropriate for participants to give their own consent.
- It is your responsibility to keep appropriate records that will enable you to demonstrate that you have obtained informed consent.
- Anonymity or confidentiality of participants must be ensured throughout.
- Data should be securely stored, and raw data that have the potential to identify individuals must be destroyed at the earliest available opportunity once they are no longer needed.
- Give careful consideration to the amount of data you need to collect – you should be able to justify your sample size, the amount of data you have collected and the nature of that data.
- Care and professionalism must be in place when recruiting participants, especially when this contact is made via gatekeepers.
- A vulnerable group is any group of individuals who have either a real or perceived lower status relative to the researcher, or have a reduced ability to comprehend the purpose of research, and for whom a negative experience of research may have a disproportionately large impact.
- Participants have the right to withdraw their research participation at any time during a project and should normally also be offered a limited period in which they can withdraw after the conclusion of a study.

FURTHER READING

Alderson, P. & Morrow, V. (2004). *Ethics, Social Research and Consulting with Children and Young People.* Ilford: Barnardo's.
This book is a really valuable guide to working sensitively with young people and children in the context of research work, with lots of practical advice.

British Psychological Society (2009). *Code of Ethics and Conduct.* Leicester: British Psychological Society.
This is a guide to the various aspects of psychological work and the ethical principles that psychologists should adhere to in the context of both research and practice. It has a useful list of further sources of guidance at the back. You can download a copy of this from the BPS website (http://www.bps.org.uk).

CHAPTER 8
DATA
COLLECTION

Once that you know what your project is going to involve from a design point of view and it has cleared the ethical approval process, you may now proceed to collecting data. However, the practicalities of data collection are not always as straightforward as they may seem, so this chapter is designed to give you some advice on how best to manage data collection once the project has begun. It will alert you to the kinds of issues that you need to be mindful of, such as professional conduct, data management and organisational issues. Advice on the transcription of data is also included here.

BY THE END OF THIS CHAPTER YOU WILL:

- Have a better idea of the issues relating to different types of data collection methods.
- Be aware of the need to present a professional presence if working off campus, and know some ways in which you can ensure this.
- Know how to transcribe interview/observational data.

8.1 INTERVIEWS AND FOCUS GROUPS

Interviewing, whether you are talking one-to-one with someone or working with a group of participants, is an art form in itself. Skilful interviewing that results in good quality data (in which your participants are talking at length on the topic that you are interested in) is easier said than done. Some people can pick it up straight away while others need to acquire the skills through practice. Either way, it is always a good idea to begin your study with a pilot interview – either a run through with a friend, or an interview with a participant that you are prepared to discard if it all goes wrong . . . and if it goes right, you are already off the mark!

With interviews, a lot depends on who your participants are going to be. Some students take the apparently easy route of interviewing people they already know on a particular topic, while others are more adventurous and seek out a special population. Many of the access issues have already been discussed, but following are some issues to consider once you are ready, with tape recorder poised.

8.1.1 Establishing trust

Your interviewee may be wary of you, and your motivations for carrying out research. This is particularly true of vulnerable groups (see Chapter 7), for example asylum seekers or homeless people. Although you may think that it is obvious that you are only a student doing a project for your degree, your participants might see you as an authority figure or expert (after all, you will appear to know more about the subject than they do). So you should tell them about yourself right at the start (this is a nice way of breaking the ice a little in any case), and say exactly why you are interested in what they have got to say. The reverse situation occurs sometimes when vulnerable participants believe that taking part in the research might be beneficial to them in ways that it will not. For example, in one study, asylum seekers believed that the student interviewing them was going to be able to use the information to support their UK residency applications. All the more important, therefore, to get it straight from the start what you are doing and who you are – and who you are not.

A student's experience . . .

> I was trying to access a specialist population and I contacted a charitable organisation who routinely advised the population that I was trying to gain access to. They were very helpful to me and I thanked them profusely and even became a little bit involved in some events. A few months later I received a telephone call from a parole officer who asked to speak to me. She then explained that the charity had given them my phone number, as there was an offender due to be released into my area very soon who also experienced the difficulty that the charity concerned worked with. Apparently the parole officer and the charity decided that because I was 'a psychologist' with 'expertise' in the area that the charity dealt with, they felt that I was ideally placed to support the offender with respect to the difficulty they experienced. I was really panicked by this call, as it was clear that they felt that I was more qualified than I was. I really didn't feel comfortable with the idea and it was a real eye opener – I had no idea how little they knew about what a psychology student (albeit a recent graduate) would be qualified to do.

8.1.2 Pacing the interview

Most interviewers begin by drawing up an **interview schedule** – a list of questions and topics that they want to cover during the course of the interview. You should have already devised this as part of your ethics proposal. How rigidly you stick to this schedule, either in terms of the order of questions, their specific wording, or whether you cover all of them, will depend entirely on your research question and what data you need to answer it. Research methods, books often specify three types of interview: **structured, semi-structured** and **unstructured.** In practice there is enormous blurring of these boundaries. Structured interviews may be little more than oral questionnaires. Entirely unstructured interviews are only really useful if you are carrying out some kind of life story research where you have no prior knowledge of the person's history. Even here you may be anticipating certain patterns, such as life phases or transitions, which will enable you to compare different interviews. However, as the next section explains, you may not actually want to phrase your questions in that way.

8.1.3 Putting together an interview schedule

The interview schedule helps to structure your session, and it also acts as a memory tool – you should have it in front of you throughout the interview. Do not feel you have to ask every question on the sheet. Your interviewee may well answer some of them unprompted, in which case you can cross them off the list as they happen. Feel free to make notes on your schedule as the interview unfolds. It is a good idea for you to explain that you may take some notes during the interview as they speak, if you are going to do this, although you should not show them the schedule beforehand in case it prompts certain answers. If you do plan to take notes during the interview, you need to remember to have multiple copies of your schedule handy, one for each data collection session.

Start by listing the main topics you want to cover in your interview. Under each topic heading you should aim to come up with three questions. More than about 20 questions in total is likely to be of little help, as it will be too difficult in practice for you to keep track of which ones you have not asked yet, and which ones have already been answered, particularly after you have conducted several interviews.

To illustrate the type of schedule that you might come up with, following is an imaginary schedule for an interview with a student to answer the research question: What does it mean when someone says they believe in ghosts?

1   BELIEF

- Would you say you believe in ghosts?
- How long for?
- Do you know other people who believe in ghosts?

2   EXPERIENCES

- Have you ever seen a ghost?
- Tell me about the experience ('how did it make you feel?').
- Other people's experiences.

3   EXPLANATIONS

- How do you account for your experience(s)?
- What is actually happening when you see a ghost?

4   OTHER PARANORMAL TOPICS

- Do you believe in ESP/UFOs?
- Do you participate in any paranormal events (e.g. ghost hunting)?

5   RELIGION

- What are your religious beliefs (if any)?
- Do you believe in the existence of a spirit or a soul?
- Do you believe in the afterlife? What do you believe happens when you die?

It is always a good idea to construct a list of prompts in addition to these basic questions – these could be mini-topics, anticipated answers, potential follow up questions or general encouraging comments or neutral phrases, that you can toss into the schedule, if your participant is a bit reluctant or strays from the subject. These prompts can, of course, be added during the course of the interview itself. For example, under *explanations* you might add things such as:

- spirits (which might mean you have to start asking some *religion* questions);
- moral judgement (e.g. why do ghosts tend to be linked to bad events, such as murders?);
- hallucinations (how can you tell the difference?);
- prompts that relate to earlier answers (e.g. why do you think you saw your grandad and not your grandma?);
- general prompts (e.g. could you tell me about that experience in more detail?).

Be prepared to tinker with your schedule from interview to interview – although take care not to stray too far from your original research question (unless you are doing something like grounded theory, which allows you to shift the focus of the study as you collect data).

8.1.4 Not asking the most obvious questions

Interviewers should appreciate the difference between their research question and their interview questions. Let us suppose you are interviewing a group of students about their dieting practices, based on your idea that young people's decisions to diet are influenced by the media; for example, what they read in magazines. Would it really be a good idea to ask 'how have the media influenced your decision to go on a diet?' Firstly, the interviewee may not know how the media has influenced them – this is something that you would be seeking to establish through your analysis of the data. Moreover, they may well not agree that they have been influenced by the media at all, but the question does not enable them to say this without contradicting you (this is known as a **leading question**), and they may not feel comfortable disagreeing with you in this context, as they may wish to please you by agreeing with your assumptions (recall that this kind of issue can be avoided, if you try not to include assumptions in your research questions in the first place). Your participant may not share your understanding of the term *media* either, as they may think that it only refers to newspapers and magazines, when in fact you may intend it to mean television programmes and advertisements too. Therefore, it is usually better to skirt around your research question by asking more specific, easily answered questions that tap aspects of the issue under discussion: for example, 'What magazines do you read?', 'What celebrities do you admire and why?', 'Is there anybody whose dietary success has inspired you?'

MAXIMISING MARKS ✔

Some good examples of bad questions

'Many people feel that, in this day and age, children have too many freedoms, have too much money and are not subject to sufficient discipline to make them respectful to others. To what extent would you agree with this?'

This is a dreadful question for several reasons. Firstly, it is just **too long.** Keep your questions short and clear. It is also a **leading question,** as it is indicating that the questionnaire is expecting some form of agreement with the statements made. (The 'Many people feel that ...' part of the introduction is also giving a clear steer to the respondent. It is also **double-barrelled** (in fact this question has multiple barrels). Double-barrelled questions are questions that are really asking two (or more) questions in one. This question should really be several, which could be phrased as follows:

- 'Do children have too much freedom to do as they please?'
- 'Do children have too much money?'
- 'Do adults discipline children enough?'

'Sir Philip Poncemby has gone on record as saying that the current bill on financial regulation goes too far. What are your views on this bill?'

This question has two main problems. The first is that it has **prestige bias:** that is, by linking a statement to the views of an influential figure, you are possibly biasing respondents to agree with their views. The other issue is that your respondents may not know anything about the bill that is being referred to – you should always **ask questions that your participants are going to be able to understand** or have appropriate knowledge of. In this case it might have been better to provide the participants with a lay person's summary of the proposals in the bill to read, and then ask them to comment on them.

'Is dinner time a period when you are not at your most alert?'

The question is **ambiguous** because, depending on where you grew up and how your family ate, dinner time may mean midday or evening. Make sure that you use terms that will mean the same thing to all people. It is also made more confusing because it is phrased negatively ('when you are not at your most alert ...').

'Chips, crisps, mashed potatoes, baked potatoes or roast potatoes: which do you think contains the most amount of fat?'

This is a poorly phrased question for two reasons. Firstly, **it lists alternatives before asking the actual question,** which is confusing and will almost certainly mean that you will have to repeat them. It is also poorly specified, as the amount of fat could depend on the portion size and on who has made the items. It would be better expressed as: *'Tell me which of the following CheapyMart own brand items contains the most amount of fat per 100 grams: chips, crisps, mashed potatoes, baked potatoes or roast potatoes.'*

8.1.5 How long is a good interview?

Unfortunately, there is no satisfactory answer to this question. Five minutes of dazzling anecdotal material may give you enough data for an entire discourse analysis but is likely to be insufficient for other forms of analysis. Two rambling and repetitive hours of questions and answers may still leave you scratching your head when it comes to analysis. As ever, it all depends on your research question – an interview is only **good** once it provides you with the data to answer the research question you have set for yourself. This is why piloting your interview schedule and wording of your questions is absolutely crucial.

A student's experience . . .

" *I did a qualitative research project for my dissertation. I set up an online web discussion to collect my data and used some stimulus material to provoke the discussion, which included some information about my research topic, and then two questions to follow it. I decided to pilot my questions first to make sure that my participants would interpret them how I wished, and would give me appropriate responses that I could use in my research. I found that participants focused heavily on the first of the two questions in their replies, when it was really the second question I wanted them to focus on. I therefore designed a single question, which orientated them to what I was really most interested in. This worked a lot better and the participants focused on what I was hoping for in their answers, so it was definitely beneficial to a pilot study, even though it involved a little extra work!* "

TOP TIP   Use the best recording equipment you can get

If you are conducting interviews or focus groups, make sure that you are using the best audio recording equipment that you can – see if you can borrow some good quality microphones from your department and check that they work with your Dictaphone (some digital voice recorders need powered microphones if they are to work properly). If you are conducting focus group discussions you may need a table microphone that can pick up everyone seated around it, or even video record the session so that you can reliably identify who is speaking. This is particularly helpful when people are speaking at the same time, as often happens in group discussions.

8.2 NOT JUST A 'BIG INTERVIEW': DISTINCTIVE FEATURES OF FOCUS GROUPS

Many of the same issues we have discussed regarding interviews may also apply to focus groups. You will need to consider how much structure you want to impose upon the discussion. This may influence the design of your focus group schedule. You may also need to check that your proposed questions are open-ended, and use terminology that makes sense to your participants. However, a focus group is more than just an opportunity to interview several participants at one time. As we mentioned in Chapter 6, there are practical and ethical considerations about running focus groups. There are also some very important theoretical issues to consider. In an interview, you might assume that a participant is describing their experience, expressing their opinion, telling a story and/or constructing an account. In doing so, the participant will often have your rapt personal attention, and feel they can speak to you in confidence. The interview is, in essence, a conversation between two people. How might this differ for the same participant in a focus group setting? Wilkinson (2003) suggests that, because focus groups involve participants interacting with each other, at least as much as with the researcher, they may produce more *naturalistic* data. They are good places to observe activities such as humour and conflict. What this means is that the data you collect from a focus group may differ in both *content* and *structure*, from that collected in an individual interview. A participant might be willing to disclose something very personal in a one-to-one interview, but be less forthcoming in a focus group setting. For this reason, some researchers prefer to use interviews to investigate sensitive topics, which may involve disclosure of personal or distressing material. You need to consider whether this may be an issue in your study. On the other hand, some participants may find the presence of others in a focus group supportive, and this may facilitate disclosure. A great deal will depend on the precise composition of the group itself, and the way in which you manage it. You may want to consider whether it is appropriate for your study to have groups that are deliberately mixed or more 'homogeneous' in terms of, say, gender, sexual orientation, age or other important characteristics.

Let us take some concrete examples. A female researcher may wish to investigate older women's experience of the menopause. She might conduct some individual interviews, on the assumption that participants will be willing to disclose more about their personal experiences one to one. If she also conducts some focus group discussions, she might find that these generate some interesting new material. Women may share a sense of solidarity and humour with each other, and be willing to disclose things they were reluctant to bring up in the interview. *Or they might not* ... Similarly, a male researcher may wish to investigate male students' views on 'heterosexual promiscuity'. He might conduct a focus group discussion, using vignette descriptions of 'a great night out on campus' to stimulate discussion. The focus group discussion might be bawdy, and give the impression that the young men taking part all shared a view that casual sex was a great idea. *Or it might not* ... Individual interviews with the same set of participants might identify a more nuanced set of perspectives, with some participants expressing reservations about casual sex. *Or they might not* ...

The thing about focus group discussions is that they are inherently unpredictable. It is rarely possible to know in advance whether focus groups or individual interviews will yield the best data for your study. You may want to find out more about focus groups before settling on this method of data collection for your study. As for any approach to data collection, you might also consider conducting a pilot before relying on this methodology for the whole of your project.

8.3 TRANSCRIBING THE TAPE: REALITY BITES!

Anyone who believes that interviews are a soft option when it comes to data collection will be in for a shock once they start the transcription process. The laboriousness of the task, and the sheer length of time it takes, lead many a qualitative project student to query their wisdom in opting for this particular method. As a result, many students often ask if their departments can provide transcription software, or even pay professional transcribers out of their own pockets. However, it is actually good practice to carry out your own transcription. So much rich detail can be lost between the recording of the interview and the production of the transcript, that the involvement of a third party may further compromise the integrity of the exercise. After all, the goal of transcription is to get as close as possible to the actual experience of listening to a recording of the interview. There are also ethical issues with the use of paid transcribers – if you are thinking of going down this route, you will need to mention it on your ethical approval form, and the panel will expect you to notify your participants that the tape recording will be accessed by a third party.

Of course we all aim for accurate transcription, but just how detailed should it be? Much spoken language consists of non-verbal 'noise' – ums and ers, laughter, coughing and spluttering, and other vocal utterances that often perform valuable communicative functions but are essentially wordless. Then there are the rhythms of speech itself – pauses, changes in tempo and pitch that we would indicate in music but not in talk. Conversation analysts have devised elaborate coding protocols for annotating all this kind of information. The most well known is the Jefferson system, which is a set of symbols that has been widely used in conversation and discourse analysis. It is quite a flexible system: nobody would expect you to use all of the symbols, and many authors use the bare minimum: (.) to indicate a pause, underlining to indicate stress or emphasis, [square] brackets to indicate overlapping speech.

Some transcription symbols (see Forrester (2002) for a more detailed treatment)

↑	marked rise in intonation
↓	marked fall in intonation
Underlined text	words that are emphasised by the speaker
:::	colons placed after a word indicate final sounds being drawn out
[ ]	overlapping speech/interruption
CAPITALS	indicating increase volume of speech
°utterance°	small circles indicate talk that is much quieter than other speech in that context
.hhh	an in-breath
hhh	an outbreath
=	used to indicate that there is virtually no pause between one utterance and the next
(comment)	researcher's comment about the talk at that point
(.)	a small pause
>speech<	faster speech
<speech>	slower speech
?	a rising intonation at the end of an utterance (such as a question)
(.4)	silence – the number indicates the duration, in seconds

Ultimately it depends on how you intend to use the information. If you are doing a fine grained conversation analysis, where timed pauses are taken to indicate discomfort or difficulty, or where the slightest cues are necessary to study the interaction between speakers, then a detailed transcription will be beneficial. For a thematic analysis, where you are simply sorting the transcript into thematic or conceptual categories, the minimal approach is much more sensible – especially if you have several hours' worth of material to transcribe.

The extract below is taken from one of the authors' transcripts of a UK television programme called 'Hot Property', showing some of the Jefferson symbols in action. It illustrates how the symbols can pick up the nuances of speech when one of the speakers is quite demonstrative or flamboyant – in this case it is the presenter of the show who is producing lots of variations of tempo and pitch in her effusive commentary. The homeowner is reduced to a rather subdued role, as indicated by her notably quiet echo of the presenter in line 200.

198   R: This the living room
199   AB: I::t's lo↑vely (.) a- (.) what >a lovely< ↑view (.)
200   R: °It is lovely°
201   AB: And do people live on those boats?
202   R: Yep (.) actually (.) on that red one
203   AB: <What are we talking about the boats> tell me about your flat
204   R: erm it (.)

A student's experience . . .

> *I had been warned by my supervisor that transcribing interview data was laborious and could take up to ten hours to do per hour of tape, depending on how 'messy' the audio quality was. I had recorded focus group discussions on a topic, but I didn't remember the conversation being particularly difficult to follow at the time, so I thought that the transcription could be blitzed in a few days. This was a real mistake, as when I listened to the recordings parts were really difficult to hear properly, and people were talking at the same time a lot more than I had realised during the actual sessions. The result of this was, with just a week to go before the deadline for my project, I was still transcribing audio tapes in the library. I had to rush my analysis and write up and I know I lost marks just because I really underestimated the amount of transcription time I would need.*

8.4 USING QUESTIONNAIRES AND SCALES

These are arguably the most commonly used methods in undergraduate psychology dissertations (if not in all modern psychological research), since they are relatively easy to administer to large samples and should lead to straightforward analysis, in the sense that scales in particular are carefully designed to yield easily interpretable quantitative data. However, they can also be problematic, if you do not put enough care into their design or appropriate use.

There are so many psychometric measures now available in the literature, or available as commercial tests, that students often find that the measures they are interested in have already been designed by someone else, and all they need to do is present the information in a way that is meaningful to participants and ethically acceptable. Sometimes, however, we are interested in a variable for which a scale has yet to be developed, or we are surveying participants on a range of behaviours that do not fall neatly into a scale as such. Designing an original measure involves a lot of work and may constitute a project in itself. We consider both types of study in this section.

8.4.1 Using existing measures

Existing measures are useful – perhaps essential – when we are examining the effect of a well-established variable, such as personality or self-esteem. It is rarely worth developing a new measure for such topics unless you are intending to explore a theoretical point that you believe existing measures fail to consider.

Once you have identified the measure you want to use in your study, you are then faced with the obstacle of getting hold of it. Many psychology departments have a 'test library' of some sort, but be aware that it may contain tests that are out of date, or lack the scoring keys or manual that go with them. Also, do not assume that it will be okay to photocopy these questionnaires – nearly all commercially available tests and assessments are subject to some form of restriction in terms of copyright. Read the small print of the terms and conditions in the manual to check this. Ask if it is possible for more copies to be purchased for you – some departments have a small budget for stocking their test cupboard, but you will need to be very realistic about your sample size (see Chapter 4). You should also check that you are allowed to administer that test as a student – some personality measures and ability tests are restricted to individuals who are qualified to administer them, although you may be permitted to use them if you are trained and supervised appropriately. However, you should always check with your supervisor or module leader – remember that some of the tests in the cupboard have been purchased for staff use only. It is, therefore, far better to stick to a measure whose components are accessible in the public domain, such as those published in journal articles.

If you are trying to find out if there is an existing measure for the variable you are interested in, begin by finding a published paper that uses the measure you are looking for and tracking down the reference (all studies in refereed journals should give a full reference for the measures they have used). There are two potential kinds of source reference:

- Another journal article that describes the construction and validation of the measure, e.g. Heinberg, L.J., Thompson, J.K., & Stormer, S. (1995). Development and validation of the sociocultural attitudes to appearance questionnaire. *International Journal of Eating Disorders*, 17, 81–89.

- A commercially developed test, only available at great cost from the publishers (and you have to be a suitably qualified individual to administer it), e.g. Costa, P.T. Jr & McCrae, R.R. (1992). *Revised NEO Personality Inventory (NEO-PI-R) and NEO Five Factor Inventory (NEO-FFI) Professional Manual*. Odessa, FL: Psychological Assessment Resources.

Through your own library or interlibrary loans, get hold of the original paper and use the items from it (along with any other useful information, such as rubric or reliability statistics). It is not always immediately obvious where this information is contained. Typically, a paper reporting a new scale will have the items listed helpfully in an appendix, so you can just copy these straight from the list. Other papers hide the items away in tables of reliability statistics or other analyses, or – particularly with short scales – they may just describe the items within the text of the method section. Keep looking! The information should be in there somewhere (although you may have to root out a few more papers, if other authors have not always referenced the very first construction of the test).

Do not forget to keep any information regarding scoring protocol – for example, which items are reverse-keyed, or whether certain items constitute discrete subscales. Very often a measure has developed quite a history within the literature, and the validity of the subscales, and their relationship to other variables, is a matter of great interest to researchers in the field.

MAXIMISING MARKS
These measures have their own histories!

It is always worth looking at later papers that have used the same measure, particularly ones by the original authors, where they may have tinkered with their own scale. To give one example, McCreary and Sasse (2000) developed a scale 'Drive for Muscularity' that measures how much effort boys and young men go to in order to develop impressively muscular bodies. Four years later, the same authors (plus a couple of colleagues) published a paper in which they argued that the scale, initially devised as a single-factor measure, is actually better described by two discrete factors – attitudinal and behavioural – and in their paper the authors specify the items that comprise each separate subscale (McCreary, Sasse, Saucier & Dorsch (2004)). A marker who is familiar with this measure would be mightily impressed if you cite the updated source and use the two subscales in your eventual analysis.

One of the biggest sources of frustration among students conducting psychometric projects is when the exact measure they need is simply not available in the public domain. Do not despair, often you can find 'short forms': validated shorter versions of commercial measures, listing the items they have selected. As an example, there are always a number of short versions of the Eysenck Personality Questionnaire in circulation (see Francis, Lewis & Ziebertz (2006), who developed a short form for German participants).

Another very useful source of psychometric test material is the IPIP – the International Personality Item Pool – that you can access at http://ipip.ori.org/ipip/. This is a website aimed at psychology researchers, that contains a huge assortment of scales, subscales and individual items, which can be mixed and matched to concoct a brand new scale. Obviously, if you are using it for this last purpose, you will need to carry out the validity and reliability checks discussed in Section 7.4.3, but you may prefer simply to use one of the existing measures already put together.

8.4.2 Designing original measures

Scale construction is a very complicated business and may well constitute the primary goal of a dissertation in itself (whole PhDs have been devoted to it), so we will not go into the process in great detail here, except to indicate one or two potential pitfalls and some places where you might pick up extra marks.

Multi-part questionnaires are very common in undergraduate psychology projects. They are often the most simple methods to conceive, but can be the most difficult to analyse. This is because they are rarely thought through, and the student may have little idea of what their actual hypothesis is, or how they intend to actually prepare the data for analysis. Following is an example of the first three items of a questionnaire to measure cigarette smoking:

1   How many cigarettes do you smoke each day?

0–5	5–10	10–15	15–20	20+

2   What age did you begin smoking?

Below 10	10–15	15–20	Over 20

3   Have you ever tried to give up? Explain your reasons below.

Let us imagine this questionnaire continues in the same vein for another 20 items. You have already set yourself a difficult task when it comes to analysing your data (and an even more difficult task of writing your results section – see Chapter 10). These three items alone constitute three separate variables. You will almost certainly be looking at some kind of regression analysis, or perhaps a series of *t*-tests or correlations. You may even have to have some kind of content analysis, particularly if you are going to make anything of the answers to question 3.

A student's experience . . .

    I was interested in people's attitudes to young people who wore different kinds of clothes. I developed a questionnaire that included pictures of people with different types of clothing style, and I also manipulated the ethnic origin of the models. I thought that it was important to look at gender too, so I added more photographs so that there were male and female models for each style and ethnic group. For each image I asked a series of questions about how the participant perceived the person wearing the clothes – in particular I looked at friendliness, aggression and extraversion, but I also asked about other personality characteristics that I thought were relevant. When I showed my questionnaire to my supervisor, she suggested I had too many variables in my design, but I couldn't see why that was a problem – I had carefully thought through all the things that might influence people's scores on the questionnaire. She tried to persuade me to make my questionnaire simpler but I thought that would leave me open to criticism so I stuck to my guns. It was not until I came to enter the data into SPSS and I ended up with so many columns that I realised that by including so many different variables (all of which were within groups), I had set myself a very difficult task for the analysis and the write up of the report. I found that I had to leave out a lot of the data that I collected just to enable me to keep track of my main research question when I came to write it up. **99**

Questionnaire constructors tend to prefer items such as questions 1 and 2, where you ask respondents to select from a predetermined set of options. It looks tidier and establishes in advance the scoring system (presumably you would code 0–5 as **1**, 5–10 as **2** and so on). In reality, however, these codes are flexible, unless you have a good reason for expecting the data to fall into a particular pattern (this age banding might reflect published norms or developmental stages). Unless you are systematically following this type of logic, it is probably better to ask your respondents simply to specify their own age, and the age at which they started smoking. It would certainly avoid the inevitable confusion faced by a respondent, in this case, who smokes ten cigarettes a day and began smoking at the age of 15!

Of course you could avoid this easily by making the bands discrete, e.g. 0–5, 6–10, 11–15 and so on. However, there is potentially a much worse problem in that, by setting the lowest category as 0–5, the questionnaire fails to identify non-smokers: we will be charitable on this occasion and assume that the student's research question required them only to select smokers!

COMMON CONFUSION **?**

Survey, scale or questionnaire?

Students who use pen-and-paper methods for their data collection are often at a loss to know how to describe these methods in their report. When does a scale become a questionnaire? A questionnaire a survey? What is the difference? The answer, as ever, is that the boundaries are blurred because the terms have been used interchangeably, and often vary according to discipline. A full blown survey, particularly the type carried out by sociologists or market researchers, will incorporate some interviews as well as one or more questionnaires. Psychologists, on the other hand, are more likely to hand out several different scales as part of a 'battery'. They may describe the whole battery as a 'questionnaire booklet'. But could they call it a survey? The simplest rule of thumb is probably the following:

Survey: a type of study design that collects a limited amount of data in a standard format from a relatively large number of people who have been selected as representative of a particular population (Robson, 2011).

Questionnaire: a broad term to refer to the pen-and-paper measure that you are handing to your participants. It may consist of a number of disparate items, eliciting qualitative or quantitative data, or a number of discrete scales. However, be careful how you use the term questionnaire – if you are simply using it to cover a set of scales, then you cannot claim to be using questionnaire *methodology*.

Scale: a discrete measuring instrument in which a set of related items or questions (usually statements on a topic) is answered on the same scale (typically a Likert-type scale). This instrument cannot be described as a questionnaire by itself.

There are many occasions on which a multipart questionnaire is necessary or desirable, as most of the time we need to collect some demographic data from our participants so some discrete items are required. Or we may be curious to discover more information about the lifestyle or habits of our sample (e.g. if we are studying marketing influences, we would need to know what kinds of media people use or where they shop). However, each item needs serious consideration. A poorly constructed questionnaire may mean that you are unable to give a good answer to your research question.

Original scale construction: while questionnaires need to be pieced together item by item, psychometric scales have their own constraints that – in theory – make them easier to put together. It is essential that your respondents use the same scale to respond to each item; typically this is a Likert-type scale of the sort illustrated in Table 8.1.

TABLE 8.1 Example of a Likert scale.

Disagree strongly	Disagree somewhat	Neither agree nor disagree	Agree somewhat	Agree strongly

You would normally score this scale from 1 to 5, although there are multiple possibilities: 1 to 7 is very common. Some authors just do away with the descriptions and simply ask respondents to indicate the strength of their agreement as a number between 1 and 10. There are arguments for and against each of these. There is a strong case for removing central options, since these are often poorly specified – in some cases they are described as 'no opinion', which of course is not the same thing as being partially in agreement! If you do decide to use a central option, do ensure that its description falls between the two poles, and is not just an opt out. Central options are often avoided because many respondents tend to sit on the fence and mark the middle value for most items – in the example above, a 4-point scale would force them to commit to agreement or disagreement. But would it be a true reflection of the person's attitude?

The hardest part of designing original scales is to know what kind of statements to include. Some people simply reuse a mixture of existing scale items or close approximations. A better way might be to produce an 'item pool' by carrying out some kind of focus group discussion, and selecting as potential items actual statements made by the speakers. This would give your scale higher ecological validity.

8.4.3 Reliability and validity

While reliability and validity issues should be considered for all psychometric scales, they are of particular importance for original scales because they are completely unknown quantities: you cannot judge their results without knowing how well they stand up to scrutiny. Researchers usually talk of internal and external reliability and validity – internal issues relate to the scale as a coherent instrument in itself; external issues consider the scale in relation to the topic it is supposed to be measuring and, if there are any, existing measures of that topic.

Reliability. The main objective of a psychometric scale is to yield a meaningful number (or numbers, if it is composed of several subscales) that reflects an individual's attitude towards something, or the strength of a personality trait or other psychological construct. That number is usually the cumulative total of all the scale 'items' (the questions or statements), so we have to take care that each item in the scale is contributing towards the meaningfulness of the total value – this is called **internal reliability.**

Let us suppose you have a scale measuring 'belief in Father Christmas' comprising the following statements:

1   There is only one Father Christmas.
2   My Christmas presents are all purchased and delivered by my parents.
3   No chimney is too narrow for Father Christmas to squeeze down.
4   Reindeer cannot fly.

Our cumulative total is a measure of how strongly respondents believe in Father Christmas, so we would expect the strongest believers to give similar answers to all the items – on a 5-point scale, something like 5, 1, 5, 1 (bearing in mind that questions 2 and 4 will need to be reverse-keyed and entered as 5 in the database). However, it may be that question 4 produces a less coherent pattern, as scrutiny of strong believers' responses indicates that some people who score as believers on questions 1 to 3 are somewhat sceptical about reindeers' aerial capabilities.

We can test internal reliability by means of Cronbach's alpha, a statistic that correlates the participant's scores on the individual items to one another and to the measure as a whole. An alpha value of 0.8 for the scale overall is usually taken to indicate good reliability. SPSS will also indicate the degree to which removal of any given item will affect that overall value – so we might find that, while our Father Christmas scale has an overall reliability of 0.73, just below the magic 0.8, the removal of question 4 would result in an overall value of 0.82. This would be grounds for dropping that particular item.

MAXIMISING MARKS ✔

Remember your subscales

You may be using a single questionnaire that comprises two or three subscales (i.e. different constructs that you are interested in assessing, such as self-esteem and extraversion). Do remember that you should calculate Cronbach's alpha for each subscale individually – do not calculate a single alpha for the questionnaire as a whole.

The other type of reliability you might like to measure is **test-retest reliability**. This is sometimes also referred to as a measure of **external reliability**, in that it compares pairs of scores from respondents taking the same measure either side of a specified time period, to see how stable a person's score is over time. For example, we might want to retest our Father Christmas questionnaire either side of the holiday period (belief might, after all, be dashed by a disappointing stocking). For this measure a standard correlation statistic will usually suffice – and we would again be expecting quite high values (0.8 or 0.9).

Validity. This is about demonstrating that your scale assesses what you intended it to. The easiest way of doing this is to conduct an assessment of **face validity**: does the scale look as though it is assessing what you claim it is? You could assess this by asking someone who is unfamiliar with your study to look at your questionnaire items and state what they think it is trying to measure.

If you have developed a new measure of a well-established psychological construct – e.g. self-esteem – you will need to ensure that it bears some relation to existing measures (these may be outdated, or developed for a different culture or age group, but the fundamental construct should be broadly similar). This is known as **construct validity** and is usually tested with new measures by including an old measure as part of the test battery. Correlations are then examined between old and new measures. Unlike reliability statistics, however, it is enough to demonstrate a significant correlation between the two measures for the new measure to be deemed reliable.

8.5 EXPERIMENTS

If you have designed your experiment well (see Chapter 4), there should be fewer problems when it comes to the data collection stage, so we have chosen a couple of mainly practical issues to focus on in this chapter.

8.5.1 Running trials and controlling variables

Compared with interviews and questionnaires, collecting data through experiments is an arduous task. Actually recruiting participants in the first place can be difficult, especially if you need a large sample. Depending on the nature of the study, it is often tempting for experimenters to run trials with as many participants as possible – in, for example, a memory study where stimuli can be projected onto a screen, or broadcast on a video or audio player. Ideally you want to keep the testing conditions equivalent for all participants, though, so if you are planning to go down this route you will need to ensure that each session has a similar number of participants (rather than, say, one session with 3 and another with 23). You may also wish to consider the possible impact that the time of day could have on your study, if you are assessing cognitive performance.

8.5.2 Using specialist equipment

One of the most enjoyable things about doing experimental projects is that it means you can finally get your hands on some of the specialist equipment lying around the department – and usually the technical staff are only too happy to help out. Sometimes, equipment is used just to facilitate the presentation of stimuli. But much of the time the equipment not only presents stimuli but also collects data, and on these occasions it is important that you know, firstly, how to retrieve the data and, secondly, what the data actually mean!

If you have been able to design a piece of software using a program such as SuperLab, eprime, DMDX, psyscope or mathlab, then this should pose no problems – although you need to ensure after each trial that the data have been stored, not just calculated. Sometimes, if you are measuring only one or two variables, it is worth keeping a hard copy of each participant's scores, just in case something goes wrong with the program at some point.

Much of the time, though, the equipment calculating data points is much more sophisticated, and designed to serve multiple purposes. For example, you may have access to equipment that measures EEG or heart rates, or even pupil dilation. The data output from such equipment can be even more intimidating than an SPSS printout, and you would need to be trained and supervised by someone who can help you to interpret the data appropriately.

8.5.3 Using confederates

Some experimental work requires the use of confederates or 'stooges' to manipulate the experimental setting (as in conformity work). You must ensure that you have fully trained your confederates and rehearsed their roles until you are satisfied that they are going to be able to behave consistently in every session. You should also try to use the same confederate(s) in all sessions, as a change in the appearance, age or gender of the confederate could cause difficulties in the interpretation of your results.

8.6 USING ARCHIVAL DATA

Archival data come in many shapes and forms and for this reason it is usually a good idea to copy them into some kind of analysable format. However, it is important never to lose sight of the research question, and it may still be important to consider their original format as well as the textual content. You must certainly never lose sight of the source of any archival information, keeping detailed records of where and when you accessed each piece of data – this will prove invaluable when it comes to writing your report.

The most likely sources of archival data for psychological research are the following:

- Traditional media – newspapers, magazines, television and radio programmes.
- Web-based material – websites/web pages, discussion forums, other online archives.
- Publicity material – advertising, information leaflets (e.g. health communication).

8.6.1 Print media

If you are accessing newspaper content through a database such as LexisNexis, you will download the material straight into a textual format. However, if you are using actual newspapers and magazines, you may need to scan textual material when doing a close analysis, e.g. discourse analysis, unless your focus is more on the visual content. In any case, it may well be important to refer to visual content – photographs, headlines, the physical layout of the story – so you will need to ensure that you keep hard copies of all your materials.

8.6.2 Broadcast media

Television and radio pose the same problems for researchers as interview data: they need to be transcribed for analysis purposes. Radio programmes are relatively easy; the issues differ little from those discussed earlier in the chapter (Section 8.3). Television programmes are more challenging because you cannot ignore the visual content. As a result, transcription becomes even more laborious, since you will need to describe changes of scene as well as spoken output. As with interview material, you will need to decide how much detail is both necessary and useful to your analysis, and this will depend on how closely you need to scrutinise the nature of the interaction between people on screen, or the interchange of verbal and visual information.

The following example is taken from the same television dataset as the extract discussed in Section 8.3, only here we have included the visual information that makes the verbal content much easier to understand and discuss. In this particular show, a young married couple is introduced to the viewers as contestants in a game where they need to estimate the cost of three selected properties. Individual interviews with the partners are spliced together, along with footage of the couple leafing through an album of wedding photographs, to construct a narrative that emphasises how much owning a property means to them, ensuring that the emotional stakes are high. So high, in fact, that the male partner, George, is eventually reduced to tears.[1] The visual effect of this process is impossible to ignore, and so it is recorded in considerable detail (the line numbers in the left column indicate spoken content).

---

[1] See Giles (2002a) for an extended discussion of some of the issues raised in programmes of this nature.

47   G (voiceover): When I met Catherine I promised her the ea::rt:h (.)
48   when we got married
      (*Close-up of hands: initially G's hand is laid over C's, then C's other hand comes to rest on G's fingers, wedding ring at centre of screen*)
49   I promised her (.) the universe (.)
      (*solo shot of G. in bedroom, real time*)
50   suppose the house would be the first s::tep (.) to giving her everything
51   <I wanted to give her> from the moment I <u>met</u> her
      (*wedding album again; solo photo of G, then one of G&C*)
52   C (voiceover): If we were in a house (.) it would totally change our <u>li</u>ves
53   (*solo shot of G. in bedroom, real time*)
      G: a j- (*closes eyes, moves head up and to right, maintaining half-smile, gradually whole body moves forward and he rubs at right eye, face briefly out of picture as he turns away from camera. Then sits bolt upright, eyes open but watery, and looks away from camera, unable to regain composure*)
54   °I'm sorry°

Notice that, again, the Jefferson transcription system is used in this extract (see Section 8.4.3 for a list of what the symbols mean). Of course it is not necessary in all studies to record so much detail of recorded speech, particularly if your emphasis is primarily on the role of the visual material.

8.6.3 Web-based data

The great advantage of web-based archival data is that it arrives in a format perfectly suited to textual analysis, so far as the manipulation of the words is concerned. However, one feature of online material is its multi-layered nature – often we travel through umpteen links in order to arrive at a specific piece of text, and this organisation can easily be lost when all data are reproduced in a Word file. Again, it is a case of deciding how much detail is necessary or useful to enable you to answer your research question. In a large-scale content analysis you would be less interested in these structural issues, but a close analysis of the virtual environment might require a thorough sense of the internet user's experience when navigating a particular website.

The most challenging issue for web-based researchers is the documentation of all the information. There is such a vast treasure trove of data in cyberspace: where do you begin and end data collection? Ultimately this is a design issue (see Chapter 4) and ideally you should specify at the outset how much data you are going to attempt to handle in the project. However, some studies are, through necessity, exploratory in nature and you may not want to constrain yourself at the outset.

Nevertheless, the important thing is to make sure that each piece of data is indexed with some kind of useful information that can make it retrievable again. Archives, and indeed entire sites, can become closed down during the course of a project, so you need to be able to indicate this in your report – in case your marker decides to check up on the source, cannot find it, and wonders if you have simply made the data up!

8.6.4 Documents and other hard copy material

Archival research often examines public information to better understand the kind of influences that operate on everyday behaviour. A typical example here is health communication research, where a psychologist might want to explore the impact of the way health information is 'framed' through its presentation in publicity leaflets – the type lying around in health centre waiting rooms or dentists' surgeries.

The issues confronted by these kinds of documents are broadly the same as for newspaper and magazine researchers. It is about maintaining a balance between formatting the textual information in a useful way for analysis, while keeping the original material on hand for further, contextual analysis – and you will almost certainly want to include some of the original material in your report, albeit only in the appendices.

8.7 OBSERVATION

As with internet data, one of the biggest challenges facing observational researchers is knowing when to stop collecting data. Of course, this decision may be taken away from you, as your gate-keeper may only allow you restricted access; in which case the challenge is to make the most of the limited time available. All the more important, therefore, is the careful construction of an **observation schedule** at the outset of the study.

Like interview schedules, observation schedules can be theory- or data-driven, depending on your research question. If the literature in your field makes it clear what variables you need to measure, or what kind of information will enable your study to be compared with previous research, then you will be able to draw up your schedule at the outset. Previous researchers may already have used a particular format that you can simply replicate in your study.

MAXIMISING MARKS ✔

Catch it on camera!

Sometimes observational research can seem an impossible task for an individual. How do we get all that information down on one schedule? Suppose we've missed something? We may have limited time in a particular setting. One way around these problems is to record the observed phenomenon on video and carry out your eventual analysis on the tape itself. Obviously you would need the permission of the participants; and you would need to ensure that the presence of the camera did not influence their behaviour. It also makes the business of establishing inter-observer reliability easier. You may of course be restricted entirely to video based material for observational purposes. For example, you might not be able to gain access to a nursery or kindergarten but videos may be available of children's play. Inevitably your report will lose some of the ethnographic richness of a genuine field observation, but you may be more interested in the minutiae of the behaviour, the children's close interaction, than in the setting itself.

If, however, you are entering a particular setting for the first time, and there is no previous research on that setting that could forewarn you what to expect, then the observation schedule will need to be built up over a series of pilot studies; during which you take extensive notes and decide what are going to be the key behaviours your data collection focuses on – and how much information you can personally record in a given time period.

Let us return to the study from Chapter 4, looking at the interaction between stand-up comedians and their audiences. Recall that there were a number of possible methods that you could use to study this topic, and a number of different research questions that could be generated. Suppose you decided to do a qualitative study of the interaction between audience members: where would you place yourself in the audience? How could you make detailed notes, let alone operate a systematic schedule?

Many observational researchers accept that there is a price to pay for being in a challenging environment and that is the potential loss of useful data; so they will disappear from the setting from time to time to make notes in a private place (typically a toilet). However, this would seriously limit the close analysis of audience activity you might want to do. How do you decide which parts of the audience to focus on? Repeated visits to the setting might be necessary before you could even begin to organise your notes into some kind of analytical format.

An essential requirement of observational research, particularly in the early stages, is that you carry out some measure of **inter-rater reliability**. This is a typical feature of quantitative observations where the phenomena you are recording are measurable in some way (even just as ticks in a check box). It simply requires bringing along a friend or course mate (find some way you can reciprocate) and getting them to complete the draft copy of the schedule that you have drawn up. There is a variety of different statistical tests you can use to measure different types of observational data – Cohen's Kappa is probably the most widely used. This is simply a measure that indicates how close your records are to one another. If there is much diversity in your completed schedules, it may require another session to refine the instrument. It will in any case be very useful to get some feedback from someone else who has attempted to use the same schedule.

8.7.1 Developing a schedule: observing group interaction

Imagine that, in your study, you are interested in the different contributions to a staff discussion involving six people from a workplace – three senior and three junior members of staff. You predict that the group's decision making will be orchestrated by senior staff despite their claims of a 'level playing field' in meetings. You have recorded the discussion on video and you can now take your time over developing a good coding schedule.

The first thing you need to ask is: *what behaviours do I need to code?* Ideally you would answer this by deciding what are likely to be the key points of difference (perhaps senior staff are more likely to interrupt another speaker, so INTERRUPTIONS would be your first category). Alternatively, you might prefer to start with a blank slate and just make notes on the video to begin with. (Bear in mind that you have a clear assumption about the outcome, so you will have to be very mindful of potential recording bias. Inter-observer reliability – preferably with a co-researcher who is 'blind' both to the status of the individuals in the group, and to your hypothesis – will be crucial in this study!)

Eventually, after a couple of run throughs of the video, you have identified a set of behaviours that you are going to code. The first thing is to sort these into VERBAL and NON-VERBAL lists. It is probably easiest to code these separately, so you can concentrate on listening in one session and on pictures in another. Then draw up a table like the one in Table 8.2.

This is, naturally, a rather crude and simplistic example – but it is something to start working with. To begin with, you might need to consider the verbal/non-verbal distinction. Is laughter – very much a physical sensation – really a verbal behaviour? Then you need to examine each of your behaviours and attempt to specify precise criteria for identifying them. What are 'signs of discomfort' and how will your co-researcher recognise them when it comes to the reliability check? Even something as seemingly basic as a head nod might produce variations in coding (a twitch might be seen as a nod). Particular attention should be paid to the problem of **non-independent** observations, where one behaviour triggers another (e.g. all six people laugh simultaneously), and multiple behaviours – for example, do you record a rapid sequence of head nods with one tick, or several separate ticks? There are no right or wrong answers to these questions: it is simply a case of making the criteria clear to your co-observer – and in your eventual report.

TABLE 8.2 An example coding schedule.

	Junior1	Junior2	Junior3	Senior1	Senior2	Senior3
VERBAL						
Agreement						
Disagreement						
Interruption						
Humour						
Laughter						
NON-VERBAL						
Head nods						
Head shakes						
Assertive body language						
Passive body language						
Signs of discomfort						

8.7.2 Some other sampling issues in observation studies

Before you actually begin data collection, it may be important to establish a rationale for when, where and how often you carry out data collection. There are a number of conventions regarding sampling that you need to consider. A distinction is often made between time sampling and event sampling.

Time sampling refers to the time periods that you are recording data: for example, if you are observing behaviour in public places there may be a number of naturally occurring variables that affect behaviour throughout the day. Imagine that you are observing shopping behaviour in a city centre. You decide to collect data on three separate occasions – on Monday, Wednesday and Friday between 9 and 11am. It looks good: you have established equivalence. But are you missing something? Another option might be to observe on Monday morning, Wednesday afternoon and Saturday afternoon. That way you would have a better cross-section of times, but suppose there is a market on Mondays that brings in lots of extra shoppers? You might still need to find a quiet period, so it might entail a fourth visit, on Tuesday morning perhaps. Of course, ultimately, it all depends on the research question – but these are issues that you will have to consider at some length.

Event sampling concerns studies that are related to specific events – a football match for instance. If you wanted to observe crowd behaviour at your local ground, the above sequence shopping times might not be much use! But what matches would you select to get the best representative sample of data? Are you seeking equivalent events or do you want a range of events? A big cup match, or a local derby against fierce rivals might elicit very different behaviours from a sleepy end of season mid-table fixture.

8.8 WORKING OFF CAMPUS

If you have been fortunate enough to gain access to a group of participants off campus, there are a number of issues that are worth flagging to you as a final set of issues for this chapter on data collection.

- **Dress codes**. Be mindful that you are both representing your university and you are in some-one else's home/working environment. Present a professional image by being respectful of any dress code that may be in place in that environment, and show respect in any case by dressing appropriately and smartly. Think carefully about clothes, jewellery and make-up – from a practi-cal and impression formation point of view. Also consider, if you are interviewing or working with very small children, whether presenting too formal an appearance could be intimidating or impersonal. If in doubt, put together an outfit that is 'layered' (i.e. wear a formal jacket over the top of something a little less formal (but still appropriate), to enable you to make your outfit less intimidating if necessary).

- **Respect and patience**. Remember that, even though you want to crack on with getting your data as quickly as possible, you must accept that you are only there because someone has given you permission, and their agenda and concerns need to come first. So if you are asked to wait a while until it is convenient for them, make sure that you do not show any signs of impatience or, worse still, begin to make demands or put people in that environment under pressure to accommodate you. For this reason it is advisable to allow plenty of time to collect your data, as you are likely to encounter some days when you will not be able to collect data at all for one reason or another. This is especially common in school contexts.

- **Communication issues**. Some gatekeepers will welcome you with open arms, only to pass you on to someone who is less pleased to have you disrupting their day. Take the time to discuss with them how to minimise any disruption and get them on board as much as possible. Also be aware that, on some occasions, the gatekeeper may have failed to brief the person concerned about your visit at all, and so you may arrive as something of a surprise. We would advise you always to get names of the people with whom you will be in daily contact when you first get permission to collect data, and contact them separately to make them aware of your study, thank them for their support in advance, and confirm any dates of any visits that you might have agreed with their line manager but that they may not be aware of. Double-check that they are okay for you to attend on those days and remember that, where it is possible to 'give something back' in recognition of their support, you should consider doing so. After all, it will also provide you with some work experience at the same time.

CHAPTER SUMMARY

- When conducting interviews, you should establish who you are and build rapport at the begin-ning of the session. An interview schedule is essential for keeping track of the session and ensur-ing that all aspects of the research question are explored. You should avoid asking participants to answer your research question directly. Focus groups are a specific means of generating data – not merely an opportunity to conduct a 'big interview'. It is worth considering the composition of your group, and the effect this may have on the data generated. Data transcription can be laborious, but there are standard ways of presenting transcribed conversations.

- Questionnaires are available commercially and via publications. It is acceptable to use a pub-lished questionnaire or develop your own. If you develop your own, you should seek to estab-lish the reliability and validity of your measure. Avoid developing overly complex 'multipart' questionnaires in which each question is a variable in itself.

- Experiments are more straightforward, but some forms of specialist equipment do not give straightforward data – you will need some support and training in how to interpret the output they present you with.

- Archival data can overcome some of the difficulties associated with transcription and also access to some populations. However, you will need to keep careful notes on where and how you obtained the data, and some copyright issues may apply.

- Observational data can require transcription, and this will also need to include non-verbal as well as verbal behaviour. Alternatively, an observation schedule, which enables you to keep track of how many times a particular behaviour has occurred, can be developed or adapted from a published source. However, it is important that you conduct some form of inter-rater reliability assessment.

- When working off campus, you should respect dress codes, show appropriate patience and deference to those who are allowing you to collect data, and make extra efforts to find out who you are going to be working with, and contact them directly to ensure that no slips of communication or resentment will occur.

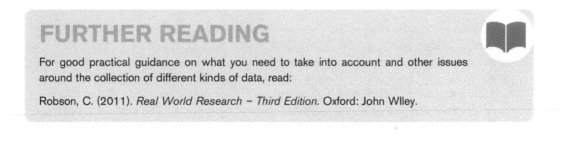

FURTHER READING

For good practical guidance on what you need to take into account and other issues around the collection of different kinds of data, read:

Robson, C. (2011). *Real World Research – Third Edition.* Oxford: John Wlley.

CHAPTER 9
DATA ANALYSIS AND PRESENTATION

In many respects, data analysis will present you with the biggest single challenge of your project. In most cases, your project is comfortably the biggest piece of independent research you have done in your course, and you may well be using sophisticated analytic methods that you have only covered briefly (if at all) in classes. Also, by the time you have collected all your data and begun analysis, you may find yourself tackling statistical techniques that you have not practised for well over a year. The biggest challenge of all, however, may be the results section of your report, at which point you will need somehow to organise all your analyses into a coherent narrative. We will discuss report writing in the next chapter, but you can make the results section (and perhaps the rest of your report) so much easier to write, if you have a good picture in advance of what your analysis will look like, and what story it will tell.

In this chapter we will go through some of the most commonly used techniques of data analysis in psychological project work, and identify some of the most important features of these methods – the numbers, or concepts, that you will need to interpret in order to make sense of your data, and to enable you to answer your initial research question or hypothesis. We will also suggest which parts of your analysis are the most useful to present in your report.

BY THE END OF THIS CHAPTER YOU WILL:

- Understand the importance of using the right analytic method to enable you to answer your research question.
- Be aware of some of the important issues relating to each of the major quantitative and qualitative methods.
- Have some useful ideas of how to present the results of your data analysis.
- Appreciate the type of information that needs to be presented with regard to each analytic technique.

9.1 STATISTICAL METHODS

9.1.1 Correlation and regression

Many contemporary psychology projects use some form of correlational statistical analysis, typically a variant of multiple regression. These techniques have become dominant because of the popularity of psychometric scales in psychological research, particularly in applied fields such as health and forensic psychology, and because this kind of research is easy to carry out with a sizeable student population. The most important things to remember, when you begin analysing correlational data, are as follows.

What are your variables?

This is not as obvious a question as it might seem. Firstly, you may have amassed a huge data file and you cannot remember which numbers went together, what concepts they measured or how they fitted into your hypothesis. Secondly, it may be that your scale needs breaking down into subtotals for your analysis to work.

To use a rather obvious example, if you have used the Eysenck Personality Questionnaire (EPQ) in your study you will not just have one single measure of 'personality' – you will need to calculate separate subtotals for each personality trait (extraversion and so on) according to the scoring key. Moreover, you should already have expressed your hypotheses in relation to these subtotals (e.g. there will be a positive correlation between extraversion and units of alcohol per week). Indeed, it would be meaningless to calculate a single overall total of 'personality', because the EPQ has been designed on the principle that personality is a complex phenomenon comprising several discrete aspects (traits).

Not all scales are quite so straightforward. The Drive for Muscularity scale was constructed by McCreary and Sasse (2000) in order to measure men's preoccupation with building muscle. It had 15 items that assessed a range of different features of this preoccupation, from thinking that your arms are not muscular enough to excessive visits to the gym. With such a diverse instrument, it is not surprising that eventually the authors found that some of the items fitted together in a logical fashion – so, several years later, using factor analysis, they identified a 2-factor structure: attitudinal and behavioural (McCreary, Sasse, Saucier & Dorsch, 2004). This means that you can calculate subtotals for attitude and behaviour (both subscales seem to be reliable; Giles & Close, 2008).

Total drive for muscularity, unlike 'personality', is still a meaningful value to use in an analysis, but the identification of different subscales may have important implications for your hypothesis. For instance, in the literature on the Theory of Planned Behaviour (e.g. Armitage & Conner, 2001) it has been found that attitudes are much easier to predict than actual behaviour. Sitting in front of your bedroom mirror and bemoaning the girth of your biceps may not necessarily drive you to visit the gym each evening. So it is useful to have subscales that distinguish the two.

Which way up are your variables?

This is one of the most vexing issues in correlational research. You believe that people who score high on 'celebrity worship' are lacking in self-esteem, which would appear to lead to a negative correlation between scores on the Celebrity Worship Scale (McCutcheon, Lange & Houran, 2002) and levels of self-esteem. When you conduct your analysis, however, you find that the relationship is significant but positive. This surprises you. But not all scales necessarily travel in the direction you would expect. You need to check your data so that you know exactly what a high score on a scale actually means. It could be that you have used a self-esteem scale in which a high score reflects low self-esteem (perhaps the authors wanted to identify a cut off point beyond which low self-esteem could be regarded as problematic, and felt that it would be more useful clinically to problematise a high score than a low one).

So this is one of the checks you need to carry out before you enter your data into correlational analyses. It could be, of course, that you have entered the data in the wrong way, or put the Likert scale the wrong way round! These are very easy mistakes to make. Another potential pitfall concerns **reverse-keyed items.** In order to prevent response bias (people just automatically ticking one end of the scale once they have guessed what it is measuring), many scales contain items that state the opposite of the scale concept. In a few scales the majority of items are reverse-keyed, just to keep respondents on their toes. Because it takes so long to enter all your data, it is very easy to forget to recode these items – and then spend hours wondering why your promising looking dataset has produced non-significant findings. Further confusion can ensue, if working out which items need to be reversed makes you forget which way up your data were supposed to be in the first place! So it is very important to get all this information right at the outset.

What associations have you predicted?

Many projects set out with deliberately vague hypotheses, such as 'there will be an association between X and Y', or 'there will be a significant relationship between X and Y'. In reality there is rarely a good reason for being so vague, unless your research is genuinely exploratory, or you have constructed an original scale (but even then you would have *some* idea of how it fits into the literature). Being vague about your hypotheses can lead to problems when it comes to the analysis – it often means you only end up analysing significant findings, which may themselves be hard to account for, leaving your discussion a bit speculative. It is always better to specify the direction of any associations, based on what has been found in previous research. This will make your analysis easier to do, and your findings much easier to explain.

The correlation matrix

If you have used correlations in your research, even if you are going to go on and present all manner of complicated regression analyses, you should present your bivariate correlations of key variables in the form of a correlation matrix. This is a table that plots your variables against each other, displaying the *r* values and, typically, some indication of whether or not the *r* is significant.

In our hypothetical example, we have plotted a number of measures relating to job performance (very loosely based on a table in Maltby, Day & Macaskill, 2007). The five measures in this study are:

Job performance – this can be described as the outcome variable. This means it is the variable we are interested in, and we are going to go on to use the other variables to see how well they predict it. (It is measured here using a line manager's rating.)

Emotional intelligence – a measure of emotional intelligence based on understanding of, and sensitivity towards, others (EQ-i; see Bar-On, 1997).

Spatial intelligence – measured using a standard mental rotation task.

Graphology – measure of 'vocational skills' based on analysis of a sample of handwriting.

Sample of work – known to be a reliable correlate of job performance (Hunter & Hunter, 1984).

The bivariate correlations are displayed below in Table 9.1. This is what the correlation matrix should ideally look like.

You can obtain a correlation matrix easily by entering the variables into SPSS – but you will need to perform a fair amount of surgery on the matrix that SPSS produces. (In any case, your lecturers

TABLE 9.1 An example correlation matrix.

	Spatial intelligence	Graphology	Sample of work	Performance
Emotional intelligence	.43**	−.26	.16	.62**
Spatial intelligence		−.15	.38**	.32**
Graphology			−.21	−.26
Sample of work				.57**

$^*p < .05$
$^{**}p < .01$

will not want you simply to cut and paste from SPSS but to construct your own table!) For one thing, the SPSS output gives you the same information twice – above and below the diagonal row of ones (after all, if you correlate emotional intelligence with emotional intelligence you will get a perfect positive correlation of $r = 1$). Half of that information is therefore redundant (not to mention the diagonal). Your matrix should end up, as in Table 9.1, without any repeated values, which means that you will have to omit one variable from your rows (here, performance) and one from your columns (emotional intelligence).

In larger data tables, probabilities are typically indicated by the use of asterisks. Two asterisks usually indicates smaller probabilities, or, if you prefer, higher significance.

MAXIMISING MARKS

Doing it APA style

A lot of psychology departments around the world ask their students to present their work 'using APA style'. We will say more about this in Chapter 10, but one thing to mention here is that staff sometimes insist that tables are presented in APA format – typically, without vertical lines of any kind, sometimes without any lines apart from the top and bottom of the table. You may have been specifically taught to draw tables this way. If not, do not worry, ask your supervisor for help – or, better still, consult the APA style guide (American Psychological Association, 2010). SPSS now includes an option that converts their tables into APA style, which might give you some useful ideas – but don't be tempted to use this as a short cut because you will still be left with the problem of dealing with all the irrelevant detail associated with SPSS output.

Multiple regression

There are several ways of carrying out multiple regression, and therefore several ways of displaying the results. In our hypothetical example, we could just regress all four variables simultaneously on to job performance, in order to examine their relative predictive power. This would give us an overall figure, R^2, that describes the relationship between the outcome variable (performance) and the four predictor variables. This is usually adjusted to account for sample size, so the actual figure you would quote in your results section would be the adjusted R^2 that is provided by SPSS. This is converted to an F statistic in order to give you a p value.

For our example, adjusted $R^2 = .59$, which was found to be significant at $p < .001$. Put another way, the predictors account for 59 per cent of the variance in job performance, which is a very high amount (much smaller R^2 statistics are usually significant).

There should usually be a good (theoretical) reason for choosing which predictors you enter into the equation, although some choose to do it by looking at the correlation matrix and ignoring non-significant correlations, in which case you would of course leave graphology out.

The whole point of multiple regression, however, is to examine the relative variance explained by the individual predictors. Our simultaneous regression analysis gives us the data in Table 9.2.

TABLE 9.2 Regression coefficients for simultaneous multiple regression example.

	Unstandardised coefficient (*B*)	Standardised coefficient (*β*)	*t*
Emotional IQ	.78	.58	5.52**
Spatial IQ	−.19	−.13	−1.20
Graphology	−.04	−.01	−.14
Work sample	2.53	.52	5.14**

Different tutors may expect to see different values cited here: some prefer unstandardised coefficients (perhaps with their standard errors – both values are provided in SPSS); others are content with the standardised coefficients, which are the coefficients converted to *Z* scores, and the ones generally cited in results sections, along with a *p* value derived from a *t* statistic.

This analysis gives us a bit more than the correlation matrix, which has spatial intelligence significantly correlated with performance. One way of interpreting the non-significant contribution of spatial intelligence in the regression equation is that spatial and emotional intelligence are underpinned by some general measure of intelligence. We could test this in a different way, by delaying the entry of emotional intelligence into the equation.

Hierarchical regression analysis involves entering the predictors in **blocks**. If we wanted to examine the predictive power of emotional intelligence independently of the other predictor variables, we would enter spatial intelligence, graphology and work sample in Block 1, and then enter emotional intelligence into the regression model in Block 2. This would give us an output like that shown in Table 9.3.

TABLE 9.3 Hierarchical regression analysis.

	Unstandardised coefficient (*B*)	Standardised coefficient (*β*)	*t*
Block 1 (adj R^2 = .31, p < .001)			
Spatial IQ	.16	.11	.84
Graphology	−.36	−.13	−1.07
Work sample	2.43	.50	3.84**
Block 2 (adj R^2 = .59, p < .001; ΔR^2 = .26, p < .001)			
Emotional IQ	.78	.58	5.52**
Spatial IQ	−.19	−.13	−1.20
Graphology	−.04	−.01	−.14
Work sample	2.53	.52	5.14**

This shows us that, even before emotional intelligence is entered into the model, spatial intelligence is still unable to account for a significant amount of the variance in job performance. Moreover, we can also see from the change in the R^2 statistic (summarised as R^2) between the two parts of the regression (each one referred to as a separate 'model') that emotional intelligence is able to account for a further 26 per cent of variance in job performance (i.e. this is in addition to the variance previously accounted for by the three other variables that have already been entered in Block 1). However, R^2 is not automatically calculated for you by SPSS: you will need to ask SPSS to provide this figure by checking the relevant box in the 'Options' subcommand.

9.1.2 Analysis of variance

Analysis of variance, usually shortened to ANOVA, is the most widely taught advanced statistical method in psychology, and is particularly useful for student projects because so many of them end up aiming to find out how two or more groups differ on some particular measure. Of course, if you only have two groups and one single measure, a simple independent t-test will suffice, but tutors will usually expect you to attempt something a little more ambitious if you are examining group differences, especially if you are interested in 'before' and 'after' measurements (pre-post-test designs). In correlational designs, your use of predictors, outcome variables and so on can be left to the last moment. However, ANOVAs are usually determined by the design of the study, so many of the important issues in variable selection are covered in Chapter 4.

One-way ANOVA

The simplest form of ANOVA involves a single factor, or independent variable, and a single dependent variable. The difference between this and a t-test is a matter of factor levels: with a single factor, ANOVA is only worth doing once you have three or more levels. Let us suppose you were interested in the effect of (classical) music on performance, and compared four groups of students on the same reading task, with four different types of music in the background. We could use this design to explore the so-called 'Mozart effect', which claims that listening to Mozart enhances cognitive performance – in the short-term at least (Chabris, 1999).

You would begin by calculating the means and standard deviations of the four groups, as in Table 9.4. A means table is an essential inclusion in any ANOVA results section.

In Table 9.4 we can see clearly that there is a means difference between the 'classical' composers Mozart and Haydn and the two later composers (Birtwistle, just in case you are wondering, is a very difficult twentieth century composer). No simple Mozart effect, however.

The ANOVA output gives you an F statistic, which you report citing two separate figures for degrees of freedom: one for 'between groups' and one for 'within groups'. You would say something like: one-way ANOVA found that there was a significant difference between the group means, $F(3, 36) = 6.39$, $p = .001$.

TABLE 9.4 Reading task means of four different music conditions.

	Mozart	Haydn	Tchaikovsky	Birtwistle
Means	74.8	74.7	66.8	63.8
SDs	9.9	6.0	5.8	5.2

So there is a difference, but where? We can conduct post-hoc tests to examine the four different groups, although you need to apply the Bonferroni correction to ensure that you do not inflate the *error rate:* since we have four groups, that means we can only accept significant intergroup differences at $p < .01$. Scheffé's test finds that, at this level, only Birtwistle differs significantly (from both Mozart and Haydn), suggesting that difficult modern music is more distracting than music from the classical period.

Preferable to post-hoc tests are *a priori* (pre-planned) comparisons that you use to test specific hypotheses. For example, we could set SPSS to compare Mozart with all the others to check the Mozart effect. Or we could predict a sliding trend, whereby the more modern the composer, the lower the reading task score. These tests are much more sensitive to means differences and so are more likely to give you significant (and more meaningful) results. For instance, pitting our classical composers against more modern ones gives $t(36) = 4.37$, $p .001$.

9.1.3 Factorial ANOVA

More commonly, for project work, you will be expected to explore the contribution of a second independent variable (henceforth referred to as a 'factor'), often a within-subjects one. We refer to factorial designs in terms of the number of factors and the number of levels of those factors. These are expressed as a multiplication in which each number represents a different factor and its value represents its levels.

2×2	Two factors, each with two levels
	e.g. GENDER (male, female) by AGE (under 18, over 18)
2×3	Two factors, one with two levels, the other with three
	e.g. GENDER (male, female) by AGE (under 15, 15–18, over 18)
$2 \times 2 \times 2$	Three factors, each with two levels
	e.g. GENDER (male, female) by AGE (under 18, over 18) by IQ (under 100, over 100)

2×2 ANOVA, independent groups

In the following example, imagine that there are 20 participants, divided equally into 4 groups (therefore, $n = 5$). Each participant has performed a computerised 'tracking task' where, using a mouse, they have been required to follow a light around the screen, keeping the cursor on the light for as long as possible. The dependent variable is a measure (in minutes) of how long the participant was able to keep the cursor on the light ('time on target'). As you can imagine, this is a thoroughly tedious exercise for the participants!

The four groups represent combinations of the two factors, PRACTICE (factor A) and TASK (factor B). The two levels of practice indicate whether the participant has practised the tracking task beforehand. They can be labelled as 1 (practice) and 2 (no practice). The two levels of task refer to the fact that half the participants were allowed to complete the tracking task by itself, and the other half were required to read out a prose passage that scrolled across the top of the screen while they performed the tracking task. The two levels of task can be labelled as 1 (single) and 2 (dual).

The first thing to present will be a table of means and statistics (Table 9.5). You could present overall totals for practice and task, but it is more meaningful, with factorial designs, to break them down into the smallest possible cells – since these are the ones that you will be using to interpret the findings of your interactions.

TABLE 9.5 Means and SDs of time on target for 2 × 2 factorial example.

	t	No practice
Single task	6.4	6.6
	1.1	1.1
Dual task	6.0	3.8
	0.7	.08

It is clear from this table that practice has little effect on single-task performance. However, there is a notable deficit in the 'no practice' group on the dual task. The ANOVA table tells us that there are significant main effects of both task, $F(1, 16) = 13.47$, $p = .002$, and practice, $F(1, 16) = 5.26$, $p = .04$. The interaction is also significant, $F(1, 19) = 7.58$, $p = .01$.

While it is clear from our means table how we should interpret this interaction, it is always helpful – for yourself as well as your readers – to illustrate ANOVA interactions by means of a **lineplot**. These are easily drawn using SPSS. Notice in Figure 9.1 how, at the level of single task, the means are similar at both levels of practice but, at the level of dual task, the lines diverge to a great extent. Where this happens, you can usually expect the interaction to be significant (although bear in mind that SPSS – its default setting, at least – uses a constricted Y-axis, and so tends to exaggerate the appearance of these effects).

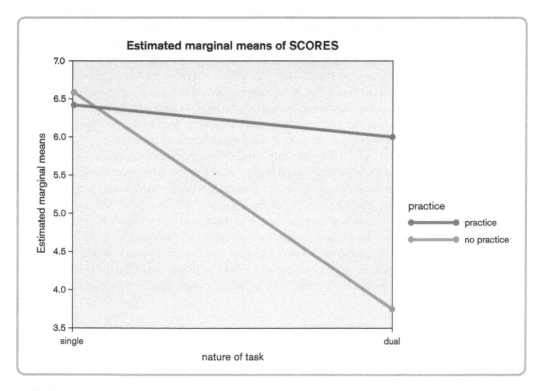

FIGURE 9.1 Lineplot for 2 × 2 ANOVA example.

9.1.4 Other statistical techniques

We have dealt so far with the most commonly used statistical techniques, but obviously there is a vast range of other quantitative methods that you may encounter and there is not enough space here to describe them all. But following we list some important issues to consider with regard to a selection of techniques.

t-tests. It is tempting, sometimes, to regard *t*-tests, *z* tests and other basic statistical techniques as 'first year stuff', to be discarded the moment you encounter ANOVA and multiple regression. However, even in most sophisticated final year projects you may still find you need to use a *t*-test, or nonparametric equivalent, to compare two groups or conditions. Often we might do this as an incidental part of a larger study – for example, you have collected data from two sources and you want to ensure that there is no significant difference between the group means.

Chi-square analysis (χ^2). A useful technique for studying patterns within categorical data. Typically these are presented in the form of a **contingency table:** the 2×2 contingency table shown in Table 9.6 displays sales figures of certain items at different times of the year. An important point to bear in mind about contingency tables is that no single item can appear in more than one cell of the table. If this is not true of your data, you may need to consider using an alternative technique.

The chi-square test compares the 'observed' (actual) values with hypothetical 'expected' values based on the row and column totals. In our example, 40 items are sold in this particular shop in January and 100 in July. The null hypothesis, if you like, is that in January 20 of those would be umbrellas and 20 ice creams, and then 50 of each in July. The value of χ^2 tells us how far away our observed data are from this 'null' situation.

In many respects, calculating chi-square is similar to calculating an interaction in a 2-way ANOVA. You still need to interpret the finding to make sense of it. But you can think of 'months of the year' and 'sale items' as two separate independent variables or factors.

Log linear analysis. Persisting with the ANOVA comparison, log linear analysis is what you need to use if your categorical design introduces a third factor, or four or five or more factors. Again, though, do not confuse *factors* with *levels*. Chi-square might work with a third level of the 'sale items' factor (raincoats perhaps), but let us suppose we added some other variable entirely, say, age: we would need to break the data down into a total of eight cells, maybe one each for child and adult. The design becomes more complicated, and so the stats need to follow. Then it becomes very much like ANOVA because you have to start thinking in terms of interactions.

ANCOVA. This is a blend of ANOVA and correlation, where you carry out an ordinary ANOVA but you hold an additional variable constant. It is particularly useful when you feel that there is a 'confounding variable' that is exerting a powerful influence on your results – age, perhaps, or IQ. ANCOVA treats that variable as a 'covariate', by analysing your data twice, once without the covariate and once with. If your *F* ratio is still significant with the covariate included, then you can rule it out as a potential confounding variable. Another common use of ANCOVA is to analyse data from intervention studies that have used a pre- and post-test design. In this instance the pre-test scores would be entered as the covariate, because you would be interested in the difference between your experimental and control group's post-test scores after controlling for their scores at pre-test.

TABLE 9.6 An example of a contingency table.

	Umbrellas	Ice cream
January	33	7
July	25	75

MANOVA. This is easily confused with factorial ANOVA, but the difference is very simple. MANOVA is simply ANOVA with more than one dependent variable. If you find that you are having to run, say, three separate 2-way ANOVAs on three different DVs (say, visual memory, spatial memory and verbal memory), you could consider combining them into a global analysis. Then you would end up with an *F* ratio that you could regard as an overall test of, in this instance, 'memory'. This is known as an 'omnibus *F* test'. You could still analyse the different types of memory separately ('univariate *F* tests'), but the omnibus test would give you a bigger picture (assuming that this is what you are interested in).

Factor analysis. This is most commonly associated with scale design, where you are interested in exploring the nature of your psychological construct, in particular the possible existence of subscales. If we take the 'Belief in Father Christmas' scale in Chapter 8, it might be that the overall Cronbach's alpha level is low because the belief construct consists of two or three separable aspects: perhaps logic, benevolence and culture. A factor analysis might help you decide which of your items best fall into these three categories. Or it might throw up a completely different structure altogether.

The key terms here are 'explained variance' (each factor that the program identifies is said to account for a decreasing percentage of the overall variance, represented as an **eigenvalue**), and 'factor loadings' (correlation of each item in the scale with each identified factor). You use the latter to sort out your items into meaningful groups: at this point the whole process becomes an interpretative exercxsise, because it is up to you as the analyst to decide what these factorial clusters *mean*.

One important decision in factor analysis is how many factors to retain. You usually do this either by examining the eigenvalues (anything lower than 1 usually is not worth keeping), or, if you have several factors with eigenvalues over 1, a graph of the eigenvalues, known as a **scree plot**. At each step, the decisions you make should be guided by the theoretical implications for the construct in question rather than the statistical information.

Structural equation modelling. With the software so available and easy to use nowadays, some supervisors might be ambitious enough to let their students loose on something really complicated. Structural equation modelling is a technique that allows you to enter any number of variables into a 'path diagram' and test a selection of models that you believe offer a theoretical account of your data. Typically, path diagrams are elaborate box-and-arrow plots with regression

COMMON CONFUSION ?

1   *What is the difference between factor analysis and principal components analysis?*
    Factor analysis is a broad term covering a range of similar statistical techniques for reducing a complex dataset to a small number of factors or 'roots' underpinning the data that need to be sensibly interpreted with regard to the measurement instruments (i.e. the scale items or other measures). The idea is that the pattern of factors will 'explain' the variance in the data. Principal components analysis is the most commonly used technique for carrying out factor analysis, but there are several different types (see Giles, 2002a: 125–126 for a brief summary).

2   *What is the difference between structural equation modelling and path analysis?*
    There is not much – both are techniques for exploring associations between different variables expressed as 'paths'. A path is simply a connecting arrow linking two boxes in a diagram, measured as a partial correlation between those two variables. A path analysis could explore as little as the paths between three variables. It is simplest to think of structural equation modelling as path analysis on a grand scale.

coefficients linking up the various boxes. They can look very impressive without actually meaning very much, so beware of using this sort of technique simply to try and blind your examiners with science! Generally you should have sound theoretical reasons for predicting particular patterns of association, and you should enter your variables into the diagram in order to examine this theory, not just because you happened to collect the data. We would strongly advise you to discuss this kind of technique with your supervisor before attempting it on your own.

Mediation/moderation analysis. If you are doing a multiple regression study, you may have heard your supervisor describing one of your variables as a 'mediator' for two other variables, or as a 'moderator'. This usually requires further analysis, and sometimes can be a way into structural equation modelling by itself. Again, we think it is best for you to discuss this type of analysis with your supervisor first, to make sure it is worth the effort of trying to carry it out.

9.2 QUALITATIVE METHODS

Students who have collected qualitative data are often presented with complex material, in the form of audio recordings, interview or focus group transcripts, or other textual data, which have to be transformed or distilled into more manageable units and communicated in a written report. Without some process of analysis or distillation, you would have little alternative than to report vast quantities of raw data, such as interview transcripts, and leave the readers to draw their own conclusions about their significance.

For student projects, the choice of data analysis is inevitably some kind of compromise, as you will rarely have the opportunity to analyse the same set of data using multiple approaches. In choosing a qualitative technique for your data collection, you need to make the best possible compromise for your study. In the remainder of this chapter we offer some suggestions to help you make your choice.

We are not going to attempt to explain how to do each kind of analysis, as that is beyond the scope of this book. What we will do is:

- highlight what is distinctive about each analytical approach, so that you can clarify which is the most appropriate for your data;
- make some suggestions as to what should typically be included in a project report using each technique;
- direct you to some further reading that will explain each approach in more depth, and illustrate the way in which results might be presented for each technique.

Some words of caution about our suggestions:

We use the words 'approach' and 'technique' interchangeably in this section, and they are often used in this way in research methods textbooks and published research articles. It is worth remembering, though, that they imply subtly different things. A 'technique' suggests a recognised set of procedures for processing data, perhaps even a recipe for 'cooking' your results. An 'approach' suggests a broader orientation to research, and a distinctive way of thinking about data. Techniques for processing quantitative data are often very clearly prescribed by statistical and mathematical principles. In qualitative research, the procedures for dealing with data are generally less rigidly determined. What really matters is that the precise technique you use to deal with your data should be compatible with the broad approach you take to research. This broad approach should, in turn, be compatible with the theoretical perspective you have adopted in the introduction to your report. Let us take a specific example.

A researcher who adopts a social constructionist perspective in their introduction would be likely to find that a discursive psychology approach was appropriate for their research. The precise technique or set of procedures that they use on the data may not be rigidly prescribed. They might choose one or more techniques from a range including, for example, subject positions, interpretative repertoires and so on. As many qualitative research projects are inductive, the decision as to which exact technique to use might only be made once the data have been collected and several different specific techniques tried out.

MAXIMISING MARKS

Coherence of approach – again!

As we have already mentioned in earlier chapters, a good project report is one in which there is a *logical coherence* across every section. That means that your choice of analytical technique should be logically compatible with the theoretical position you have established in your introduction and the nature of your data. Be sure to check that this is the case when selecting an analytical technique or beginning your analysis.

9.2.1 Content analysis

Whether your content analysis is deductive (i.e. coded into categories chosen in advance of the analysis) or inductive (coded into categories developed in the process of analysis), there are some key things you need to communicate when you present your findings.

If you have not already done so in the method section of your report, you need to make clear the nature of the sample selected. Let us take the example of the student project we mentioned in Chapter 4, the content analysis of messages posted on a discussion forum about polycystic ovary syndrome. In the method section, it was made clear how the sample was obtained, and how many messages there were overall.

Messages were sampled from those posted online on a UK PCOS discussion site between 1 October 2006 and 31 January 2007.

The aim was to sample the first 30 messages in each forum, while retaining threads of related messages intact. Using both these criteria, 277 messages were downloaded for analysis.

Each message was coded using a content analysis framework according to the topics it referred to. The framework included symptoms of PCOS, psychosocial aspects identified in previous research and those included in the polycystic ovary syndrome health-related quality of life questionnaire (PCOSQ). Further categories were developed inductively from the data. Figure 9.2 shows the percentage of messages which referred to each category of concern.

In the results section, the report listed the categories used (or developed) in the content analysis, and showed the number of messages coded in each. There are no hard and fast rules that state exactly how you must do this, but some content analysis studies use tables and/or graphs. For example, Figure 9.2 shows how it was done in the PCOS study.

You should provide a verbal narrative or description to accompany the graph or table, for example:

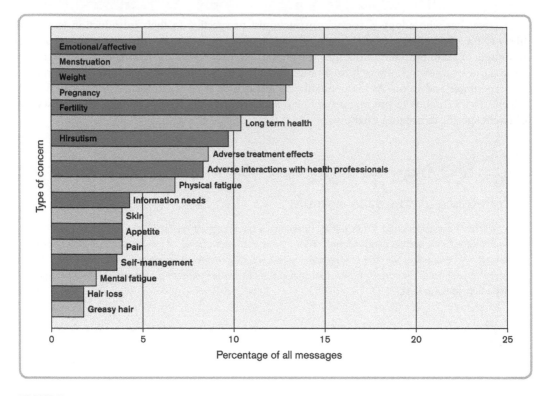

FIGURE 9.2 Example of a content analysis graph.

The topics most frequently referred to in the messages were emotional/affective issues (22.3 per cent of all messages), menstruation (14.4 per cent), weight (13.4 per cent), pregnancy (12.9 per cent), fertility (12.3 per cent), long term health (10.5 per cent) and hirsutism 9.7 per cent). However, these were closely followed by concerns not reflected in previous research with clinical samples and/or the PCOSQ question-naire. These included additional symptoms such as mental (2.5 per cent) and physical fatigue (6.8 per cent); appetite difficulties (3.9 per cent) such as cravings and binge eating; non-menstrual pain (3.9 per cent) such as headache; skin problems (3.9 per cent), including acne, and hair loss (1.8 per cent).

Adverse treatment effects such as unwanted drug side effects were referred to in 8.6 per cent of mes-sages. Adverse interactions with health professionals, for example, being treated unsympathetically by their doctor, were referred to in 8.3 per cent of messages. 4.3 per cent of messages referred to informa-tion needs and 3.6 per cent to self-management concerns such as difficulty adhering to exercise, dietary or medical regimes.

Can you think of anything else that could be added to make the results still clearer? You may have noticed that some bars in the chart shown in Figure 9.2 have verbal labels on the outside (right hand side) of the bar. These represent categories that the researcher developed inductively from the data. The other bars, with verbal labels inside, represent categories that the researcher had in their analytical framework before they coded the data. In the report, a key could be added to the figure, and this could be explained in the narrative that follows.

This is just one example of how you might present a content analysis, but it is by no means the best or only way. Because there are remarkably few published qualitative studies in psychology that have used content analysis, there is considerable scope for you to develop your own format of presentation, based on close reading of those studies that are available in print. The key issues to remember are:

- Be *transparent* about how the analysis was done – which categories (if any) were pre-determined and which developed inductively?
- Ensure that there is sufficient information clearly presented in your results section, to allow the reader to see the most important *patterns* in the data.

9.2.2 Phenomenology

As we discussed in the chapter on designing your study, phenomenological research focuses on the nature of individual *experience*. In the interests of coherence as regards the conceptualisation, design and execution of your study, *before* you begin data analysis, you need to ensure that the data you have collected are appropriate for a phenomenological approach. *Are they first person accounts of experience?* Assuming that they are, the following are some suggestions to help you get started with analysis.

Reports of phenomenological research often identify key *analytical* themes that capture the experience being investigated. Although the analysis presented in published papers may be very convincing, there is rarely enough space in the article, for the authors to explain exactly how they got from the raw data to a list of themes in their results section. We only have space here to provide an overview of the processes you might undertake, but we hope that this brief snapshot, with some further reading, will be enough to encourage you to begin your analysis.

Giorgi and Giorgi (2003) give an excellent description of four basic steps they recommend for researchers doing phenomenological analysis.

The first step is to read the entire description given by the participant. Having the discipline to do this means that you attend to everything in the experience being given. It can help you counter the temptation to skim over or ignore parts of the data that may seem mundane, irrelevant or not sufficiently 'psychological'.

The next step is to segment the data into 'meaning units'. Giorgi and Giorgi (2003: 1455) suggest that you do this by inserting a slash (or other dividing marker) at every point where you detect a 'transition in meaning'. To give a concrete example, this might mean inserting a marker in the transcript, when a participant (let us say in our study of stroke survivors) moves from talking about the, person they used to be, to talking about the, person they are now, or between talk about loss and talk about gain. You will need to label each meaning segment with a word or phrase that captures its contents. It may seem obvious but, in the example just given, the first meaning unit might be labelled something like 'the person I used to be', and the second 'the person I became'. Or the segments might be labelled 'what I lost', and the second 'what I gained'.

The third step is to transform the meaning units, to make them more appropriate for a published report. This might involve making the meaning more explicit, more generalisable and/or more 'psychologically sensitive'. Giorgi and Giorgi (2003: 1455) point out that this does not mean turning participants' personal accounts into jargon terminology, but it does mean making apparent the psychological significance of their experiences.

The final step required is to develop a structure that gives an overall shape to the meaning units and the relationship between them. This is the 'tip of the analytical iceberg' that you get to see in a published paper. It is usually a number of analytical themes that capture, as concisely as possible, what is 'typically essential' about the experience under investigation (Giorgi & Giorgi, 2003). In the case of our study of stroke survivors, this might be a list of themes that capture what it is like to survive a stroke. This list should enable the reader to understand the experience in question, without having to read the entire set of transcripts for themselves.

COMMON CONFUSION

?

Description versus analysis

As you will have learned from research methods classes, and/or from reading methodology texts, doing qualitative research involves more than simply *summarising* what participants tell you in an interview. While for some methods you will need to *begin* by summarising, chunking or turning into codes/bullet points, the content of your data, this description alone is rarely enough.

Most qualitative research in psychology involves not just describing what is in the data, but recognising *patterns* in them, and the social/psychological *significance* of these. You should bear this in mind when completing your analysis and writing your results section.

If you write a purely *descriptive* results section, this can read rather like a glorified version of '*He* said, *she* said, then *he* said, *then* he said, then *she* said'. This does not offer the reader much more than they could have gained by simply reading the raw data.

An *analytical* results section will offer the reader a perspective that they would not have achieved by simply reading the raw data. It will be supported by extracts of raw data, but these will be chosen carefully to support rather than 'bulk out' the results.

9.2.3 Interpretative phenomenological analysis

With some minor variations, IPA is very similar to other phenomenological approaches, in the type of data used and in the format for presenting results of the analysis. When considering whether your data are appropriate for IPA, bear in mind that many IPA studies are based on data collected in semi-structured interviews, even though some phenomenological researchers prefer data that are arguably more spontaneous, naturalistic or contemporaneous.

The analytical process in IPA is rather similar to that used in phenomenology. For example, the first step in IPA should always be to read and re-read the data transcript – excluding nothing at first, as it may turn out to be relevant.

In IPA, it is often recommended that you begin by making analytical notes in the margins of your transcript. You may wish to change the page layout of your transcript so that you have bigger margins and room to fit these notes in. Some researchers like to use software packages to manage this process, but the important thing to remember is that these packages do not do any of the thinking or analysis for you. A printout of your transcript might work just as well. Perhaps as a compromise, use the 'insert comment' function in a basic wordprocessor package to link your notes to the raw data.

Researchers often begin in the left hand margin of the transcript, by making a note of meaning units. You do not have to use slashes to mark the boundaries between meaning units, you just need to attend to and make a note of every chunk of meaning that is presented. There is quite a bit of variation in what counts as a meaning unit at this stage of IPA research. Some researchers prefer to see these left hand column meaning units as 'descriptive codes'. When doing preliminary coding for IPA, simply convert what the participant is saying into bullet points in the left hand column of the transcript. This is a very time consuming process, and can introduce a frustrating delay in getting to the 'real' analysis, but they feel that it is a useful form of discipline in attending to every conceptual unit the participant is presenting.

Other researchers make a note of a smaller number of more select meaning units. This may work well if you are a confident user of the methodology. If you are less confident, you may prefer to be more pedantic and over inclusive in your coding, at least until you have had some feedback from your supervisor on a sample of coded transcript.

The codes in the left hand column of the transcript are often very descriptive, perhaps even in the same language that is used by the participant. You might think of this column as 'what the participant is telling me about their experience'. By contrast, in the right hand margin, researchers usually make a note of more 'analytical' meaning units. You might think of this column as 'what is the (psychological) significance of what is being said?'

The next step in IPA is usually to look across an entire transcript, or perhaps across several interviews, in order to extract more general or overarching 'master themes'. These might be based upon a single interview, or drawn from analysis across several transcripts. It is these master themes that are likely to form the basis of your results section.

A cautionary note about 'steps' in analysis

You may have noticed that in our descriptions of phenomenological analysis and IPA, we have referred to *steps* that you might follow to guide your analysis. We have done this because it is often reassuring to have a set of clearly defined steps to follow, especially if you do not have much experience of using a particular technique. It is worth remembering, though, that real data analysis is rarely this straightforward or linear. Researchers often need to move back and forth between steps, to add to or refine their analysis. For example, you may find that you need to reread an entire transcript, part way through coding it, even though you read it entirely at the outset. You may also find that some great analytical insights occur to you while you are still doing your preliminary read through of the data. Rather than chastise yourself for leaping ahead, why not make a note of this insight, and the place in the transcript that triggered that idea? You can then get on with reading the data, knowing that you can return to your inspirational insight later.

9.2.4 Discourse analysis

So far we have discussed how you might extract analytical themes from interview transcripts, or other first-person accounts of experience. Discourse analysis can be used on the same sort of material, but it can also be applied to just about any form of talk or text. The 'analytic units' produced by discourse analytic research vary widely according to the precise approach adopted. They might include, for example, discourses, repertoires or subject positions. We cannot do justice to the range of approaches in discourse analysis here, so we present a brief overview and suggest that you do your own further reading.

You need to begin by reading and rereading your data, with a focus on both *content* and *process*. In other words, you need to attend to *what* is being said, and also *how* it is being said. The precise nature of your analysis will depend on the broad approach that you take. For example, Willig (2003) distinguishes between discursive psychology and Foucauldian discourse analysis. If you choose to take a discursive psychology approach, you are likely to be interested in the *action orientation* of talk: how your participants are *doing* identity, jealousy, heterosexuality, etc. in the course of interpersonal communication. If your interest is more in the operation of power, and the relationship between talk and social institutions or practices, you may adopt a more Foucauldian approach. Actually, there are no clear boundaries between these two broad approaches, and you may choose to develop a hybrid of the two that works for your specific project. Willig (2003) provides a more detailed comparison of these approaches and a worked example. Whichever you decide, following are some ideas to get you started with your analysis.

The concept of *interpretative repertoire* was developed by Wetherell and Potter (1988), to account for variability in talk, even from the same speaker/interviewee. To take a specific example, Rachel Lawes, in her study of talk about marriage, found that participants drew upon two different interpretative repertoires: the 'romantic repertoire' – theoretical, idealised constructions of marriage and the 'realist repertoire' (Lawes, 1999). It was not the case that participants had signed up to, or believed in, one or other of these views of marriage absolutely. It was that they were able to draw on one or other at any given time, and drew on both at different times in their interview. You might begin your analysis by looking for ways in which your speaker(s) draw on different repertoires throughout the data transcript.

Another way to consider *variability* within talk, is to think about the way speakers position themselves. For example, in Paul Stenner's work on couples talking about jealousy and infidelity, Jim and May, a soon to be married couple, each construct different *subject positions* for themselves in the course of single interview (Stenner, 1993). Jim begins by positioning himself on a high moral plane, as someone who does not believe in jealousy between sexual partners. He constructs the expectation of sexual fidelity as an instance of selfish possessiveness, something he just can not understand in others. When this position becomes untenable within the conversation – Jim is about to get married after all – Jim shifts to a different subject position, that of 'selfless person blown about by the winds of everyone else's desires' (Stenner, 1993: 6). This position enables Jim to explain why he is acting in apparent contradiction to his high moral principles. While it might be tempting to see the analysis of evidence that Jim is a liar, or at best an untrustworthy source of information about his relationship, it is perhaps better seen as an example of something we all do in conversation. We all construct subject positions for ourselves, that make sense at that particular time and place. It is argued by many discourse analytic researchers that this is a key way in which the process of identity (or identification) is achieved. You may like to examine your data to see if you can identify different subject positions taken up or constructed by speakers within it.

A core concept worth considering to give *context* to your analysis is that of *discourse*. In the study referred to above, Paul Stenner refers to ideas that prevail in wider society, that enable Jim and May to position themselves as they do in their interviews. The permissive discourse (widely available in Western industrialised societies) allows Jim to separate sexual activity from *emotional* infidelity. The sexual liberation discourse allows May to position the less sexually experienced Jim as simply catching up with her level of experience, rather than committing an act of infidelity. When analysing the data you have collected for your study, it is worth considering the social context in which the data were generated, and the range of discourses that may influence participants' talk.

There are many other variations on discourse analysis, with some important and subtle distinctions between them. We recommend you read as many relevant texts and published papers as possible, in order to become familiar with the range of approaches. This will enable you to pick the one that is most appropriate for your own study.

9.2.5 Narrative psychology

As we discussed in the chapter on designing your study, narrative designs are particularly focused on stories generated by participants. Narrative researchers use a wide range of data sources. They may, for example, collect their data in a deliberately storied format. You might have data that is shaped in this way if, for example, you conducted a semi-structured interview which asked participants to tell you about their experience in a chronological sequence. On the other hand, you may have data that is more 'free form', perhaps collected from an online or archival source, such as a weblog. In checking that your data are appropriate for narrative analysis, you need to consider the broad approach you mean to take in your study. Some narrative research projects draw on ideas from phenomenological research, and treat narratives as descriptions of *lived experience*. Others draw on ideas from discourse analysis, and treat narratives as *constructions*, which can tell us a great deal about processes such as identity or power relations within society. If you mean to use narratives as part of a broad phenomenological approach, you may need to check that the narratives are first person accounts; that is, participants talking about their own experience, rather than that of other people.

We will not attempt to do justice to all the variations on narrative research in this brief discussion, and you would be wise to do some further reading if you want to adopt a sophisticated approach. What we will do here is make some simple suggestions that may help you to get started in thinking about narrative analysis.

Perhaps not surprisingly, the first step will be to read and reread the data, immersing yourself in them as far as possible. During this reading you may begin to notice, not just what participants are saying, but also the 'shape' they give to their account. This means that you are attending to both the *content* of the story and its *structure* (Murray, 2003).

At the most basic level, you may wish to identify those sections of data which relate to explicit or implicit *stages* within the participant's story. For example, in a study on the experience of stroke survivors, you might want to identify those sections of a transcript which relate to life before a stroke occurred, those at the time of the stroke, immediately after and so on. You may even have shaped the interview this way yourself, by asking questions about these particular stages in that explicit order.

The stages you look for in your data could be ones that you had in mind in advance, such as, for example pre- and post-stroke, but they might also be developed inductively, from stages constructed by the participant. Someone who has survived a stroke may have their own sense of different stages in the experience. For example, they might describe a stage such as 'when I was still in denial', and another such as 'when I really started to accept what had happened'. It can be more difficult to identify stages that were not part of your original assumptions, but being sensitive to these possibilities may ultimately make your analysis more rich and interesting.

You might focus in more detail on the *description* of each stage. What characterises the participant's experience at that stage? Or the way they describe or construct it? For example, how does the description of being in 'denial' differ from the description of 'starting to accept it'? Having repeated the process for all the different 'stages' in the account, you might *compare* them to see if there are significant differences. This will begin to advance your analytical work from mere description to *analysis*.

Another issue you might focus on is the *transition* between stages. What is being described when a person moves from 'being in denial' to 'starting to accept it'? What characterises these transitions? It might be, for example, that the participant is describing certain factors that facilitated (or even forced) the transition from denial to acceptance. You might, by comparing different transitions within one person's narrative, or comparing the narratives of different people, be able to suggest why some transitions are different from others.

This last suggestion draws attention to another important aspect of narrative analysis – the importance of linking individual narratives to *context* (Murray, 2003). How does the narrative provided by an individual person, in an interview for example, fit into what we know about the rest of that person's life? And how does it relate to ideas (narratives, perhaps discourses) in wider society? Let us take the example of an individual stroke survivor, who describes being forced to accept that he had lost part of himself when he found himself no longer able to drive. If we look at his account of life before his stroke, we may find that he describes himself as the breadwinner for his family, and the person on whom his wife depended for car transport. This context may help us understand why the loss of capacity to drive is a key turning point in his narrative. If we also consider societal norms about gender and marriage, we may understand the implications that a stroke can have for an individual's masculinity.

MAXIMISING MARKS ✔

Theoretical relevance of narratives

If you use a narrative approach to analyse your data, consider why it is appropriate. Be sure to explain this in your report. Work out whether you think any narrative patterns in your data are due to:

- The way in which the data were collected;
- The way in which participants actually experienced the events in question;
- The way in which available discourses are 'story-shaped'.

These answers are not mutually exclusive, but it is worth considering which are most convincing for your data.

9.2.6 Conversation analysis

To check that your data are appropriate for conversation analysis, you need to consider whether they are naturally occurring verbal interactions, recorded and transcribed in sufficient detail to allow close scrutiny of features such as *adjacency pairs* and *overlaps*. It can be very tedious to transcribe audio recordings in such detail, but it is essential for a successful conversation analysis. Assuming you have data that meet these requirements, the following are some suggestions for steps you might take in conducting a conversation analysis. We refer here to an excellent account given by Drew (2003) and, if you intend to use conversation analysis, we strongly recommend that you read the original in full.

It is assumed that participants in conversation are not merely communicating but are engaging in *action*. The first key question for analysis might then be: what action is being achieved in the talk? At first this might seem obvious. In the case of a study by Toerien and Kitzinger (2007), the conversation was ostensibly a preamble to a beautician plucking the eyebrow hair of a client but, as it turns out, there is more to this than first appears. As you read and reread your transcript, consider alternative possibilities for the action, that participants are engaged in. What action is one speaker engaging in at any given point, what are they saying and how?

To develop your analysis, you should identify where the *turn* to speak moves from one speaker to another. Look at what *precedes* each turn. How did the speakers get to this point? And what is it that *facilitates* the changing of turn? How does the second speaker *respond* to the first? Once again, it might seem obvious that participants are simply exchanging information but, if you take seriously the assumptions of conversation analysis, you may see that the talk is doing more than transmit information. By examining the detailed patterns across a whole conversation or encounter, it may be possible to identify *common features*. These may become yet more apparent when you compare the patterns you can see across different interviews or transcripts.

By taking this broader perspective, the authors of the 'eyebrow pluck' study we mentioned above were able to conclude that the social process being achieved in the conversation was that of emotional labour. They argue that this is a competency expected of beauticians, in addition to various technical skills applied directly to the female body (Toerien & Kitzinger, 2007). The social context for this specific conversation is one in which women are disproportionately represented as both providers and consumers of 'beauty' services, so the analysis tells us something of real interest about femininity, and how it is achieved through such apparently banal encounters as eyebrow plucking. Other studies using conversation analysis have taken a similar approach, using fine grained analysis to show how, for example, neighbour complaints made to a telephone hotline can shed light on the operation of racism in everyday life (Stokoe & Edwards, 2007). You might like to consider what the conversational exchanges in your project data tell us about the social process that your study set out to explore.

9.2.7 Thematic analysis

As we discussed in the chapter on designing your study, thematic analysis is a very flexible technique. It can be conducted on any qualitative material so, if your data do not quite meet the criteria for, say, conversation analysis or IPA, thematic analysis may be appropriate. Thematic analysis is also an 'accessible' method – one that is generally easier to learn than some of the other more specific techniques we have mentioned. Two factors – flexibility and accessibility – are good practical reasons why you might opt to do a thematic analysis, but it is also worth considering positive academic reasons for using this approach. A very clear case for the strengths of thematic analysis is offered by Braun and Clarke (2006). The authors point out that, rather than being a 'fallback' method for researchers who do not want to do IPA or discourse analysis, thematic analysis offers distinctive benefits of its own. For example, because thematic analysis does not specify too narrowly in advance what your analytical focus will be, it may allow you to work inductively to produce a rich description of the phenomenon you are studying. This may also mean that you are able to include social and contextual factors in your analysis, alongside issues that are more obviously psychological. We recommend that you read Braun and Clarke (2006) and consider how you can make a positive case for doing thematic analysis in your qualitative research project.

To *do* thematic analysis, you will need to read and reread your data, actively attending to what is being said. You may note interesting features of the data, and label these with words/phrases that capture their meaning. These initial codes can be collected together into linked groups or themes, which can be labelled appropriately. Themes can then be reviewed, checking that the titles you have given them really encapsulate their meaning, and that the themes really capture what is in the data you have examined. It is quite likely that you will need to generate new themes to account for some data.

Although it is true that thematic analysis can provide a rich description of the topic under investigation, it is worth bearing in mind that a good psychology project generally requires a bit more than description alone. This is true of a design using thematic analysis as much as any other qualitative approach. Try to step back from your analysis and check that you have done something more than just 'bullet point' or paraphrase what your participants have said. In order to ensure that you have interpreted rather than just described your data, you might, for example, consider how the themes derived in your analysis answer specific research questions, or relate to theoretical or contextual issues. Good examples of thematic analyses that manage to do this are provided by Braun and Clarke (2006), along with other criteria you might use in checking the rigour of your work. This paper is particularly worth reading, if you are thinking of undertaking your own thematic analysis.

9.2.8 Grounded theory

You may recall, from the chapter on designing your study, that grounded theory is a methodology for both collecting data and analysing them. A full blown grounded theory study design would be one where you collect some data, do some analysis and then begin data collection again. If you are able to do this in the course of your dissertation project, you will be somewhat fortunate. As many undergraduate projects are so time limited, you may have to restrict yourself just to coding a single dataset, using grounded theory techniques for *analysis*.

GT, more than any other qualitative approach, is one where there is the greatest level of prescription about steps and procedures. We are not able to cover all these in this chapter, and recommend that you read at least one original account of the process, for example Charmaz (2003). To get you started thinking about this form of analysis, we suggest that you bear in mind the following key ideas.

Grounded theory analysis should be *inductive*. In other words, analysis should begin with the *data*. This may seem to be stating the obvious but, by starting with the data, we mean suspending your preconceptions about what you think will be, or perhaps ought to be, in the data and allowing yourself to work from the 'bottom up'. You will need actively to read your data, and begin to chunk them into meaning units. One of the most reliable ways to do this is to work line by line, making sure that you do not succumb to the temptation to skip lines, because they seem irrelevant or insufficiently exciting. This process of identifying and labelling individual chunks of meaning is sometimes referred to as *open* coding (Charmaz, 2003).

Once this initial coding has been done, it is usually suggested that you examine your list of open codes, to see which are the most frequent and/or most significant. Rather than stop at this point to write your report, as a grounded theory researcher committed to the principle of *constant comparison*, you need to go back to your raw data to see which of your 'long list' of open codes makes the best conceptual sense. This process of comparing preliminary/open codes with the data is often referred to as *focused* coding (Charmaz, 2003).

As initial labels or codes are subjected to this constant testing against the raw data, your original 'long list' may become shorter and more conceptually refined. Eventually, you may feel that you have reached a point where your analysis matches your data, and not only describes but *conceptualises* it. At that point you may begin to develop a short list of *categories* that account for the phenomenon you are studying. This list of categories, and perhaps the relationships between them, may then form the basis of the *grounded theory* specific to your individual study.

MAXIMISING MARKS

The cyclical 'art' of grounded theory analysis

If you are not already familiar with grounded theory, it may well have occurred to you, after reading our brief description: *How do I know which open codes are most significant? And how do I know when I have achieved a conceptual analysis?*

There is no easy answer to this question, and we cannot tell you how you will know when to stop in your own particular analysis. Grounded theory is a set of principles and techniques that informs how researchers may go about their analysis, but there is still a lot of personal judgement involved, making GT perhaps as much an art as a science.

Published explanations of grounded theory do offer some suggestions to help you make analytical decisions. For example, you may be advised to aim for *saturation* of your categories. This means that you should keep on coding and refining category labels until no more changes are required to make sense of your data.

Our best advice is to read as many original published accounts as possible, then start doing some open coding. Discuss with your supervisor how to advance your analysis if you start to feel stuck or overwhelmed. If either of you need some very detailed guidance on procedures, two excellent sources of specific techniques to follow are the books written by Corbin and Strauss (2008) and Charmaz (2006).

COMMON CONFUSION ?

Guiding principles or required procedures?

If you read some books on grounded theory you may get the impression that all the steps and procedures they describe have to be followed in precisely the way set down in the text. Some people find this reassuring – and of course that is one reason why we have recommended that you read some original texts. Some researchers like to know where to start with their analysis, what to do next and so on. Many students want to feel confident at the end of analysis, that they have done it 'right' and can prove how they got from the raw data to the end product. On the other hand, some novice readers may find the level of detail regarding grounded theory procedures overwhelming, and/or the level of apparent prescription stifling. Some students may be so discouraged that they choose not to undertake a grounded theory analysis at all.

If you feel discouraged or overwhelmed, it might help to know that the authors who developed grounded theory cannot agree on exactly how to do it. There are at least two broad schools of thought regarding grounded theory research – both are accepted as legitimate within the social sciences. One of these emphasises the importance of following set analytical procedures in order to process data appropriately. The other is more permissive – emphasising the general inductive principles of grounded theory, and is less prescriptive of how exactly the analysis should be done. As a student undertaking an independent research project, you have every right to decide which approach to take, so long as you and your supervisor agree it and you can explain why you have made the choice you have.

9.2.9 Presentation of qualitative data analysis

Just as there is a degree of flexibility in the choice of specific procedures for dealing with qualitative data, there is also considerable variation in the way that qualitative researchers present their results. Some published papers use differing combinations of headings within their reports, including results, findings, analysis and discussion. Some reports present 'results/findings' separate from the discussion section, others combine these together. If you read through a range of published articles using the same analytical technique, and even within the same journal, it will become apparent that these variations are quite legitimate. Once again, because there is a very strong inductive element to most qualitative analysis, and your findings will arise out of the data, it may not be possible to anticipate the exact content or structure of your results in advance. So the suggestions we make here for the content and structure of your results section is a very broad guide only. Read published articles that have used your chosen technique and discuss a plan with your supervisor before you complete your analysis and draft the results section of your report.

Presenting analytical themes

Most reports of phenomenological, IPA, narrative and thematic analytic research have a results or findings section in which the themes are *listed* and *described*. Authors typically take each theme in turn as a subheading. They describe the theme, then present data extracts to illustrate and elaborate it.

Some published studies seem to present themes in an apparently arbitrary *order*, and some organise themes into a sequence (e.g. chronological order). Variations are legitimate, providing you can make a convincing case as to why they work for your specific analysis. For example, if you are doing a narrative study, it may make sense for you to present themes sequentially, as they relate to the stages, episodes or phases within your participants' stories/narratives. Even if you are not doing a study that is explicitly narrative in approach, you may want to present them in the order that presents the most coherent picture of your findings.

You may notice that some published papers present a *hierarchy* of themes and subthemes. This may reflect overarching 'master' themes that have subsidiary parts. For example, in a study where there was a theme of 'problems due to healthcare experiences', this might have several subthemes, such as 'problems getting appointments', 'problems having intrusive investigations', and 'side effects from treatment'.

Finally, some papers use their themes to develop a *diagram* with boxes and arrows, showing apparent *relationships* between themes. The results of grounded theory research are sometimes presented in this way, suggesting that the researcher has developed a model, or 'middle range' theory from the data. This is a legitimate variation of grounded theory, and it is sometimes applied to the findings of other qualitative approaches. If you feel that a diagram is appropriate to represent your analysis, think carefully about what is implied by placing analytical themes into boxes and drawing arrows between them. This is often suggestive that you have identified a *process*, and perhaps *causal relationships* between phenomena. You may well have done so, but perhaps discuss with your supervisor how confident, or *tentative*, this model should be.

Using data extracts

You will have seen that published papers typically only include a few data extracts to illustrate each analytical outcome, and that extracts are never presented one after the other, without the researcher's description and narrative explanation in between. Be judicious when selecting your extracts – only use those that best make the point you wish to illustrate, even if this means that some material is left 'on the cutting room floor'.

COMMON CONFUSION ?

Adequate versus excessive use of data extracts

A good report will only include those data extracts that illustrate and clarify the points made in the author's analysis. This does *not* mean that you should include every extract that supports every theme or concept you have identified.

When a marker sees a project report in which there are long lists of data extracts, with very little commentary in the student's own words, they may conclude:

- The student has produced very little analysis.
- The student lacks confidence in their analysis.
- The student has a poor understanding of the conventions of academic writing.
- The student has poor editorial skills.

This type of report is unlikely to be awarded a good mark.

Using tables for themes

Published papers sometimes present themes in table form, even when the table has only one column. More typically, a table of themes may have two (or even three) columns, indicating overarching themes and subthemes. This is quite acceptable, but be aware that having too many columns (and layers of subthemes) may mean that you do not have enough space to discuss every one of the themes in depth. Discuss this with your supervisor and work out how many themes you really have space to discuss before getting too carried away with your table.

Providing an overview of your sample

You may like to provide a description of the sample from which your data were collected. This might be a description of relevant characteristics (e.g. age, gender or ethnicity), so that the reader can assess the extent to which your findings might be representative of a particular group or population. In some published papers you may have noticed that this information is reported in the form of a table, listing the exact characteristics of each participant. The exact format is a matter of choice for you and your supervisor, but bear in mind that a table might provide such specific information about individual participants that it makes them identifiable. This could be a significant problem if you have promised participants anonymity in return for their cooperation.

Tables showing themes across participants

Markers and some other readers may like to know that the themes you present in your findings are drawn from participants across the range of your sample, and not just based on only one or two interviews. One way to show how participants' responses are represented across themes is to present a table like the one shown in Table 9.7.

TABLE 9.7 Distribution of themes across interviews.

	Anna	Bernard	Charles	Deirdre
Theme 1: Carefree life before stroke	✓	✓		
Theme 2: Hectic time when stroke occurred		✓		✓
Theme 3: Confusion immediately following stroke	✓	✓	✓	✓
Theme 4: Hopelessness on receiving diagnosis		✓	✓	
Theme 5: Uncertainty about likely recovery	✓			✓

Ticks indicate theme was extracted from interview indicated.

Not all published papers do this, and not every researcher or reader considers it necessary. Think about whether, and how, this might enhance your report.

Indexing extracts using pseudonyms, participant numbers, line numbers, etc.

Published papers vary in the extent to which they index data extracts to individual participants or events. If a study was based on a sample of 12 participants, it may be useful for the reader to see how many extracts have come from participant or interview number 3 for example, mainly to assess how well the analysis considers material from the whole range of participants. Some authors prefer to give participants pseudonyms rather than numbers, on the basis that this makes them more memorable and helps the readers navigate their way through the analysis. Other authors argue that giving participants fake names in this way does nothing whatsoever to enhance the presentation. Whichever you decide to do, beware using pseudonyms that might reveal a participant's true identity, if you have promised anonymity as part of your research briefing. Supposing you interviewed 12 final year students and used pseudonyms with the same letter and ethic origin as participants' real names. Students to whom you have given unusual pseudonyms might be identifiable as a result.

Most papers refer to extracts by the numbers of the lines in the data transcript. If you do this in your report, make sure that the numbering you use is consistent, both within the report and any appendices, such as raw data transcripts that you might include.

Special requirements for presenting discourse analysis and conversation analysis

Most of what we have said so far relates to presenting the thematic content of your analysis. You will be aware, though, that some approaches focus at least as much on the natural *structure* of qualitative data as on its content. This is particularly true of studies using discourse or conversation analysis.

Superficially, the results/analysis section of a discourse analytic report might look similar to one from any qualitative study. Authors often take a subheading within the results section for each discourse, repertoire, subject position, etc. then describe it, then present one or more data extracts to illustrate it. However, there is an important difference:

- Discourse analytic researchers place special emphasis on discourse as a *process*. They try, as far as possible, not to reduce their data to isolated units. Consequently, the data extracts presented in a discourse analysis report are usually *longer* than in other types of study, and each extract is usually discussed at greater length.

- Conversation analysis researchers also present long data extracts, and discuss them at length. Because the conversational *exchange* is especially vital to the analysis, researchers are more likely to focus at least as much on processe such as turn taking and overlaps between speakers, as on the thematic content of the talk.

9.2.10 Some general points about presentation of qualitative findings

Using published examples to help you shape your results section

It should be obvious by now that reports of qualitative research studies, using very different analytical approaches, can appear superficially very similar. At first glance, the formula of themes as headings, followed by explanation and description, followed by illustrative data extracts can seem almost universal. There are, however, important differences between papers when you read them more closely. For that reason, it is not wise to base your own analysis and presentation on a rigid template you have adopted from just one or two published chapters or papers. We recommend that you read as many published papers as possible for your chosen technique. Try to pick out what, if anything, they have in common, and any differences between them. Consider why the authors may have chosen to present their specific findings in just that way. Choose the method of presentation that is compatible with your chosen approach, and best fits your data or research question.

How writing for assessment may differ from writing for publication

Some university departments require students to write up their dissertation report in the exact format required for a specific journal. This is a useful skill to develop if you intend to pursue a career in research, and of course you will have had the opportunity to read and compare numerous examples of research articles published in this format. However, your department may expect you to write in a different format, specifically for undergraduate dissertation projects. There are good reasons for this, when we consider the different purposes of published articles as opposed to reports submitted as part of your degree assessment.

When authors publish an article in a journal, they are typically seeking to communicate their theory or findings to other researchers. Although their work may be critiqued by reviewers and readers, it is generally assumed, by the time the paper goes into print, that the authors are skilled researchers who knew what they were doing when they conducted the study. When students writes a dissertation report, they are not just seeking to communicate research findings, but also to demonstrate subject knowledge, and skills in research and academic writing. The report needs to provide evidence of the student's knowledge and skills, that markers can assess, in order to award a mark or grade. For this reason, it is often necessary to include materials in a dissertation report that would not normally be included in a published article. This might include, for example, appendices containing the interview or focus group schedule used, or evidence of ethical approval. In terms of presenting your analysis, your supervisor might expect you to include data transcripts, or lists of codes produced at early stages of the analysis. You might find it helpful to include a worked example showing how some data were coded, to demonstrate the process by which you derived your results. To ensure that you produce a report that evidences your knowledge and skills, without being overly inclusive, we recommend that you check with your department, your project guidance documents and your supervisor, to find out their specific requirements. You may also find it helpful to talk through with your supervisor your plan for presenting the analysis and results, with a rationale as to why you have planned to present them in that format.

MAXIMISING MARKS

The format of your report

Read published papers that have used your chosen technique, but also check with your department for the specific format you must follow for your dissertation project reports. A report written for assessment may need to differ somewhat from one written for publication.

Ways to show that your analysis is rigorous

Qualitative researchers do not always apply terms such as validity, reliability or generalisability to their work, but there are still accepted grounds for assessing the quality or *rigour* of qualitative analysis. The precise concepts and terminology used depend on the specific approach to analysis adopted, but you should ensure that you address rigour at some point in the methodology, results/analysis or discussion sections of your report. This might include, for example, describing specific procedures you adopted to ensure the appropriateness of data coding, or to check the match between your analysis and the data; or how you decided that your analysis was complete. Some analytical approaches offer specific techniques for doing this. For example, in reports of thematic analysis, authors may mention that two or more researchers coded data independently, compared their results and produced an agreed version. Grounded theory researchers may discuss using *constant comparison* between the data and the analysis, and discuss how the analysis was complete when *data saturation* or *category saturation* was achieved. In phenomenological research and work using IPA, one way to assess methodological rigour might be to *check with participants* if the analysis really captures their experience. Finally, in both IPA and constructionist research, the researcher's subjectivity plays an important role in the analysis. For that reason researchers often include a discussion of *reflexivity* within their report, to enable the reader to assess what part this may have played in shaping the findings. When planning your analysis, and your presentation of it, consider which of these concepts are compatible with your chosen project and technique. Discuss with your supervisor how they would expect you to address these issues in your report.

MAXIMISING MARKS

Methodological rigour

Consider which definition of methodological rigour is most compatible with the theoretical perspective you have adopted for your study, and your chosen analytical technique. Incorporate a discussion of rigour when you present your analysis or discussion.

CHAPTER SUMMARY

- It is essential to make sure that you are entering correlational data correctly – each psychometric scale has its own scoring protocol–and you should check for reverse-keyed items and what items correspond to each subscale.

- A factorial ANOVA design is primarily constructed in order to test interactions between factors or variables. Make sure that you can interpret these correctly – a lineplot often helps you and your reader to understand the analysis.

- Deductive analysis of qualitative data may offer more certainty about how to approach this, but inductive analysis allows you to discover new insights that were not part of your original conceptual framework.

- Many different approaches to qualitative analysis involve segmenting your data into smaller chunks of meaning, which can be used to identify thematic content. Some approaches, such as conversation analysis and discourse analysis, pay more attention to the structure of talk and the social processes occurring within the data.

- Some techniques, such as grounded theory, explicitly require the process of data analysis to be cyclical, but this principle can be applied to most other qualitative approaches.

FURTHER READING

As qualitative methods tend to be less familiar to many students than quantitative ones are, the following are some examples of published papers using specific qualitative approaches. This is not an exhaustive list, just some suggestions to get you started. Use your literature searching skills to identify others that may be more relevant to your specific project.

Phenomenology

Ek, K., & Ternestedt, B.M. (2008). Living with chronic obstructive pulmonary disease at the end of life: a phenomenological study. *Journal of Advanced Nursing*, 62(4), 470–478.

Karlsson, A., Arman, M., & Wikblad, K. (2008). Teenagers with type 1 diabetes – a phenomenological study of the transition towards autonomy in self-management. *International Journal of Nursing Studies*, 45(4), 562–570.

Interpretative phenomenological analysis

Eatough, V., & Smith, J. (2006). 'I was like a wild wild person': understanding feelings of anger using interpretative phenomenological analysis. *British Journal of Psychology*, 97, 483–498.

Lavallee, D., & Robinson, H.K. (2007). In pursuit of an identity: a qualitative exploration of retirement from women's artistic gymnastics. *Psychology of Sport and Exercise*, 8(1), 119–141.

Discourse analysis

Capdevila, R., & Callaghan, J.E.M. (2008). 'it is not racist. it is common sense'. A critical analysis of political discourse around asylum and immigration in the UK. *Journal of Community & Applied Social Psychology*, 18(1), 1–16.

Day, K., Gough, B., & McFadden, M. (2003). Women who drink and fight: a discourse analysis of working-class women's talk. *Feminism Psychology*, 13, 141–158.

Narrative psychology

Hemsley, B., Balandin, S., & Togher, L. (2007). Narrative analysis of the hospital experience for older parents of people who cannot speak. *Journal of Aging Studies*, 21(3), 239–254.

Hok, J., Wachtler, C., Falkenberg, T., & Tishelman, C. (2007). Using narrative analysis to understand the combined use of complementary therapies and bio-medically oriented health care. *Social Science & Medicine*, 65(8), 1642–1653.

Conversation analysis

Stokoe, E., & Edwards, D. (2007). 'Black this, black that': racial insults and reported speech in neighbour complaints and police interrogations. *Discourse & Society*, 18(3), 337–372.

Toerien, M., & Kitzinger, C. (2007). Emotional labour in the beauty salon: turn design of task-directed talk. *Feminism & Psychology*, 17(2), 162–172.

For a detailed guide on how to conduct a conversation analysis, we would recommend that you read the following document, which is freely available on the internet:

Forrester, M. (2002). A guide to conversation analysis. Published on the Higher Education Academy Psychology Network website http://www.psychology.heacademy.ac.uk/html/extra_material.asp

Thematic analysis

Malik, S.H., & Coulson, N. (2008). The male experience of infertility: a thematic analysis of an online infertility support group bulletin board. *Journal of Reproductive and Infant Psychology*, 26(1), 18–30.

Walsh, S.P., White, K.M., & Young, R.M. (2008). Over-connected? A qualitative exploration of the relationship between Australian youth and their mobile phones. *Journal of Adolescence*, 31(1), 77–92.

Grounded theory

Abrahamsson, K.H., Berggren, U., Hallberg, L.R.M., & Carlsson, S.G. (2002). Ambivalence in coping with dental fear and avoidance: a qualitative study. *Journal of Health Psychology*, 7(6), 653–664.

Holt, N., & Dunn, J. (2004). Toward a grounded theory of the psychosocial competencies and environmental conditions associated with soccer success. *Journal of Applied Sport Psychology*, 16(3), 199–219.

CHAPTER 10
PREPARING THE REPORT

That is it. You have designed your project, collected and analysed all your data, and all that remains is to write the report. Simple, is it not? Well, in some cases your work may have hardly begun. Even if you have done everything relating to your project single-handed from design to analysis, with just a couple of cursory supervisory meetings, what you will ultimately be judged on is your ability to write a coherent, competent report with all the important details in the right places and with a general air of authority and professionalism. In this chapter we will give you some advice on how to achieve this.

BY THE END OF THIS CHAPTER YOU WILL:

- Consider some of the broad aspects of report writing and style.
- Have some useful ideas about how to organise various sections of the report.

10.1 REPORT WRITING STYLE

The first part of this chapter discusses the overall style of report writing in relation to psychology as an academic discipline. The style for typical psychology projects is the scientific report format. It is unlikely that your examiners would expect you to present your report in any alternative format, although there is a lot of flexibility within science! But typically you would expect a psychology report to consist of four broad sections: an introduction, including an extensive review of relevant literature; a method section with comprehensive details of the data collection process; an analytic section, usually headed 'Results', although qualitative researchers usually prefer 'Analysis'; and a reasonably lengthy discussion.

Around this main body of the report are a number of optional features, although it is fair to say that all project reports will include an abstract or summary, a reference section and at least one appendix (if only a copy of an ethical approval document, but these usually include things such as your interview schedule or questionnaire). You may also have a table of contents with page numbers, and an acknowledgements or dedication page. Other features will depend on the idiosyncrasies of the department or course, but these will be made clear to you in your course project guide or by your supervisor.

One of the most difficult things for final year project students is that, by the time you come to start writing your report, it may be over a year since you last handed in this type of assignment. The report writing training in psychology degrees is usually confined to practical classes and, on many courses, students are only required to produce a handful of research reports over the first two years of the degree. Some of these will be written, if not as a team, in parallel with fellow students who have been collecting data together. Your final year project may use a methodology or analytic technique that was not covered in your practical classes and so you might never have had the chance to write a report that required you to write up such a technique.

Psychology students will differ to a greater or lesser extent in terms of training for report writing, but in most cases today they will have been encouraged, if not instructed, to adhere to the guidelines produced by the American Psychological Association (these will be referred to henceforth as the 'APA style'). These guidelines were produced primarily for the authors of professional journal articles, but they are extremely detailed and it is usually felt to be good practice for students to follow them, with varying degrees of flexibility.

The APA guidelines (APA, 2010) cover everything from how to report statistical tests to how many inches your paragraph indents need to be. How strictly you need to adhere to the formatting aspects of APA style will vary enormously both between and within psychology departments. Some lecturers are real sticklers for APA style and complain about things such as paragraph indents, while others may not even be familiar with APA style at all, wonder why their students should be following an American style, indeed encourage you to break the rules! So, as elsewhere in this book, we ask you to check with your department first, if in any doubt, and use the guidance provided by it.

However, there are some fairly universal principles that underpin all psychology reports, whether APA directed or otherwise. For instance, the referencing style used by APA derives from the Harvard Library system of citation: namely, that you cite author surnames and dates of publication in the text itself and include full source details in an alphabetically arranged reference section at the conclusion of the report. We would expect this format to be followed by all psychology degree courses, but we still advise you to check if you have been instructed otherwise earlier in your course. Indeed, many journals that psychologists publish in (in areas as diverse as biology, nursing and cultural studies) have different formats altogether.

MAXIMISING MARKS

Watch your grammar!

This might seem like a strange consideration for scientific report writing, but it is helpful to be aware of some of the conventions of narrative when it comes to telling the story of your research. For instance, your teachers will probably have requested repeatedly that you write 'in the third person', because this is the conventional form for a scientific report. So, avoid all use of *I, my, we* and *our;* and use *it* or *the researcher* where possible, even if you are referring to yourself.

You may, on the other hand, have been told that you can write 'in the first person' if you are doing a qualitative project. It is important to be careful not to lose an authoritative tone. Writing a report in the first person runs the risk of slipping into 'Dear Diary' mode if you repeatedly refer to what you did ('I decided to … I conducted … my participants …'). What qualitative researchers mean here is that you should write *reflexively:* acknowledge the role that you play as a researcher in your study; perhaps explain your theoretical perspective, your interaction with the interviewees or whatever. The use of first person pronouns will most likely be confined to a couple of paragraphs rather than sprinkled liberally throughout the report.

The other grammatical convention to be aware of is *tense.* Again, you are likely to have been told repeatedly to 'use the past tense for reports'. This is because you are narrating an account about events that happened in the past (you carried out a piece of research and then wrote it up). However, this advice can be taken too literally, to the point where students write *everything* in the past tense, including things that have not yet happened!

Be sensible: if something does not sound right when expressed as a past event, that is probably because you need to find another tense to write in: the conditional (*It was thought that participants would find the first section difficult*), the subjunctive (*It was important that the participants wore protective clothing*), or the perfect (*Many studies have been conducted using balance beams*).

Perhaps the trickiest tense issues are encountered in the method, where you are required to describe things such as tests and scales that have been published in the past but are still in use. If you say something like *The Fear of Ghosts scale consisted of 24 items* then it sounds as if you constructed it specifically for this one study (and it will never be used again). On the other hand, if it is a previously published instrument, you should really refer to it in the *present* tense, because it is theoretically available for use in the same format, and readers might wish to use it themselves in their own research (and not just in a replication of your study).

10.2 THE MAIN BODY OF THE REPORT

It may be helpful to think of the report as a story. At each stage in the process you need to think about your readers. What have you told them so far? What do they need to know? If you mention a particular term on page 2 that you do not actually define until page 5, why might this be a problem for them? It is always a good idea to have a mental picture of your most important reader – and in many cases this is not your personal supervisor but the second marker. They will not be familiar with your topic, even though they will usually be reasonably familiar with the broad area and/or methodology, so they may need to have many things spelled out that you might not feel necessary to spell out to your supervisor. Imagine them reading each page; what might go through their mind as they try to unravel the intricacies of your study?

10.2.1 Introduction

In most cases, the introduction to your project can be broken down into discrete sections:

- opening paragraph: a brief introduction to the project, setting the scene;
- extensive literature review, itself perhaps broken into subsections;
- 'The present study': a more formal introduction to the project, along with the rationale;
- closing statement, formal or otherwise, in which you make research predictions, hypotheses, or outline the study aims.

The opening paragraph

Your opening paragraph is important because first impressions count. You want to engage your reader immediately. Blindly launching into the literature is not a good idea, if your reader has not quite worked out what the project is all about. Never leave the title to do all the work for you. And forget the abstract entirely – you must never think of this as the first paragraph of the report (see Section 10.3.1).

Let us suppose that you are writing up a project about attitudes towards public transport. You could start the report by presenting it as a study about environmental behaviour: perhaps with a fact such as 'In 2008 in the UK 84,907 journeys were made by car on a single day', or a similar statement about declining usage of the railway. Or you could move in a bit closer and begin by talking about the literature. 'With the environment high on the political agenda, psychologists have begun exploring the ways that the public can be persuaded to use *greener* forms of transport.'

An opening paragraph usually fails if it casts the net too wide or too narrow. A wide opening might begin 'The first omnibus made its journey from ...', or whatever. Or 'Attitudes are the ...' In the first example, you would need to make up an awful lot of ground to get from the birth of public transport to the focus of your own project! In the second, your reader is likely to miss your point, thinking that your project is simply a technical exercise on the methodology of attitude testing. Conversely, a narrow opening takes you straight into the literature without any kind of scene setting. 'Attitudes towards public transport have been studied by ...' You really need to explain, briefly, why it is important to carry out another study on attitudes towards public transport. Think of yourself as having to sell the importance of your study: why should we care? (Remember the 'So what?' test from Chapter 1.)

Unless citing the source of a piece of factual information, or perhaps an overview of a specific body of literature, it is a good idea to avoid references at this stage of the report. It is possible to write an excellent opening paragraph that does not contain a single reference (indeed, many APA journal articles open in this fashion). It certainly is worth trying to write it without using references, then adding one or two if absolutely necessary to back up a claim. One other tip is, as with the abstract, to leave writing the opening paragraph until the rest of the report is finished, which may give you a clearer overview about the findings and the general direction of the whole.

You could conclude your opening paragraph by making some statement about your own study. In any case, you should certainly indicate, briefly, how you have structured the rest of the introductory section at the end of this paragraph, so that the reader knows where you are going to take them. This is particularly important if you are prone to drifting off the point or waffling. If the reader has been set up with a *schema* of your introduction structure, they are likely to be more tolerant of brief deviations and occasional instances of waffling prose. But beware of spending too long outlining the plan of your introduction here. Remember, it should be brief: just a sentence or two, no more.

Literature review

We will not say too much about literature reviewing here, partly because it has already been covered quite extensively in Chapter 3, but also because it is almost certainly the element of report
writing that you are already quite familiar with. The important thing to consider when planning
the literature review is *organisation*. You have probably consulted dozens of research articles and
books; you have a long list of references that you wish to include; but you have only so many words
allocated to this section into which to cram them all. You might decide to break your review into
subsections, organised by theme (environmental behaviour, attitude testing, persuasion or whatever). If you go down this road (and we know some supervisors dislike it, so check first) you need
to make sure that you structure each subsection very carefully so that the reader understands why
you are reviewing this particular literature, and how it connects to the other subsections.

If you do not wish to organise your literature review by subheading or theme, an alternative
strategy is to organise your literature into chronological order, telling the story of how research relevant to your project has progressed from the earliest ideas and findings through to contemporary
research and theories, remembering to be evaluative in your account rather than just descriptive.

MAXIMISING MARKS

Signposting

One of the most common complaints by readers of student projects is that they cannot work out
where the report is going. Frequent changes of topic, abrupt openings or conclusions, or the inclusion of spurious detail: all these can baffle your reader without accompanying explanations. It is
therefore important to use plenty of *signposts* in your writing. For instance, you can indicate where
each part of your review is about to go:

> This section begins with a broad overview of research on environmental behaviour, followed by a
> more specific review of the literature on public transport use.

Then, afterwards, you can conclude the section by pointing out the road ahead.

> Although there are few studies that have considered attitudes towards public transport, there is a
> considerable literature on attitudes towards recycling.

Sometimes, a brief explanation is all that is necessary.

> This study will be considered in some detail because of a number of methodological shortcomings.

Summaries are also useful, since they reinforce the point you have made just in case your reader has,
for whatever reason, missed it.

> To summarise, then, the small literature on public transport use consists mainly of qualitative
> focus group studies, while the recycling literature has mostly relied on attitude scales.

If all this seems rather prosaic to you, not to say pedantic, remember you are writing a technical report
and not a novel. Having said that, you are telling a story all the same – and the worst thing that can
happen is that the reader loses track of the plot!

The present study

At some point in your introduction you will need to shift from reviewing the literature to explaining the purpose of your own study (usually referred to as 'the present study' to avoid confusion

with the completed studies you have been reviewing – and also to avoid using the first person). This will certainly need to be *signposted* and you may wish to create a separate subsection (typically entitled something like 'the present study', or 'rationale').

Although you should introduce your study here in a bit more detail than in the opening paragraph, you have to be careful not to introduce extraneous detail that would ordinarily be covered in the method. What you really need to do here is to explain what makes your study different from the others you have reviewed so, if the difference is a matter of methodology, then you will need to indicate, broadly, how you carried out your study.

Another very important function of this section is to provide a critical argument, or *rationale*, for your study. This will usually be some explanatory statement, such as 'since the existing research has mainly consisted of focus group analysis, the present study was designed using a psychometric scale'. Or, 'after reviewing the literature on the theory of mind protocol, it was decided to replicate Johnson (1998) but to introduce confusion through the use of a distractor task'. Or, 'using the phenomenological interview technique of Cross (2002), IPA was used in the present study to explore the experiences of potholers ...' This might seem like 'giving away' some of your method in advance, but it is crucial detail if your hypothesis or research question is going to make any sense. It also gives your reader a clear sense of direction, as, at this stage in the journey, they should already be able to anticipate the outcome.

The closing paragraph

You have set the scene, reviewed the literature, explained the rationale – all that remains is for you to make some sort of advance prediction or to articulate a clear study aim. It is very important to get this right because, if you do not know what question you are asking, how do you know if you have got the answer?

Traditionally, students are taught at this point to *state a hypothesis*, typically using future tense. In some cases you will have been asked to state the null hypothesis (e.g. 'there will be no significant difference'), followed by the 'alternative' hypothesis (i.e. the one you are expecting). Numerous commentators have pointed out the absurdity of this convention (Cohen, 1994), but if your supervisor insists on it, make sure that you include it, as this is another aspect of project work that varies from department to department.

In most cases, however, you are best advised simply to make some sort of research prediction, e.g. 'it was anticipated that the dogs would display superior search skills to their owners'. Without this kind of statement, it is impossible to know whether to employ a one- or two-tailed inferential test, and it is equally impossible to know how to interpret the outcome! Incidentally, unless you have good reason to just state 'there will be a difference', you should avoid making open, two-tailed predictions, even if your one-tailed rationale is somewhat speculative.

Of course, if you are conducting a qualitative piece of research, it may be impossible for you to make any meaningful research prediction of this type. Instead, you should give the reader some indication of what things you will be looking for when you conduct your analysis. An open-ended interview-based study using IPA or grounded theory might necessitate a bit of broad-mindedness here, but even those methods require you to have some kind of study aim: a theoretical model of the phenomenon under investigation, or a set of salient themes common to the participant group. The aims of your project might be stated in the following way:

● 'To explore the experience of ...'

● 'To investigate the discursive construction of ...'

● 'To develop a model of ...'

COMMON PITFALLS

The ambigious referent

> It was hypothesised that the participants in Group B would display slower reaction times than those in Group A.

Whenever you find yourself writing a sentence like this one, ask yourself: has the reader been introduced to groups A and B yet? It is unlikely that you will have given a clear description of your study design (and procedure) before the end of the introduction, and the reader will not have any idea what the difference is between groups A and B. In fact, it is best all round if you can give your groups meaningful labels rather than abstract letters or numbers (e.g. 'the mnemonic group' versus the 'control group'). An easy way to lose marks is to slip into using your own shorthand for referring to your groups, rather than using their full titles.

> Group A filled out the memory cards while waiting to receive the treatment.

Let us suppose this is the design section, at the beginning of the method. Have you explained '*the memory cards*' yet? Unless memory cards are a frequent instrument in the research literature, and have been fully explained in your introduction, it is unlikely, as you would usually wait till the method for such detail. How can you get around this apparent dead end? The answer is that the reader is clearly not ready to hear about 'the memory cards' yet: leave this detail for the procedure section (or move materials into pole position in the method).

Just being clear about what you are looking for will help the reader to evaluate your study once you get to the analysis section.

10.2.2 Method

The method section is one of the most challenging parts of the report for psychology students. This is because, traditionally, report writing is taught using a strict four part format: a design section, where you explain the dependent and independent variables; a participants section; a section headed 'Materials'; and a procedure. Many students arrive at university with this format irreversibly fixed in their minds and may have it reiterated in level 1 laboratory classes. Many university lecturers still cling to these 'classic' subsections as containing everything they expect to find in a good method. For this reason, as usual, we ask that you check your supervisor's expectations before taking our advice. If they expect to find a list of materials, even if you are doing a discourse analysis, then you are best off putting one in!

The problem with this four part format is that it only really works if you are writing up an *experiment*. It is unsuitable, frankly, for any other type of project. An interview study analysed using qualitative methods is unlikely to have any *materials*. Many of the procedural aspects could be covered in participants, or under design. A study using questionnaires, or psychometric scales, has *measures* rather than materials; again the procedure is better covered in one of the other sections. It is therefore important to regard the method section as highly flexible in the way its subsections are organised.

Pick up a contemporary issue of a psychology journal and you will find all manner of different method sections. Just by way of illustration, the first three papers in the May 2008 issue of the BPS's *British Journal of Psychology* produced the pattern of subsections as shown in Table 10.1.

TABLE 10.1 Examples of subsections used in published psychology reports.

Bould and Morris (experiment on emotion recognitiwon)	(*General method*: Introductory section outlining broad design and data collection procedures) *Participants* *Stimuli* *Stimuli grouping* *Procedure*
Morrison and O'Connor (experiment on rumination and attentional bias)	*Participants* *Measures* *Procedure*
Steptoe et al. (survey panel study of positive affect and health outcomes)	*Participants* *Measures of positive and negative affect* *Other measures* *Procedure* *Statistical analysis*

At the same time, there are certain fundamental characteristics of all studies that will need to be covered in your report. The remainder of this section, then, takes you through the must have details. What we cannot do, though, is tell you exactly how to organise your method depending on the type of study you have done: each study is different and your supervisor should be able to advise you on this.

Design

An interesting characteristic of modern psychology papers is that they rarely have a separate design section. You often find a section headed 'Design and procedure' or 'Design and participants', but the fact is that it is hard to describe the design of a study before you have actually described its various components; so we are back to ambiguous referents such as Group 1 and Group 2 again! Also, it is not always clear how to describe the design of a non-experimental study, other than 'a correlational design', 'an interview study' and so on. Such information barely requires a separate subsection.

In a qualitative study, it may be useful to clarify whether the study is inductive or deductive (or perhaps both). Depending on the precise approach you have adopted, it may also be relevant to indicate whether the data were collected contemporaneous with the phenomenon under investigation, whether the data were first person accounts of experiences, and whether they were archival or collected specifically for your project.

Participants

The vast majority of undergraduate psychology projects will involve human beings as participants in some capacity. Nevertheless, there are a few students who will use archival or other (e.g. media) data for psychological ends (content or discourse analyses, perhaps). Very occasionally, students carry out discursive studies using media interviews, and list each of the interviewees on the TV programme as their 'participants'. This is a clear example of a project where a participants section is redundant, if not plain silly, since none of the interviewees have actually taken part in your study: their interviews were conducted for a different purpose, and you are using it as secondary data in your project.

What about an observational study, though? Here, even if you are wearing a T-shirt reading 'Researcher', and all the observees are fully aware of their participation in a study, it would only make sense to describe them as participants if you were observing a very small number of people at close quarters (think of a *Big Brother*-type setting with you logging information behind the screen). On the other hand, if you are hanging around a busy public space, it would make little sense to describe your thousand or so passers-by as 'participants'. The rule of thumb is whether your participants (or perhaps, in a child study, their parents) have formally consented to take part in your study: if they have not, then they are not truly study participants and do not merit a section to themselves.

Participants, sections vary enormously in length, depending on the size of the sample. A questionnaire completed by 100 undergraduates is unlikely to require much participant detail – most researchers collect some form of demographic information to give the study some social context, but beyond age and gender, the amount of this type of information will depend on your research question, the nature of the sample, your hypotheses and so on.

Where you are conducting a small-sample study, for example an IPA or thematic analysis with six or so individual interviews, you would be expected to tell us much more about your participants. We might expect to hear a little of their personal histories: after all, if you have selected them for such an exclusive sample, there ought to be a good reason! Perhaps they are all people with a particular diagnosis; then it will be important to know about their 'aetiology', their course of treatment, time since diagnosis and so on. If they are a sample of drug users, tell us about how long they have used drugs, what drugs they have used, and the context in which they take drugs.

The participants, section should also include information about selection and recruitment. How did you obtain your sample? Students have a habit of writing 'opportunity sample' to cover any group of participants larger than ten but, unless you have managed to capture a lecture hall for a questionnaire blitz, it is more likely that your sample is a *volunteer* one, particularly if you are using an organised participant 'pool'. It is also important to tell us about the ethical procedure here as well – what sort of information participants were provided with (consent forms, debriefing, etc.). You might also add that you received ethical clearance through your departmental committee, or whatever formal system approves projects at your institution.

Materials or measures?

Naturally, if your study is experimental in nature, you will have a nice set of 'materials' to report in a specific subsection. These will be the stimuli you use in your experiment: slides projected on a screen or computer; picture cards; word lists; vignettes or film clips; edible solutions; anything, in short, that is used to obtain your dependent variable(s). Provide enough detail about these stimuli so that readers could, if they wished, replicate your study. You may need to include some illustrative examples, or at least include some examples in an appendix. If you are using materials that are themselves derived from a previous study, you can omit some of the detail, so long as you give the reader enough source information (and of course a citation to the original study).

You should also include any form of technical apparatus in this section (although feel free to create a separate subsection headed 'Apparatus' if you prefer). Again, you should include sufficient detail of any original piece of 'kit' designed especially for your experiment so that a reader could order an equivalent contraption from their technician. If it is a standard piece of equipment, simply record information such as the model number and basic technical details, so that the reader could order one from a manufacturer.

If your study is not experimental but still quantitative in nature, we recommend that you put all your data collection materials under 'Measures', to avoid any confusion. It is common for people to scrape the barrel in order to satisfy the demand for 'materials': pens, pencils, paper, chairs, tables, sheets of paper and all manner of household items are included that have nothing directly to do with the data you are collecting.

The bottom line with measures, as indeed with materials, is that you describe in some detail everything you have used to obtain the raw data that are entered into your statistical analysis. Your reader will expect to find a clear connection between each measure listed and a column in one of your data tables.

Like sets of stimuli or apparatus, the amount of detail you provide will depend on the origins of the measure. An original questionnaire or scale will require a lot of detail because the reader will have no other source to consult should they wish to replicate the study. For a previously published scale, it will be enough simply to reference its source and to give a general idea of the sort of items it contains, its subscales (if any), its scoring system (e.g. five-point Likert-type scale) and, ideally, some measure of reliability (typically Cronbach's alpha).

Settings and schedules

If your study is an observation, as suggested previously, you may not have a participants, section, and it is unlikely you are using any 'materials' as such, other than a checklist or other proforma attached to a clipboard. In this case it is probably a good idea to use different types of subsection, broken up using headings such as 'Observational setting' in which you give a comprehensive description of the space in which you are collecting data, and 'Schedule' or other formal means of compiling data. You may wish to reproduce your exact checklist (or perhaps refer the reader to an appendix).

In qualitative studies, data collected are often a product of the interaction between the researcher and participants. This interaction begins from the moment you attempt to recruit people to take part, so details of recruitment materials, such as invitation letters, posters, emails and participant information sheets, can be listed here (with links to the original documents in the appendices).

For interview studies and focus group research, the setting may also be relevant, particularly if you are interviewing people in their own homes. However, here you will certainly have a detailed participants, section and you may wish to include that kind of information there. You will certainly need a section in which you describe your interview *schedule* or focus group guide though, including a list of questions, topics or themes, and some idea of how you conducted the interview or focus group itself.

Procedure

This section is most appropriate for experimental studies, where you will have a clearly defined procedure, independent of the testing materials or measures, that is followed by each participant (or each member of an experimental condition). As with 'materials', the key thing to bear in mind is how relevant the details are to the collection of data: does it matter how close participants sat to the screen, how far apart the chairs were placed, and whether participants marked the paper with a pen or pencil? However, things such as the sequence of events, or measures, are important, and any precise, standardised verbal instructions. It may also be worth clarifying whether interviews were conducted face-to-face, as opposed to on the telephone, and whether participants were interviewed one-to-one, or in the presence of others, such as friends, relatives or carers. Do beware, though, of an undergraduate tendency to fill this section with a long quote consisting of the standardised instructions: here it is important that you tell the reader exactly what happened, not what was *supposed* to happen.

For other types of project, the procedure section is optional, as many procedural details can be better contained within other sections. Qualitative researchers might wish, however, to include a section called 'Analytic Procedure' in which they detail the steps taken as part of a systematic technique, such as IPA or thematic analysis. If you do not include this detail in the method you will certainly need it for your analysis section.

Pilot studies

If you have used a pilot study in order to refine your project design, then you should report its findings somewhere in the method (again, the worry that you should only report data in the results leads some students to the wrong conclusion here). If the pilot study is very extensive, then you could report the findings formally but, in the vast majority of cases, it will be a small sample 'dry run' of some aspect of the study that you have conducted in order to check whether the experimental procedure works, or how long it takes your respondents to fill out your questionnaire, or even just a simple rehearsal of an interview schedule before 'the real thing'.

In each case, you should at least mention, in an appropriate subsection of your method, that you have piloted the materials, or the procedure, and provide details of any changes you made as a result of the pilot. If nothing else, this gives your reader some explanation of how you came to set the timings for your stimuli, or the order of questions, or any aspect of your methodology that might otherwise seem random or spurious. Often, pilot studies are sufficiently successful to warrant keeping the data and entering them into the final analysis. If this has happened to you, make sure you report that you carried out the pilot work anyway (for the reasons listed previously).

Sometimes, mini-studies are conducted as part of the data collection process that you do not want to report formally – for example, a focus group that is used to collect statements to use for a psychometric scale. You still need to report this study, in the same way that you need to get ethical approval in order to run it. You can choose to have a separate subsection in the method, or you can just report it in a paragraph under measures, materials or procedure – wherever seems most appropriate. Be careful, though, not to confuse your reader by mixing up the details with those of your main study (by lumping the participants of your focus group in with the respondents who eventually completed the final version of your scale, for example).

Data preparation

Often researchers like to use the method section to describe how raw data were prepared for subsequent analysis. The reader does not really need to be told, as in so many undergraduate laboratory reports, that 'the data were collated and entered into SPSS', but it may be that complex transformations were necessary, or that the data were recoded or reorganised in some way.

Often students are reluctant to put statistical information in the method, believing that all this type of detail belongs exclusively to the results. Sometimes, though, it is helpful at this stage of the report to tell the readers that your experimental groups did not differ significantly in IQ (along with relevant inferential statistics), or that your sample broke down into specific percentages according to occupation, or some other characteristic, maybe even expressed diagrammatically (with a pie chart, for instance). Any statistics relating to specific measures should be reported here, such as reliabilities; there is no need even to leave means and standard deviations (of psychometric scale measures) until the results. We have even seen factor analyses reported under measures as a means of identifying subscales.

10.2.3 Results/analysis

We will not say much about results in this chapter, because most of the relevant information has already been covered in Chapter 9. As with all the sections, it is vital that your information is carefully and clearly organised, so that the reader knows exactly where to go in order to find out how you have answered the research question. Illustration should be kept to a minimum: you would expect to find a selection of tables but no more than a couple of graphics. Endless pages of scatterplots might *bulk out* a thin report, but your reader will almost certainly skip them in a huff, wondering when you are going to get down to the important business of relating what you have found.

10.2.4 Discussion

On the face of it, the discussion should not be the most difficult section of the report to write. Nevertheless, it turns out very often to be the most challenging section to write and serious marks can be won and lost here. Students typically leave it until the last minute and do not know what to put in it, especially if they have obtained non-significant results It is frequently clogged up with all manner of speculative ramblings about whether time of day, external noise or participant gender might have affected the results, without displaying any evidence from the data or any sensible reason as to why this might have been the case. Indeed, some departments ask project supervisors not to give students feedback on drafts of their discussion, because, irrespective of supervisor input to study design and analysis, this is the one section of the project that truly displays independent thought.

In the next section, we give you a few ideas for improving the discussion section.

Opening paragraph

As with the opening of the introduction, it is important to set the right tone at the beginning of the discussion. Your reader has waded through all the nuts and bolts of your study, has some sense of how the research question has been tackled, but at this point they want to hear your account of how the research question has been answered. So the first paragraph of the discussion should be a general statement about your findings – whether your hypotheses (if you have them) are supported, what the salient features of your analysis are and so on.

Try to avoid any 'statistical language' (i.e. names of inferential tests, p values – indeed, any numerical information) in this opening paragraph. You could in fact use this statement as part of your abstract (see Section 10.3.1). Apart from anything else, it helps your reader – and possibly you – recap the most important parts of the results or analysis section, and relate them back to the predictions or aims that you stated at the end of the introduction.

As always, to get a sense of how to write a good discussion opening, it is worth checking the first paragraph of the discussion in a few published articles.

Accounting for findings

The next part of your discussion should ideally be a more detailed consideration of the main findings, broken down into themes. Preferably you would begin with your main hypothesis or aim and then consider increasingly minor subthemes. The main purpose of this section of the report is to *account for* your findings, usually with regard to theory and/or previous research. This may well involve a fair few references to the literature you reviewed in the introduction.

After the first page or two, discussion sections diverge according to whether the study findings were expected or unexpected. If you supported all your hypotheses, or the data fell into place exactly as you had anticipated according to previous studies on the topic, then the main purpose of this section becomes a discussion of the **theoretical implications** of your findings. That is, how do your results fit with the existing theoretical ideas in the area: what are they indicating? Remember that you constructed a theoretical framework in your introduction – now is your chance to review it in the light of what you found, and even suggest how it could be amended to account for the results of your study. You should do this regardless of whether your results were consistent with your expectations or not. A common mistake students make is to immediately launch into an inquest into why they did not find the results that they wanted, and to assume that they must have done something wrong methodologically. Before you engage in this critique of your method, assume, just for a brief moment, that your results are perfectly valid. If that really is what is going on, what does this say about all those studies you reviewed in your introduction? Perhaps there are weaknesses in *their* methods, rather than in yours!

When you do move into a critique of your own study, it is important not to let your discussion turn into a list of excuses for *what went wrong*. There will always be aspects of a study that could benefit from a little 'tweaking' – even if you have carried out a rigorous pilot. These aspects should always be described as the **limitations** of your methodology, never as 'weaknesses'. You need to weigh up these limitations while seriously considering the possibility that your predictions were not justifiable in the first place. This may be because the literature has led you to false conclusions (indeed, you may have played devil's advocate to some extent, by stating a hypothesis you wished to disprove – otherwise known as the Popperian approach to science).

COMMON PITFALLS

Fishing

Fishing occurs frequently in the discussion section of student reports. It usually takes place when the author has run out of sensible things to say about the study findings, or has one hour left before the submission deadline and needs to make the discussion look like a reasonably substantial piece of writing. In most cases no attempt has been made to verify the claims by returning to the data and carrying out some post-hoc analysis. You need to have *some* reason for considering these factors as interfering variables: even anecdotal material might convince a reader that these suggestions are worth taking seriously.

Following are some of the fish frequently caught during this activity – unless accounted for, they should be thrown back into the water immediately!

The results were non-significant because:

1   *Participants were tested at different times of day.* Okay, perhaps natural biorhythms account for the variance. Is there any reason to suppose this? If not, and you really do feel that the morning participants were sluggish and unfocused compared with the ones you tested later in the day, why not simply compare the means of the morning and afternoon groups? At the very least, you should report your observations of the morning participants' behaviour in the discussion.

2   *There was external noise during the study.* How exactly did the external noise affect participants' performance? Did noise affect some participants and not others? If so, is it possible to compare their data?

3   *There were too few participants.* A sitting duck, rather than a fish, for a critical reader. Why did you not manage to recruit more? Is the study underpowered? (This is something you can test and present data for.) Was there some aspect of the recruitment process that did not work? Unfortunately, in most cases, students under recruit because they begin data collection too late and end up having to settle for underpowered samples. In fact, it is probably *never* a good idea to say that your study had too few participants (after all, inferential statistical tests account for sample size in their formulae, so it really is a case of simply stating the obvious).

4   *Only student participants were used in the study.* This looks, on the face of it, a reasonable argument – after all, many critics have argued that the routine use of undergraduate samples invalidates a lot of psychological research. But the critics have usually explained *why*; you, too, should think of ways a non-student sample (and give us some examples of realistic comparison groups) might perform differently on the topic in question.

Alternatively, there may be something beyond your study design that interfered with your findings. It is always important that you present the reader with some *evidence* for your suggestions here. Do not feel, however, that each suggestion needs to be backed up by evidence from your dataset; the discussion is a great opportunity for you to present some anecdotal material (if you have kept your research notebook up to date and used it to record your thoughts and observations during the study, you should find some useful discussion material there).

Suggestions for future research

After discussing the outcome of your study and its relationship to theory and previous research, you should move towards a consideration of ways that future research might take your findings forward. Again, there is likely to be some divergence between predictable and unpredictable sets of findings. Predictable findings ought – if the research question is carefully rooted in the theoretical literature – to generate a clear path of future inquiry. Unpredictable findings are harder to follow up. It really depends what you have concluded in the previous section of your discussion. Do you tinker with the methodology? Focus on a different population? Rethink the hypotheses/broad study aims?

In either case, you should once again avoid the kind of 'fishing' outlined above. Suggestions for future research should have some valid basis. Is there any point in extending the age range of your population? What might it serve to achieve? How would you expect a younger or older sample to be different from the present sample? This is particularly true when simply adding participants or extending from students to non-students.

You should also take care not to suggest comparisons that you can not already make from the data you have collected. If it really would be interesting to 'compare males and females' on a particular measure, is there anything to stop you returning to your data and doing just that?

Closing remarks

You can choose to round off your report with a separate subsection headed 'Conclusions', in which you reiterate the project aims, the hypotheses or research question, the methods, broad findings and implications, and some sort of closing statement. Or you can do all this in a final paragraph. Whatever you decide, it is always better to give the report a sense of completion rather than leaving your discussion hanging in mid air.

10.3 SUNDRIES

10.3.1 Abstract

In the old days, lists of journal article abstracts were housed in huge bound volumes on dusty library shelves: the researcher had to sit there poring through the fiendishly complicated cross-referenced indices. There was no hyperlink to the full text article. The poor old thing (or the weary and bad tempered librarian) had to climb a ladder to find the appropriate volume, brush off the dust and plonk it on the table, waking up the dozing student on the next desk.

Then came the glorious invention of CD-ROM and the arrival of PsycINFO and various other versions of search tools that enabled researchers to enter any word or phrase they liked and extract all the abstracts containing that word. You still had to go to the library, up the ladder and fish out the hard copy volume, but at least you knew that the effort would be worth it. Today, abstracts are often the only part of the online journal that non-subscribers have access too, so they still serve a useful function.

What all this is leading up to is a reminder that the abstract is a fully self-contained piece of writing. Indeed, it is best not to think of the abstract as the first section of the report at all, but as a summary that has, literally, been *abstracted,* or removed, from the rest of the report. Therefore it is very important not to behave, when writing the first paragraph of the introduction, as though the reader has already been introduced to the key concepts of the research and the study aims.

Abstracts vary enormously in recommended length (although usually they are somewhere between 100 and 200 words), so you need to check with your supervisor about what is expected in your department. As a general rule, though, your abstract should contain most, if not all, of the following pieces of information:

- a brief rationale for the study;
- basic information about study design, or measures used;
- description of participants;
- short statement containing the main findings of the study;
- brief implications of the findings.

Generally speaking, try to avoid references in your abstract, unless your study is heavily reliant on a previous source (e.g. it is a partial replication of a published study, or it is directly testing a theory or research finding). Likewise, avoid citing inferential statistical detail such as p numbers, although if there are descriptive statistics that summarise your findings these are suitable abstract content (e.g. 56 per cent of participants failed to complete the tasks in time).

Generally speaking, the two most common sources of error in writing an abstract are superfluous background (e.g. chunks of literature review used as rationale), or ambiguous referents (undefined jargon, labels, acronyms and so on). Just think of the poor reader trawling through pages of archived abstracts, trying to work out what you mean by 'group A' and 'group B'.

10.3.2 Referencing

As mentioned earlier, most psychology departments recommend that students use the referencing system of the American Psychological Association (APA), or, more broadly, the 'Harvard system'. Both are based on the principle that, each time you refer to a figure, claim or statement cited in another source, you reference the source *in the text* by way of the name and date. Then you provide, at the end of your work, a detailed list of sources in alphabetical order of the first author surnames. (Other referencing systems use superscript numbers, numbers in square brackets, and so on, in the text, and the reference list at the end may be organised according to order of citation – you have probably seen these in some journal articles, although these systems are rarely found in psychology journals, which frequently request that you format your paper according to 'APA style'.)

In the following section, we have differentiated between the source information you cite when referencing sources in the text, and the detailed information to provide in the alphabetical list of references.

Citations in the text

Usually it is sufficient just to cite a single source as evidence to support a claim, or as information for the reader.

A full review of the literature can be found in Percy and Wood (2008).

You might want to cite that source as an example (note, by the way, how the 'and' becomes an ampersand when put inside parentheses):

Studies that have used this technique (e.g. Percy & Wood, 2008).

However, you might wish to elaborate and cite some of these other studies:

Studies that have used this technique (Percy & Wood, 2008, 2009).

When you cite several studies, use semicolons to separate them, arrange them alphabetically according to the first author names, and arrange works by the same first author chronologically. So:

Carol Percy and colleagues have conducted several studies (Giles, Percy & Wood, 2006; Percy & Wood, 2008; Wood & Percy, 2008).

A word about gratuitous 'stacking' of sources: it may look big and clever to list half a dozen or so sources in a single set of parentheses, but it is rarely necessary unless you are writing a comprehensive review paper, and is often done simply to appear 'scholarly'. Wisely, the BPS Style Guide (British Psychological Society, 2004) recommends that you never cite more than three studies at any one time. A statement such as:

A full review of the literature can be found in Wood (2007).

will usually suffice if you have lots of examples that just repeat the same type of information.

Sometimes awkward academics publish more than one work a year under the same name(s). If you need to cite both works, then you need to refer to them by letters, e.g.

One year, David Giles clearly had too much time on his hands (Giles, 2002a, 2002b).

Do not forget to remember which letters refer to which sources when you draw up your reference list!

Where three or more authors are named on a publication, the standard practice is to include them all in the first citation, e.g. Giles, Wood and Percy (2006), but thereafter only to cite the first author followed by *'et al.'* and the year, e.g. Giles *et al.* (2006). If there are six or more authors, use the *et al.* construction throughout. However, in both cases you should include all authors with the full entry in the reference list.

Also, do not forget to add page numbers when you reference a quotation in the text.

The study used a 'rather unusual and regrettably cumbersome' method (Wood & Percy, 2005: 567).

The reference section

The following formats should be familiar to you.

Journal article

Sandfield A., & Percy C. (2003). Accounting for single status: heterosexism and ageism in heterosexual women's talk about marriage. *Feminism & Psychology*, 13, 475–488.

Book

Wood, C., Littleton, K., & Sheehy, K. (Eds.) (2006). *Developmental Psychology in Action*. Oxford: Blackwell.

Book chapter

Rockwell, D., & Giles, D.C. (2008). Ready for the close-up: celebrity experience and the phenomenology of fame. In Hart, K.R. (Ed.) *Film and Television Stardom* (pp. 324–341). Newcastle-upon-Tyne: Cambridge Scholars.

Other sources include: dissertations, newspaper and magazine articles, conference papers and non-academic reports (e.g. to funding bodies). The format varies according to the nature of the source, but for a typical example of a conference paper:

Giles, D.C., & Close, J. (2007, August). *'Lad Magazine' use, drive for muscularity and dating.* Paper presented at the annual conference of the European Health Psychology Society, Maastricht, the Netherlands.

Online sources are more complicated. Very often the material you cite has landed on the web via an offline source (e.g. a journal article), or lacks a named author or publication date. The rule of thumb is that you give as much information as is necessary for a reader to locate the material, so typically you would conclude with the words 'Retrieved 14 August 2008, from' followed by the URL information in the address bar. For example:

European Commission (n.d.). *Searching for Health Information on the Internet – 2005.* Retrieved 14 August 2008 from http://www.euser-eu.org/ShowCase.asp?CaseTitleID=858&CaseID=1824& MenuID=

Do not forget to check these references before you submit your project, just in case they have changed – the site itself may no longer exist!

10.3.3 Titles

The title of your project may seem like a personal matter, or even a trivial issue. It should certainly be unique. All we can advise, therefore, is that you do not give your examiners a bad first impression by using an inappropriate or clumsy title. In our experience, if a title is badly worded (and especially if there are spelling, grammar or punctuation errors) then it is a bad omen of things to come. After all, if you cannot put the effort into getting your title absolutely perfect, what hope is there for a random sentence in the middle of the discussion?

Good titles fall into two classes: the informative (tells you exactly what is in the tin, so to speak), and the eye-catching. You could play safe by choosing the first option, but you need to make sure that you do not mislead the reader by claiming that your study is about bullying when it is actually about aggression, or that you fail to mention the important point that your participants' wartime reminiscences relate specifically to World War II from a group of 80-plus adults, and so on. A paper recently published in the otherwise excellent journal *Current Directions in Psychological Science* was entitled simply 'Speed-Dating', telling the reader precisely nothing about the study (we still had a look, just out of curiosity – maybe that was the idea).

It is helpful to be relatively brief, however, so do not try and pack too much detail in. A good recent example from the *British Journal of Psychology* is:

Memory for curvature of objects: Haptic touch vs. vision

This title does not muck around: only nine words long (including an abbreviation) You do not need to be an expert to know straight away that you are dealing with two basic experimental conditions and what the research question is likely to be. One way of thinking of a title (for a quantitative study) is simply to list your variables and the investigated relationship between them.

Eye-catching titles typically cleave into two parts separated by a colon. Here is one from another BPS journal, *Psychology and Psychotherapy*:

'I feel like a scrambled egg in my head': an idiographic case study of meaning making and anger using interpretative phenomenological analysis

The second part on its own would seem rather dry, but the authors have used a striking quote from their data to bring the title to life and tempt the reader to explore further. If your study is purely quantitative, or you cannot think of anything particularly witty or clever to represent it, stick with the previous option, and just give it to the reader straight.

10.3.4 Appendices, etc.

This final section consists of all those bits and pieces that surround the main body of your project report. We will not say much about these because departmental protocol around them is so idiosyncratic, and you will almost certainly be given detailed advice by the member of staff responsible for coordinating the final year dissertation.

However, it is always important to respect your appendices, and not to treat them as a dumping ground for extraneous information to pad out a worryingly thin report. Appendices should be carefully organised and clearly labelled, and each appendix should be referred to somewhere in the body of the report itself (as a rule, if there is not anywhere in the report where you can say 'see Appendix 4', then it is probably the case that Appendix 4 is unnecessary). They should include all the detail that your supervisor (or your department) has asked for and no more. Be aware that sometimes it is necessary to include such things as scale items in the method section, and that you should not force your reader to keep constantly leafing through the report to find important information in the appendices. Appendices should always be clearly labelled with a number and a meaningful, descriptive title.

Typically, your report will include a contents page, where you list all the different sections of the report and the page number they begin on. (Do not forget to add the page numbers first!) This is particularly useful for appendices, since the other sections of the report usually occur in a predictable order and are relatively easy to find. Sometimes you might be asked to list your tables and figures separately.

Finally, you are likely to be invited to include a page headed 'Acknowledgements'. In our experience, this is a very useful place to thank your supervisor. Usually students go on to thank all sorts of other people (romantic partners, friends, parents, dogs and deities), but your supervisor should come first and foremost. Also, if you have been given lots of help by technical or administrative staff, it is a good idea to mention them next. Take care, though, when mentioning other members of teaching staff, especially if someone has helped you without your supervisor's knowledge!

10.3.5 And finally . . .

You have finally finished your discussion, labelled your appendices, concocted your abstract and put all the references into the right format. What happens next?

Student 1: You look at your watch. Three hours till the deadline. Reprographics might just be able to turn it round in an hour if there is no queue, so that gives you one hour to print the whole thing off (assuming you can find a free printer in the open access room) and then there will be an hour until the hand-in office closes and you lose 10 per cent (or whatever your department docks for late submission). Best get a move on.

Student 2: You look at your watch. Twenty four hours till the deadline. But Reprographics might be a bit busy, given that a sizeable minority of your 150 fellow psychology final year students will also be handing in their projects at the last moment. So you had better print it off and get it down there pronto. No time to mess around.

Student 3: You look at your diary. A week till the deadline. Plenty of time, then, to carefully check through your work, beat the queue to Reprographics, and then deliver it to the hand-in office – a gently glowing beacon of calm in a sea of utter chaos on deadline day. As you head off to celebrate, you pass Student 2, who is relatively calm but is about to lose several marks for sloppy presentation. Much later, on your way back from the student bar, you run into a tearful Student 1, who, instead of waiting in the long queue at Reprographics two hours after sorting out the printer jam, handed in his thesis, dog-eared and tenaciously held together by a sequence of staples – in a transparent document wallet.

Finishing on time is essential. Finishing ahead of time is much better. There is a world of difference between a piece of work that has been properly proof-read, checked for mistakes and generally made sense of. Almost all substantial pieces of writing contain a multitude of errors from simple typos (you know the right spelling but just missed a keystroke) to awful, mangled sentences that nobody could make head nor tail of. Typos are relatively easy to spot (spellcheck may be drawing your attention to them anyway); syntactical horrors are not. These can only be detected by painstakingly reading the text – perhaps out loud – to ensure that the sentences flow, and that what you are trying to say will make sense to the reader. Best of all, get someone else to read it through. Swap your report with a fellow psychology finalist and maximise both your marks!

It goes without saying that there is no short cut to well-presented work. Your efforts will be rewarded if you plan carefully, setting deadlines in advance and sticking to them. These rules still apply if you are only required to submit your work electronically. Often students think that they can relax a little as they no longer have to worry about the printer breaking down, running out of paper or ink, or the reprographics shop closing a few minutes early. However, you still have to worry about failure of your computer equipment, including USB drives, and your internet access failing either at home, or because there is a server problem on campus. Also, online submission systems are often overloaded on the day when final year projects are due, and this may mean that the system will crash or be painfully slow at uploading your assignment. As with the student who gets their project to the assignment handling office well before the deadline, you should aim to be the student who submits their work electronically the day before it is due, when the online systems are running smoothly, and you still have some time to fix any problems if they arise. Failure of technical equipment is usually not accepted as an acceptable reason for an extension, and most universities will only accept extension requests in advance of the coursework deadline. You should also be aware that many departments also require you to submit both an electronic and a hard copy of your work (the electronic copy is used to detect possible plagiarism). If you submit one, but not the other, by the deadline set you may find that your work is marked as late. So make sure that you are aware of all the requirements for submission well in advance of your deadline.

CHAPTER SUMMARY

- Your abstract may be the first piece of writing in your eventual study report, but it should be the last thing you write. Do not think of it as the introduction: it should be able to stand by itself in a remote database.

- You may have learned that the method section has to consist of design, participants, materials and procedure. But those subheadings are not appropriate for all types of psychological report: make sure you use subsections that are meaningful for your study.

- Take some time over your discussion: this is often 'knocked off' at the last minute, but will benefit enormously from careful thought and preparation, and could well earn you some extra marks – first impressions count but so do last ones.

- Proof-read your report before getting it bound – it is pointless losing marks for poor presentation.

FURTHER READING

As mentioned in the chapter, the follow text is a good source of guidance when preparing your report in terms of what to put in each section and how best to phrase your ideas.

American Psychological Association (2010). *Publication Manual of the American Psychological Association, Sixth Edition.* Washington, DC: APA.

CHAPTER 11
DISSEMINATING YOUR RESULTS

Once your dissertation has been bound and sent off to be marked, and you have recovered from the celebrations, waited for it to be marked, celebrated again (or commiserated, but we will come back to this later), possibly even gone out and got a job or started a postgraduate course, you may well be contacted by your supervisor and asked the question: 'Have you thought of publishing your project?'

What should you answer? No? This might be seen as a snub by your supervisor, who has put in long hours helping you through difficult analyses and thorough pruning of your overlong literature review. It may mean that your supervisor replies 'Okay, well do you mind if I publish it?' and the possible risk of them getting all the glory for your hard work (although *authorship* is another topic that we will return to). It may also simply mean that, if neither of you bother, a useful finding goes unreported to the scientific community.

If, on the other hand, you reply 'yes', you are potentially involving yourself in a lot of hard work. Is it worth it? That really depends on whether: firstly, it will ever be useful in your career; and, secondly, how much pride you are likely to have in seeing your work in print in an academic journal or an alternative outlet. Hopefully, in this chapter, we will give you some advice should you decide to say 'yes'.

BY THE END OF THIS CHAPTER YOU WILL:

- Appreciate the value of disseminating your study findings.
- Have a good idea of the potential outlets for disseminating your research.
- Understand better some of the practicalities involved in academic publication.
- Be able to decide whether it is worth disseminating your research after all!

11.1 DISSEMINATION OUTLETS

Where you decide to publish your findings will depend on *why* you are doing it, and *who* you want to tell your story to. On the face of it, if you have taken the decision independently to tell the world about your research, the most obvious place might seem the national media. Why not? It is your research, and perhaps you want to reach the biggest possible audience – via national TV and newspapers. However, try to recall the last time you heard a news item that began 'A psychology student has just made an earth shattering finding in their final year project'.

Media coverage is probably not the first thing you would think about as an outlet for your research. It might come later, but only as a result of having published the findings in a more formal context, such as a journal or conference, and there are some tips later in the chapter for handling what can be quite an eye-opening experience for a novice researcher.

In the meantime, and especially if your supervisor is driving the publication process, it is far more likely that you will need to navigate your way through the choppy waters of academic publishing. By far the easiest route is to publish your findings in the form of a **poster** at a psychology conference (or perhaps at an appropriate specialist conference – your supervisor would advise on this). However, this can take quite a long time to organise. You usually need to submit proposals for conference presentations several months before the conference takes place, and you are usually expected to be physically *at* the conference in order to present your work. This entails quite a lot of forward planning, and you should usually only submit a paper or poster if you can guarantee that you will actually be available to attend. Bear in mind, also, that, by the time the conference takes place, you might well be doing something completely different with your life. You do not want to be macheteing your way through a rainforest on a charity mission when you suddenly remember you are supposed to be presenting a poster at a conference in Brighton!

Submitting your work to a psychological journal involves a lot of hard work at the initial outset, but once it is 'in press' that is the end of the process (unless you are called upon to do any media work once it finally sees the light of day). There is, however, a much higher likelihood of rejection, so it really depends how ambitious you are, and in particular how useful it is likely to be to have a publication on your CV. If you do not think you will ever be considering a career in academia, or research of any kind, it is probably not the most rewarding dissemination outlet.

COMMON CONFUSION ?

Does it have to be a first?

Many supervisors will not dream of suggesting that you publish a project that has failed to clock up a first-class mark. Others will happily offer to patch up a 2:2. There really is no direct correspondence between the quality of a final year project and its *potential* publishability, except that a 2:2 would need a substantial amount of work to be prepared to publication levels in even the most modest outlet. But that does not mean to say that the *data* are not publishable in themselves, just that you have not written it up very well. Even first-class projects need a lot of revision, albeit for presentation purposes. However impressed examiners are with your work, there is often a big gap between undergraduate research and professional research. The project with the best chance of publication, therefore, is one that has been carried out as part of a large-scale funded project involving several researchers. One-off studies are harder to publish, however well presented, but do not let that put you off!

If you have carried out some research that you think might be useful to a non-academic audience – for example a charity or a workplace – you might consider presenting your findings either in the form of a presentation or as a report, depending on the organisation you are involved with. In any case, it is good practice, if you have relied on an external organisation in any stage of your project, to send them a summary of your findings once you have completed your report.

11.2 PUBLISHING IN AN ACADEMIC JOURNAL

A published paper in an international peer reviewed journal, with your name on it, is the epitome of success in academia. It is almost certainly the route your supervisor would suggest if they consider your work (at least your data) to be of publishable quality. However, the road to journal publication is long and arduous, and can involve much torment, so it is best to be aware of the trials ahead, if you have decided to take this particular route.

First of all, the rejection rate is high. Some papers get rejected several times by different journals before they finally find a home. Even then, they may have to undergo substantial revision before they are finally accepted. This is partly because standards are high in the academic publishing world. It is also because there are simply not enough journals to go around. It is difficult to get publishers to take on new titles because even the long-standing and successful ones do not bring in a lot of money, and so there is high competition for space in all but the lowliest of publications. Also, psychologists are notorious for being critical of one another's work.

Second, publishing in a journal means lots of hard work revising your project. However closely you have stuck to the APA guidelines, however high a mark it has received (if you are waiting till that point before publishing), it is unlikely to be in an appropriate format for an academic journal. Extensive appendices, for one thing, are rare in journals. Your literature review is likely to be too long. Your discussion may need a severe trim. Even then, there may be lots of rewriting ahead: often very good projects look less good once you try to repackage them as journal articles, which are typically written by professionals with many years of experience. You are competing with professors in top departments with vast research funding, and your reviewers can rip to shreds what seem like perfectly justifiable aspects of your project.

At this point, how far you proceed may well depend on whether your supervisor is prepared to take on any aspects of the writing process themself. Unless you are very confident of your writing ability, your familiarity with the formats of academic publication, and the methodological rigour of your research, it is best to leave the bulk of the work to them. Either way, they will expect to be named as an author, and the order in which your names will appear is significant, as it is assumed that the first author has made the greatest intellectual contribution to the published piece. So in some case this would legitimately be your supervisor, especially if they suggested the project to you, gave you a lot of support and guidance, and also substantially rewrote it for publication. However, if you led on the ideas front, were proactive, and remained heavily involved in the drafting of the potential published version of the paper, it may be more appropriate for you to be named as first author. In any case, this is a discussion that you should have early on, so that there are no misunderstandings or assumptions made on either side (see Common confusion box 'Order of authorship').

It is also worth bearing in mind at this stage that academic journals do not pay for articles. The journal editors receive a small sum towards their efforts, but authors are rewarded with nothing but the prestige value of their work appearing in print. Such is the nature of academic life!

11.2.1 The publication process

Even if your supervisor is happy to do most of the work from this point, it is still worth knowing the ins and outs of the publication process, which is broadly similar across different journals, or at least those that are considered 'international' (i.e. published by major publishing houses, with editorial board members from a variety of countries), and 'peer reviewed' (they only accept papers once they have been reviewed by experts in the topic area of the research).

First of all, you need to select an appropriate journal for your research. The most common reason for rejection is that the author has sent the paper to the wrong journal. Therefore it is essential that you are familiar with any journal you would like to publish your research in. Read the contents of the most recent issues carefully. The website of the journal should include a page headed 'guide to authors', where it will list the type of articles it accepts – for project work, the most likely successful outcome is a 'brief report' or short report, of a single study. If a journal prefers papers that knit together the findings of several studies, it is best avoided. However, the only sure way of finding this out is to send the editor a brief email describing your paper and ask whether it is likely to be appropriate for the journal.

It is always a good idea to be aware of the hierarchy of academic journals, which is based on something called **impact ratings.** Every year or so, a set of figures is released (causing much excitement among researchers!) based on the number of *citations* obtained by each journal (i.e. the number of times other journals have cited work published in that journal). Academic psychologists are constantly striving to have their work accepted in the highest ranking publications, so your supervisor will obviously prefer you to aim for the highest possible outlet that seems sensible. Sometimes, however, they are happy to publish in more specialist journals that have smaller audiences but which are prestigious enough within that particular field. Check with them as to the best place to begin. One rule of thumb, though, is: always start with the highest ranked journal, because you will get the best feedback from those journals even if you are rejected. Then you can revise your work accordingly and stand a better chance of acceptance in a slightly less prestigious publication.

COMMON CONFUSION ?

Order of authorship

Who decides who goes first in the list of authors on a paper? It might seem surprising to discover that order of authorship can be a real can of worms in the academic world, and that wars – well, minor vendettas – have been started because Professor So-and-so went third instead of second (at these times, academia does rather take on the appearance of a grown-up playground). There are ethical recommendations surrounding authorship. These concern how much work merits the inclusion of an author, what sort of contributions are considered marginal and only worthy of acknowledgement, and so on. They do not say much about order of authorship. Typically, it is the writer of the paper who goes first so, if your supervisor has left it up to you, it is only fair that you are first author. However, departments will have their own conventions and it may be standard practice – particularly with undergraduate projects – that supervisors are always first authors (it might be worth checking this out before doing extensive work on the paper). Sometimes, particularly if your project was part of a larger piece of research, there will be an authorship arrangement that is written down as part of the grant proposal. However, in this case, your supervisor should mention it before the paper is written. If in doubt, do not be afraid to ask.

It might seem tempting, especially if you have got a high mark, to submit your project as it is, with just a few minor tweaks here and there. However, it is much more sensible to select your outlet first, and then tailor your paper to that specific audience. The potential readership of a journal will vary from undergraduate students to leading world experts in your specialist field. Most important of all, your reviewers will be chosen from among those readers. It is always worth second-guessing who your referees might be, and keep them in mind while writing your paper.

Once you have selected an appropriate journal, you will need to locate its website and find the link to 'Instructions to Authors'. There you will find all the submission information you need, including the presentation details (how to organise your Word file, whether to include a title page, whether to put tables and figures on separate pages, etc.), the name of the editor, and information about journal style. Many psychology journals simply request that you format your paper 'using APA style', but often publishers have their own in-house style that they prefer for reasons of consistency and identity. The biggest difference is often in the formatting of the reference list, so take care to follow this to the letter (Sage and John Wiley, to name but two big publishers of psychology journals, have quite distinct styles of formatting references that are subtly different from APA).

Once you have rewritten and reformatted your paper you will then need to find, through the journal website, a link to the electronic submission site. Most leading journals today invite authors to submit using an automated system where you upload a Word file, which is then converted to a pdf for the reviewers' benefit. However, a number of specialist journals still ask you to send your Word file direct to the editor's email address where it will be dealt with.

If your journal uses an automated system you should receive an immediate receipt of submission, and possibly a second response a few days later to tell you that your paper has been entered into the review process. This is not a formality, however; in that period, the editor will have glanced through your paper and made an initial decision about whether it is worth sending your paper for review. There are many reasons why they may decide not to bother: chief among them is that you have selected the wrong outlet for your work (and in this case a good editor should recommend an alternative). However, they may simply not like the look of it: it does not meet their very high standards; your sample size is too small; your research question is not of interest, and so on. In this case you should simply forget them and move on to the next journal on your list, which may have a completely different reaction altogether.

Once your paper is formally entered into the review process, there will be an interval of varying length before you hear back from the reviewers. The reviewers themselves will be two or three academics with expertise in your area (or as close as possible) who will give your paper a thorough, often painstaking, review and make suggestions as to whether the paper should be published or not, and, if so, whether there are any revisions or additions to be made. Given that most the people involved in the review process are academics who are busy with teaching and research of their own, and that several potential reviewers may be unavailable, or forget to send in their review on time, it could be six months before you hear anything.

Eventually, one day when you least expect it, you will receive an automated email (or perhaps an email from the editor) that describes the outcome of the review process, followed by a number of observations or recommendations. At the foot of the message will be the reviewers' comments themselves, which may be short and pithy, or unbelievably detailed and nit-picking. It is very important to read these reviews as *constructive criticism*. This is usually how the reviewers intend their remarks to be taken. Good reviews can contain reams and reams of recommended revisions: bad ones can be mortifying. However, there really is no alternative but to take criticism on the chin, swallow your pride, and just get on with what the editor asks you to do (or, in the case of rejection, move on to the next appropriate journal).

11.2.2 Reading and responding to reviews

It is often difficult to judge what the outcome of peer review actually means. This is because there are a number of different conventions in terms of what journals expect from their authors (and reviewers), of the number of different outcomes that can be recommended, and of the pragmatic requirements of the journal. Some journals are so popular that they have to reject large numbers of high quality papers, even those with glowing reviews, to prevent their 'in press' waiting list from getting out of hand. In fact, after having waited up to six months to hear the outcome of the review, even if the outcome is (unusually) an immediate acceptance, you may well still have to wait another year before it actually appears in print. That is simply how long it takes for the publication process to grind through the gears.

There is a range of potential outcomes that you can expect for a paper.

Your paper is accepted outright.

This is an unusual outcome for a major journal, since it usually suggests that it has very little material, and rather low standards of presentation (or reviewing). Your reviewers should usually have found *something* to quibble about. Nevertheless, some small, specialist journals will accept papers and then make a few small changes at the production level without requiring any formal resubmission.

Your paper is accepted subject to minor revisions.

This is the best outcome. The editor (and, presumably, the reviewers) like your paper, are happy with its presentation and will publish it. However the reviewers will have picked up a few points that could benefit from revision: perhaps you have missed a key reference somewhere in the literature review; maybe you have included one data table too many, or failed to account for an anomaly in the results, or failed to provide some methodological information. Whatever, you will just need to add the missing material and put the revised version back into the process, where it should simply be a formality that you will eventually get a letter thanking you and telling you that your paper is now 'in press'.

Your paper is accepted subject to major revisions.
Your paper is rejected but a resubmitted version will be considered.

This is where things start to get rather more complicated. The editor has decided that the paper is suitable for the journal, but needs substantial revision before it can be published. However, different journals express this in different ways, and it can be terribly confusing for authors (and reviewers!) to be told that the paper is 'rejected' when in fact the editor is quite keen on it. Inexperienced authors frequently give up at this stage, pointlessly, without realising how close they are to getting published! Where this outcome differs from the previous 'minor revisions' one is that you will usually need to rewrite a sizeable portion of the paper and include a supplementary file with a detailed description of how you have addressed the referees' criticisms. If one of the reviewers has raised substantial concerns, it may even be returned to them for approval.

Not surprisingly, this outcome will further delay the time it takes for your work to appear in print. Sometimes it may never appear: the reviewer still has major concerns, or another reviewer is brought in who does not like it either. On the other hand, sometimes they are perfectly happy with your resubmitted paper. There really is no way of knowing how this sort of outcome will proceed, except that, with some experience, you can learn to 'read between the lines' and anticipate whether the editor really wants to see your work in print or not. At the end of the day it is *their* decision, whatever the reviewers say.

COMMON CONFUSION

?

What do you *mean* 'it's not in APA style'?

Reviews can be painful experiences even when they are quite positive. Some reviewers are very pedantic, picking out all manner of minor or trivial points in your paper (this is particularly annoying when recommending rejection, since in that case they really *are* trivial points). One of the most common, and irksome, comments is that 'the paper is not in APA style', when you have sat there with the APA style guide, painstakingly ensuring that every indent and table border corresponds with its exact specifications. Usually what the reviewer (or editor) means by this is that there is something in your paper that is not consistent with the guidelines, but there is, it has to be said, a certain hubris involved in not specifying what exactly. You just have to grin and bear it: get out the guidelines, go back through the paper, try and work it out for yourself – or ask your supervisor, who may be just as mystified.

Your paper is rejected.

This is the worst outcome, especially since the editor has taken the time to commission reviews (although it may seem galling at the time, an instant rejection is not so bad once you have recovered from the shock). It usually means the reviews are bad, although, as suggested earlier, some editors may reject after receiving quite favourable reviews, if they have a big editorial logjam and need to clear some space (in this case they should really recommend alternative publication outlets). At least you have received some feedback that you can digest and address before sending your work elsewhere.

But let us assume that this is not the case, and that your paper has been accepted. The first thing you can do is to add a new section to your CV – 'List of Publications', along with your paper, in standard APA reference format, along with (in press) where you will eventually have the year of publication. There will then be a wait before you are sent the 'proofs' of your paper to examine. These consist of a pdf file in the form that your article will eventually appear when it is in print – it is quite exciting to see it in its formal setting for the first time! There will usually be a list of queries from the copy-editor – typically missing references, dates that do not match up between the text and the reference list, misspelled names, typos, missing words and other minor errors that you need to check and correct.

Today, many journals publish 'in press' papers on their websites, which does rather take some of the fun out of the old system where, one day, a package arrives in the post containing a copy of the journal with your article inside. But it is still nice, once the actual issue appears on the website, to be able to amend the publication details to the entry in your CV.

A student's experience . . .

> ❝ I got a high mark for my project and, because I wanted to go on and study at postgraduate level, I asked my supervisor about publishing in a journal. She helped me turn my report into a publishable paper and we sent it off to a journal that she had published in before. Two months later I received an email that told me that our paper had been 'rejected' but that they would consider a revised version. It sounded like an awful lot of work, especially since one reviewer had been very critical of the project, and, because my supervisor was on research leave, I decided to forget all about it. Besides, I had been unable to obtain funding for a PhD and I was starting to consider other avenues. Six months later my supervisor got in touch and asked me what had happened to the paper. By then I had obtained a research assistant

post and I was feeling much more positive about my future, but I replied that it had been rejected and that I thought some of the criticism was a bit harsh. She read the reviews and said 'that's nothing, you should read the hammering that my first paper got!' She suggested some reasonable amendments and we resubmitted it. Several weeks later the journal accepted the paper subject to minor revisions and that was it! Shortly afterwards I applied successfully for a PhD studentship and subsequently found out **"** *that my one publication had given me the edge over the other candidate.*

11.3 PREPARING AND SUBMITTING A POSTER OR ORAL CONFERENCE PRESENTATION

If you do not feel ready to undertake the work required for a print publication, presenting at a psychology conference is a lighter and often more enjoyable option. It is a good way of seeing how the academic world works on a 'day out' and may be a good opportunity to meet other people at a similar stage in their academic careers, particularly if you give a poster (many posters at conferences are presented by postgraduate students). It also often gives you a chance to meet some of the people whose work you have been writing about in your dissertation.

Conferences, like journals, come in all shapes and sizes. The biggest ones are international conferences, such as the European Congress of Psychology, which takes place every other year in a different European capital and attracts thousands of psychologists from all over the world. It lasts for the best part of a week and at any given time there may be a dozen papers being presented and a couple of poster sessions, some in different languages. It will be held in a huge conference centre filled with publishers' stands, other psychology related commercial representatives, and even the occasional art exhibition. It can be a very daunting experience. Other conferences, typically with a specialist theme, may last for just one day and may require little more than a short train journey.

Probably the most suitable conferences at which to present your research are medium sized ones, such as the annual conferences organised by the various divisions and sections of the British Psychological Society. They even do one specifically geared towards undergraduate students – see http://www.bps.org.uk/smg/meetings-and-events.cfm – and one for postgraduate students – http://www.psypag.co.uk. Or you might prefer the BPS annual conference, a rather larger affair but still small enough to have a friendly atmosphere and attract a number of postgraduates.

Conferences are usually advertised on the web many months before they take place. Indeed the deadline for submissions is usually at least three or four months in advance, and sometimes much longer (especially for big international affairs). You are usually required only to submit the abstract of your paper – whether oral presentation or poster – which makes for a very attractive alternative to writing for a journal! Bear in mind, though, that some interdisciplinary conferences, such as the International Communication Association annual conference, actually demand that you submit, at some point, a full blown research paper that they will publish in the *Conference Proceedings*. Make sure that you check this well in advance since you might then change your mind about the whole thing! Even where you just submit the abstract, you can list the presentation (or poster) in your CV under 'List of Publications' (follow the standard APA format for referencing conference papers).

11.3.1 Oral presentations

An oral presentation (sometimes also, rather confusingly, referred to as a 'paper') is exactly what you might expect: you stand in front of a seated audience and talk about your research for 15 minutes or so. Depending on the conference, the size of the room and the topic of your paper, your audience could be crammed in, or there will be three people and a dog. In either case, you will be expected to appear as professional as possible both in your delivery and in the content of your presentation.

The conference website will provide all the information you need to be able to prepare your presentation. Most oral papers are not expected to last more than 20 minutes, which usually includes time for questions, and is a much shorter interval than might appear. Most presenters will use PowerPoint or similar presentation software – you may well have had practice using this type of format at some point in your course but, if not, the best advice is not to 'crowd' the information in your slides, and not to have too many. It is tempting, as a novice researcher, to add lots of extra slides in case you struggle to find things to say and run out of steam after 10 minutes. But if you do, make sure your 'extra' slides have nothing very important on them!

In any case, it is always a good idea to bring along a number of handouts (either copies of your slides, or – in the case of qualitative studies – a couple of sides of quotes). It is always difficult to gauge how many you need, given the huge variability in audience size, but 20–25 is usually a good number. If people are really interested in your talk they will be able to get in touch, since your email address will usually be included in the conference delegates' pack.

The space for questions after the paper itself is potentially the most nerve-racking aspect of the conference presentation. Again, it varies enormously depending on your topic and on the number of people at the presentation. The disappointment at finding such a small audience may soon be replaced by relief at the friendly and supportive atmosphere that often arises when so few people are involved. Generally speaking, if you are obviously a recent graduate, audiences will be fairly kind to you. The worst experiences are those when your supervisor is well known and has some of their rivals in the audience: it is not unknown for such unpleasant individuals to attack their opponent's theories or methods through their students!

It is always worth having a trial run through your presentation beforehand with one or two fellow students (and maybe your supervisor), to anticipate any difficult questions. Then again, it can be equally disappointing when a huge lecture theatre packed with delegates fails to find a single thing to ask you! Never mind, it is all over – and you can enjoy the rest of the conference without having to worry about your own performance!

11.3.2 Poster presentations

Giving a poster at a conference might appear a less daunting experience than standing up and talking to a crowd of eminent psychologists. However, posters usually involve rather more advance preparation, and these days they can expose you to just as much carping criticism as an oral presentation, particularly where the conference organises 'plenary' sessions where poster presenters are expected to give a short talk about their research.

Generally speaking, though, posters are the least painful options for undergraduate project dissemination. The poster itself is usually expected to be about A0 in size and is mounted on a board that enables people to wander past and read it at their leisure. You could, in theory, print out your poster on about 12 sheets of A4; 20 years ago this might have sufficed, but today it will look cheap and scrappy compared with the others, most of which will be on a single sheet of laminated cardboard with the author's university logo proudly at the top. You will need to use your university's reprographics service to get this quality of work (your department will often be willing to fund the cost of this or make a contribution towards it).

The format of posters can vary depending on the topic being presented, but a good poster gets the balance right between eye-catching visuals (graphs, photos or other illustrations) and text. Text should be informative but kept to the bare essentials. Think about summarising your literature review, method section, results and discussion into key ideas and statements that can be presented as a sequence of bullet points rather than as paragraphs of detailed prose. Your supervisor will have examples of their own posters that you can look at for inspiration. However, you can get quite creative in how you present your data and work. Remember, however, that you must not use images of your participants without permission. It is better to 'mock up' a photograph of your study for the purposes of illustrating your poster.

Typically, the posters form part of a continuous display somewhere in the conference venue – like a refreshment room where delegates are going to be milling about in between the talks – although at a big conference there may be quite a fast turnover and you need to be fully aware of the time slot that you have been given to present. Otherwise, just turn up at the start of the conference, when the poster boards are being put up, stick or pin up your masterpiece, and then leave it until you are actually required to go and stand alongside and field queries.

Some conferences have quite tightly organised 'plenary' sessions during which presenters may be required to give a short oral presentation to an amassed group of delegates. These sessions can be quite chaotic, but at least your poster remains on display while people come around to look and maybe to chat. It is always a good idea to have a pile of handouts (perhaps just a miniature version of the poster), which you can leave for people to collect if you need to leave your poster for a moment. Some presenters pin a plastic document wallet full of handouts underneath their poster for this purpose.

There is often a prize for the best poster – a rare opportunity to actually make some personal money out of research! The winner is usually one that combines a good, clearly presented research study with eye-catching visuals, so you are encouraged to use your imagination (and humour if appropriate). Try not to overload the poster with text: delegates should be able to get the gist of your study and its findings in less than a minute's perusal. If they are interested they will, hopefully, stay a bit longer!

11.4 THE MEDIA

Finally, here are a few tips and hints for dealing with any media coverage that your paper might generate. It is, in theory, possible for you to go straight to the press with your findings, bypassing academic publication sources altogether. However, the media will usually be much more convinced by research that is published somewhere, than studies that have simply 'been carried out', even at prestigious institutions. They will quickly get wind of the fact that you are a student and not a senior academic, and may become sceptical. Or, if you are a good salesperson and convince them otherwise, the university will get its name plastered all over coverage of unpublished research and your department may not be best pleased (especially if it is controversial, or slightly dubious science, neither of which have ever stopped certain media outlets).

By far the most likely media coverage you will have will arise, not from the project itself but from published reports. Both the publishers of journals and the organisers of conferences inform the media about their proceedings in regular 'press releases'. These are carefully put together weeks in advance of the issue or conference. The articles, or conference papers, are scrutinised for their newsworthiness (or 'sexiness', given that some topics, such as gender differences in relationships, are always more attractive to media outlets than others, such as logical reasoning). Those deemed to be most newsworthy to the media will be chosen as 'highlights' for the press release.

If yours is one of the chosen papers, the publisher, or conference organiser, will usually contact you in order to get your approval. Not all academics enjoy dealing with the media, and some actively avoid it, whatever the nature of their research. First, you will be sent a copy of the draft press release that relates to your paper, usually an A4 sheet with three or four short paragraphs describing your research in a way that is comprehensible to a non-psychologist (or non-academic).

You will usually find something in the press release that is not quite right: a finding has been misinterpreted, or worded in an ambiguous fashion; a statistic is misleading; you have been mis-quoted. Yes, you will have been quoted – press releases usually contain a couple of lines from your paper followed by '… as Dr Percy says', or starting 'Dr Wood claims that …' This is a ploy to make your research seem lively and up-to-date (given that by this time it may well be two or three years old). It also enables journalists to cut and paste their reports: it is surprising how many press cut-tings appear after a conference that have simply rehashed the press release!

Once the press release meets with your approval, you will be expected to provide contact details (including your mobile number if you are going to be at a conference), and you should be avail-able during a specified period for journalists to contact you, if they need further details. In most cases, this consists of nothing more than a few phone calls where the journalist wants a bit more information. Sometimes they are miles wide of the mark, and rather disappointed that you do not have quotes from a study that is clearly experimental or psychometric in nature. At other times, they are so keen to present your findings that they will interview you at length. Very occasionally they will be so interested that they will ask you to go to the radio or television studio (often at the crack of dawn the next day!) to take part in a live or recorded interview.

When a paper generates media interest it is often the case that one high profile story (particularly in a daily paper or on a national news website) will spark a flurry of activity. You may do 2 inter-views one day and 12 the next, and even more the following day – this is because, for most forms of media, other media are their main source of stories. So, if the ball starts rolling, you may have to prepare yourself for a long campaign!

Whatever the outcome, it is always exciting to see your name in lights, even if they have not quite got their facts right. You can always comfort yourself with the thought that newspapers are here today and gone tomorrow. Unlike journals, it is unlikely that people will be picking up your misquoted words in a week's time.

All the same, it is worth being prepared for unflattering coverage, and the best way of doing this is to ensure that you do not say anything ambiguous or potentially misleading when you are being interviewed. Journalists often try and stray from the topic, get you to discuss individuals (celebrities for instance), or to comment on news issues that you have not done any research on. The simplest response in these cases is simply to reiterate your study findings, and not to be drawn into making comments that you do not have any direct evidence for.

A student's experience . . .

> My project had looked at the experience of being a victim of crime. I had given out a questionnaire to students about petty crime on campus and found some surprising differences between males and females, so my supervisor encouraged me to present the findings at a national psychology conference. I was summoned to the conference press office on the day of my talk because a daily newspaper wanted to interview me. I was really thrilled to be asked about my study but a bit nervous because I had heard stories about being misquoted. Halfway through the interview the journalist asked me to comment on an incident that had taken place overnight in which a well-known TV presenter had had a lot of personal possessions stolen from the family home. He asked me what psychological impact this incident would have had. I replied that my research had only explored campus-based crime and that people living in their own homes would have very different experiences. I was worried afterwards that the paper would just twist my replies to make up a statement

about the celebrity's experiences. I entered the newsagents nervously next morning and tentatively leafed through a copy of the paper. There was a big story about the celebrity, with a huge photograph, but thankfully no mention of my research. Unfortunately there was no mention of my research anywhere else in the paper! **"**

Many organisations now offer media training for academic researchers, so if you are thinking about a career in academia, and you are researching in an area that is likely to be attractive to the media, it may be worth taking one of these courses so that you are prepared when the time comes. Ask your supervisor about this and the possibility of departmental funding (although this is likely to be available only if you are staying on to do postgraduate research).

CHAPTER SUMMARY

- The most common dissemination methods for psychology project findings are presenting papers and posters at psychology conferences, and writing articles for peer reviewed scientific journals.

- Deciding on the best dissemination method will depend on a number of factors – the amount of effort you are prepared to put in, your own level of confidence and your career ambitions.

- Journal articles in psychology run a high risk of rejection but, if you learn how to 'read' the criticism, they can be a very useful first step if you are hoping for an academic career.

- Psychology conferences can be very valuable experiences, and giving a paper or poster can be good fun – and not too intimidating!

- If your research has high media appeal, you may well be approached at conferences by journalists from the press and TV. Enjoy your brief glimpse of the limelight, but take care to avoid being drawn into discussing topics not directly connected to your own research.

FURTHER READING

We would recommend the following two books if you are considering any form of written dissemination:

American Psychological Association (2010). *Publication Manual of the American Psychological Association: Sixth Edition.* Washington, DC: APA.

Nichol, A.A.M. & Pexman, P.M. (2003). *Displaying Your Findings: A Practical Guide for Creating Figures, Posters, and Presentations.* Washington, DC: APA.

CHAPTER 12
EMPLOYABILITY AND YOUR PROJECT

Throughout this book we have made various passing references to the skills and competencies that you will either acquire, demonstrate or develop as a result of completing your psychology project work. As supervisors, we are often extremely proud of the abilities and achievements of our project students, and we will write about you in glowing terms if providing references when you are applying for jobs or further study. However, usually we are only invited to write job references for you if you are shortlisted for a post you have applied for. You only get shortlisted if you have written a strong application in which you have been able to relate your knowledge and experience to the person specification and job description for that post. Too often students fail to do this, which is frustrating given the wealth of experience that your final year project alone will have given you.

The purpose of this final chapter is to give you some insight into the job application process and offer advice on how you can use your project to enhance your CV and job applications, to maximise your chances of being offered the job you want.

BY THE END OF THIS CHAPTER YOU WILL:

- Understand the significance of the person specification in the shortlisting process.
- Be aware of the range of skills and competences that your project work will have equipped you with.
- Learn how best to demonstrate that you match the person specification in the context of your application form or CV based job application.
- Understand how you can refer to your project experience in interviews.

12.1 APPLYING FOR JOBS

When students complete their degrees, there is usually strong competition for suitable jobs, and this can and does often lead to rushed job applications as students respond to a mixture of panic that they will lose out on the best jobs, financial pressure to earn some cash, and competition between friends to see who will secure employment first. Our first piece of advice would be to stay calm, and think carefully about what types of work you want or need to do next, so that you can achieve your medium and longer-term career aspirations. There is a balance to be achieved between wanting to earn a reasonable wage, getting strategically important or high prestige jobs, and keeping an open mind about what kinds of job will give you the skills that you need to acquire. However, the first and most important piece of advice we would give you is to remember that you are now a graduate (rather than a student) and this means that you can and should be applying for 'graduate level jobs'.

COMMON CONFUSION

?

What is a 'graduate level' job?

A graduate level job is simply one that requires you to be educated to degree level in order to do that job. The easiest way to see if the job you are considering is graduate level is to look at the person specification, and see if an undergraduate degree is listed as an 'essential' requirement.

A student's experience. . .

I was thrilled when I found out that my hard work had paid off and I had managed to get a first class psychology degree. I knew that I wanted to be an educational psychologist in the long term, and so I applied for jobs that would give me some experience of working with children who had learning difficulties, as I did not have much experience of that on my CV. I was shortlisted for and offered the first job I applied for, which was working as an hourly-paid classroom assistant in a local school. My intention was to do this for a little while to earn some money and get some experience whilst I looked for other opportunities. The post itself didn't require a degree, and so I guessed that I was successful because I had a strong academic background. However, the work was exhausting – I often worked longer hours than I was paid for, and the type of work I did didn't really stretch me or make use of my psychology. I quickly fell into a dogsbody role, and was so tired at the end of the day I couldn't face applying for other jobs. The pay was basic, and was not enough to enable me to live independently from my parents. I realised I had to leave when they suggested that I needed to apply for and complete a GNVQ if I was serious about a career doing what I was doing. I already had a first class degree but clearly they didn't see any relevance between my degree and my work, and to be honest neither did I. When I realised I was in a (slightly sub) GNVQ level job, I realised I had made a mistake and left to apply for further study.

The best way to identify what kinds of work experience you need is to look at the **person specification** of the job that you ultimately want to apply for and make a list of the qualifications, skills and experience that they expect applicants to have. Then you need to think about what kinds of job would enable you to meet those requirements, and begin to look at advertised positions in those terms, by looking at the job description and other information about the organisation. At this point it may be useful to talk to your university careers advisor and/or recruitment agency to see what types of job they think you could be successful in at this point in your career.

12.2 SHORTLISTING

Graduates often do not understand why they are not shortlisted for interview. As far as they can tell the job appears to be made for them. Do they (the employers) not know that your project was exactly on a topic which is directly relevant to the job they have advertised? Did they not see that you have a first/upper second class degree? Why are they ignoring you?

Now, what we are going to do is offer you a little bit of an insight into what it is like to shortlist candidates for a post. Employers spend a long time thinking about and drawing up a person specification: a list of essential and desirable attributes of their ideal candidate. They are then required to produce a shortlist of applicants, which is based on exactly **how closely they match this list of attributes.** You have to understand that the panel are only going to look at whether you match this, not whether you could potentially do the job. If you do not meet all the essential criteria on the person specification, then the job is not the right one for you.

Often your application will be amongst a pile of 20, 30, or even 100–200 applications for a job. What you have to do, if you want your application to stand a chance against this competition, is ensure yours is sufficiently detailed and well presented; and you also need to make the job of the panel as easy for them as possible. That is, you need to explain clearly how your skills and experience map onto the person specification for the job and, if you can do that by covering the points in the same order that they appear in the person specification list, so much the better. If you can demonstrate the desirable elements as well as the essential ones, then make sure that is clearly stated. Most importantly, start your personal statement or covering letter (depending on whether you are filling in a form or sending in a CV), with a statement to the effect of, 'As you can see from my application I meet/exceed the person specification for this post in the following ways...' and then go on to explain exactly how your qualifications and experience **do** meet the specification. This way the appointments panel does not have the job of trawling through the pages of your application trying to work out the relevance of what you have listed on the form or CV. You have to remember that they may not be familiar with the types of job or course you have mentioned in passing, and so you will need to unpack this for them. Shortlisted candidates routinely use their personal statement in this way, and take a great deal of care over their phrasing and presentation. Remember, if the panel has received a lot of applications, they will be looking for the 'easy discard' – reasons why they do not want to take your application any further. A lazy or poorly expressed application will provide them with this reason. Particular 'pet peeves' of shortlisters include:

- applicants who do not bother to complete the application form properly (especially not really completing the personal statement section properly, or at all);
- applicants who just staple a CV to the application form because they cannot be bothered to fill in the form;
- applicants who do not follow the instructions for completing the application form that were clearly provided;
- applications from candidates who ignore the person specification.

12.3 TRANSFERABLE SKILLS FROM YOUR PROJECT

So, each of you will be slightly different from each other in terms of your prior and ongoing work experience, but the one thing that all psychology graduates have in common is your experience of completing the final year research project. It is important to reflect at this point on the different transferrable skills of which you can now claim to have direct experience. Below is a list of the more obvious skills and abilities that you can now lay claim to (a * indicates a skill that will only apply to certain types of project):

- locating published sources;
- critically reviewing ideas;
- developing independent ideas;
- generating predictions about events;
- collecting data;
- analysing data;
- presenting data in appropriate formats;
- interpreting data appropriately;
- scoring, coding and transcribing skills;
- use of psychometric tests*;
- liaising with the public;
- liaising with outside organisations and stakeholders*;
- communicating ideas effectively to lay audiences orally and in writing;
- project management skills;
- time management skills;
- ethical awareness;
- problem solving;
- risk assessment;
- working with specialist populations* (e.g. children, older people, etc.);
- report writing;
- summarising complex ideas succinctly and accurately;
- teamworking skills*;
- responding to direction and constructive criticism (from your supervisor);
- developing good working relationships with senior colleagues (staff);

12.4 MAPPING YOUR SKILLS ONTO A PERSON SPECIFICATION

Most application forms, if not all, include a section entitled either 'personal statement' or 'other relevant information', or similar. You will recognise this section when you see it, as it is usually a large empty box around one page in length. Often applicants are unsure about what they should put here. For example, it looks very similar to a box you will have completed when applying to university in the first place, and back then you just had to talk enthusiastically about why you wanted to study the course you had applied for. However, if you write enthusiastically about why you really, really want the job in that box this time, you are unlikely to be shortlisted; because (and altogether now) the shortlisters are only interested in whether or not you meet the person specification. So clearly what they are expecting to see in that box on the form is a narrative that explains, point by point, how you more than meet the specification, and then any other relevant information you think may swing things in your favour. Remember not to come across as too needy ('I really need this job because...') or too arrogant ('Your team will benefit from my involvement because...'). Just be very factual and confident, and a little bit of background about why you are interested in developing a career in this area is also helpful, but again, try not to overdo the enthusiasm levels or overstate your knowledge of the area.

Below we have reproduced a typical person specification for a graduate level research assistant post, to show how far your project work can be used to demonstrate appropriate skills and experience in a graduate level job. Hopefully you can see straightaway how, if you have embraced the dissertation experience in full, you can easily write a narrative about how you can demonstrate competence with respect to many of the skills on this list.

We would encourage you to take a few moments now to practice writing out the ways in which you think that you meet (or will meet when you graduate) the person specification shown here, making references to the transferrable skills list from your project work and your other skills and experience from your CV. You may surprise yourself!

Person Specification - Research Assistant

Attributes	Essential	Advantageous
Education/ Qualifications	• Good degree (1st class or 2.1) in an appropriate subject.	
Experience (paid and unpaid)	• Sound knowledge of research methods relevant to psychology.	• Experience of working with children.
Research/ publications Special interests	• Desire to publish conference or journal papers related to psychology and/or education. • Up-to-date knowledge and understanding of topic under investigation.	• Experience of giving conference papers or publishing research papers.
Job-related skills/ Aptitudes	• Excellent communicator, organised approach to work, confident in working independently and as part of a team. • Self-motivated and able to take initiative and to work both unsupervised and to close direction.	• Flexible approach to work.
Interpersonal skills	• Excellent communication skills will be essential, both in terms of verbal communication and written communication. • Must be a team player and able to work towards a common research goal.	
Other requirements	• May be required to work outside of normal 8.30am to 5:00pm hours, including weekends, on occasion. • Willingness to travel to other organisations.	

A student's experience. . . .

> My personal tutor had advised me to apply for some research assistant posts but when I looked at the job description, I was put off as the responsibilities of the posts seemed to be much greater than what I was expecting and they were certainly more than I had previously done in my part-time work or volunteering. I was convinced that the job was intended for much more experienced individuals than me. However, my tutor made me sit down and look at the person specification, and she showed me that I met all the essential criteria and reassured me that the posts were intended for recent graduates. And after a few applications and interviews I was finally offered a post! I love my job now and can't imagine doing anything else. I'm even thinking of doing a PhD!

12.5 YOUR PROJECT AND THE JOB INTERVIEW

If you are fortunate enough to get shortlisted and are invited to interview, you can still draw on your dissertation in this context. For example, many graduates will arrange for their dissertation to be smartly bound and then bring a copy to the interview with them in case the panel shows an interest and would like to take a look at their writing. Another thing to be aware of is that you can make your interviewers' lives easier for them by answering their questions as clearly as you can, providing an example of an instance when you actually demonstrated that you could do the thing that they are asking you about. For example, if they ask you about your ability to manage difficult situations, you should try to think of a specific occasion when you had to do exactly that, and then talk them through what you did and whether or not it was successful. Your project experience will provide you with many examples that you can use in this way to good effect. It is worth thinking about some likely questions you may be asked at interview and how you can illustrate your responses appropriately. For example, nearly every interview includes a question along the lines of 'what would you say are your areas of strength and weakness?' Your project work will have taught you a lot about yourself, where you can still improve, and where you surprised yourself!

CHAPTER SUMMARY

- If you want to be shortlisted for a job, it is essential that your application explicitly addresses how you meet the person specification for that post.
- Focus on applying for graduate level jobs that will provide you with relevant opportunities and experiences, and be aware that securing a post like this will take a little longer than if you apply for jobs that do not require you to have a degree.
- Your dissertation project will equip you with a wide range of transferrable skills that you can relate to many graduate level jobs.
- Use the 'personal statement' section of the application form, or your covering letter if you are applying with a CV, to explain exactly how you meet the person specification; and practice doing this for different jobs you are interested in.
- Use your project work to illustrate your answers in interviews, and consider taking a copy of your dissertation with you for the interview panel to see.

REFERENCES

Alderson, P., & Morrow, V. (2004). *Ethics, Social Research and Consulting with Children and Young People*. Ilford: Barnardo's.

American Psychological Association (2010). *Publication Manual of the American Psychological Association*, Sixth Edition, Washington, DC: APA.

Armitage, C.J., & Conner, M. (2001). Efficacy of the theory of planned behaviour: a meta-analytic review. *British Journal of Social Psychology*, 40, 471–499.

Bar-On, R. (1997). *The Emotional Quotient Inventory (EQ-i): A Test of Emotional Intelligence*. Toronto, Canada: Multi-Health Systems, Inc.

Braun, V., & Clarke, V. (2006). Using thematic analysis in psychology. *Qualitative Research in Psychology*, 3, 77–101.

British Psychological Society (2004). *BPS Style Guide*. Leicester: British Psychological Society.

British Psychological Society (2009). *Code of Ethics and Conduct*. Leicester: British Psychological Society.

Burke, R., & Barron, S. (2007). *Project Management Leadership*. Available from burkepublishing.com

Capdevila, R., & Callaghan, J.E.M. (2008). 'It's not racist. It's common sense'. A critical analysis of political discourse around asylum and immigration in the UK. *Journal of Community & Applied Social Psychology*, 18, 1–16.

Chabris, C.F. (1999). Prelude or requiem for the 'Mozart effect'? *Nature*, 400, 826–827.

Charmaz, K. (2003). Grounded theory. In Smith, J.A. (Ed.), *Qualitative Psychology: A Practical Guide to Research Methods* (pp. 81–110). Thousand Oaks, CA: Sage Publications.

Charmaz, K. (2006). *Constructing Grounded Theory: A Practical Guide through Qualitative Analysis*. Thousand Oaks, CA: Sage.

Cohen, J. (1994). The earth is round (p < 0.05). *American Psychologist*, 49, 997–1003.

Coolican, H. (2004). *Research Methods and Statistics in Psychology – Fourth Edition*. London: Hodder Arnold.

Corbin, J., & Strauss, A. (2008). *Basics of Qualitative Research: Techniques and Procedures for Developing Grounded Theory*. Thousand Oaks, CA: Sage.

Day, K., Gough, B., & McFadden, M. (2003). Women who drink and fight: a discourse analysis of working-class women's talk. *Feminism and Psychology*, 13, 141–158.

Drew, P. (2003). Conversation analysis. In *Qualitative Psychology: A Practical Guide to Research Methods* (pp. 132–158). Thousand Oaks, CA: Sage Publications.

Fisher, A. (1993). *The Logic of Real Arguments*. Cambridge: Cambridge University Press.

Forrester, M. (2002). *A Guide to Conversation Analysis*. Published on the Higher Education Academy Psychology Network website http://www.psychology.heacademy.ac.uk/html/extra_material.asp

Francis, L.J., Lewis, C.A., & Ziebertz, H. (2006). The short-form revised Eysenck personality questionnaire (EPQR-S): a German edition. *Social Behavior and Personality*, 34, 197–204.

Giles, D.C. (2002a). Keeping the public in their place: audience participation in lifestyle television programming. *Discourse & Society*, 13, 603–628.

Giles, D.C. (2002b). *Advanced research methods in psychology*. London: Routledge.

Giles, D.C., & Close, J. (2008). Exposure to 'lad magazines' and drive for muscularity in dating and non-dating young men. *Personality and Individual Differences*, 44, 1610–1616.

Giorgi, A., & Giorgi, B. (2003). Phenomenology. In Smith, J. (Ed.), *Qualitative Psychology: A Practical Guide to Research Methods* (pp. 25–50). Thousand Oaks, CA: Sage.

Hart, C. (1998). *Doing a Literature Review: Releasing the Social Science Research Imagination*. London: Sage.

Heinrich Heine Universität Düsseldorf, Institut für Experimentelle Psychologie. G*Power 3. Retrieved 9 September 2008 from: http://www.psycho.uni-duesseldorf.de/abteilungen/aap/gpower3

Hemsley, B., Balandin, S., & Togher, L. (2007). Narrative analysis of the hospital experience for older parents of people who cannot speak. *Journal of Aging Studies*, 21(3), 239–254.

Hunter, J.E., & Hunter, R.F. (1984). Validity and utility of alternative predictors of job performance. *Psychological Bulletin*, 96, 72–98.

Lawes, R. (1999). Marriage: analysis of discourse. *British Journal of Social Psychology*, 38, 1–20.

Madill, A., Gough, B., Lawton, R., & Stratton, P. (2005). How should we supervise qualitative projects? *The Psychologist*, 18(10), 616–618.

Maltby, J., Day, L., & Macaskill, A. (2007). *Personality, Individual Differences and Intelligence*. Harlow: Pearson.

McCreary, D.R., & Sasse, D.K. (2000). An exploration of the drive for muscularity in adolescent boys and girls. *Journal of American College Health*, 48, 297–304.

McCreary, D., Sasse, D.K., Saucier, D., & Dorsch, K.D. (2004). Measuring the drive for muscularity: factorial validity of the Drive for Muscularity scale in men and women. *Psychology of Men and Masculinity*, 5, 49–58.

McCutcheon, L.E., Lange, R., & Houran, J. (2002). Conceptualization and measurement of celebrity worship. *British Journal of Psychology*, 93, 67–87.

Murray, M. (2003). Narrative psychology. In Smith, J. (Ed.), *Qualitative Psychology: A Practical Guide to Research Methods* (pp. 111–131). Thousand Oaks, CA: Sage Publications.

Percy, C., & Murray, S. (2007). *The Psychosocial Impact of Polycystic Ovary Syndrome: Using On-line, Non-clinical Data to Shed Light on What Most Concerns Women About this Chronic Condition*. Paper presented at the The British Psychological Society, Division of Health Psychology, Annual Conference, University of Nottingham, 12–14 September.

Prussing, E., Sobo, E.J., Walker, E., & Kurtin, P.S. (2005). Between 'desperation' and disability rights: a narrative analysis of complementary/alternative medicine use by parents for children with Down syndrome. *Social Science & Medicine*, 60(3), 587–598.

Robson, C. (2011). *Real World Research – Third Edition*. Oxford: John Wiley.

Smith, J.A., Jarman, M., & Osborn, M. (1999). Doing interpretative phenomenological analysis. In Murray, M., & Chamberlain, K. (Eds.), *Qualitative Health Psychology: Theories and Methods* (pp. 218–240). London: Sage.

Stenner, P. (1993). Discoursing jealousy. In Burman, E., & Parker, I., (Eds.), *Discourse Analytic Research: Repertoires and Readings of Texts in Action* (pp. 94–132). London: Routledge.

Stokoe, E., & Edwards, D. (2007). 'Black this, black that': racial insults and reported speech in neighbour complaints and police interrogations. *Discourse & Society*, 18(3), 337–372.

Tabachnik, B.T., & Fidell, L.S. (2007). *Using Multivariate Statistics: Fifth Edition*. Boston, MA: Pearson Education.

Toerien, M., & Kitzinger, C. (2007). Emotional labour in the beauty salon: Turn design of task-directed talk. *Feminism & Psychology*, 17(2), 162–172.

Wetherell, M., & Potter, J. (1988). Discourse analysis and the identification of interpretative repertoires. In Antaki, C. (Ed.), *Analysing Everyday Explanation: A Casebook of Methods* (pp. 168–183). Thousand Oaks, CA: Sage Publications.

Wilkinson, S. (2003). Focus groups. In Smith, J. (Ed.), *Qualitative Psychology: A Practical Guide to Research Methods* (pp. 184–204). London: Sage.

Willig, C. (2003). Discourse analysis. In Smith, J. (Ed.), *Qualitative Psychology: A Practical Guide to Research Methods* (pp. 159–183). Thousand Oaks, CA: Sage Publications.

Wood, C. & Terrell, C. (1998). Poor readers' ability to detect rhythm and perceive rapid speech. *British Journal of Developmental Psychology*, 16, 397–413.

APPENDIX
ANSWERS TO THE ETHICAL SCENARIOS

1 **Adhya's study.** People walking past in the corridor may see who has signed up and make assumptions about them, especially about their sexual activities. It may be assumed that they are sexually active – something that could cause problems for some people within their families or community. Even if only email addresses are used, it may still be possible to discern people's identities. Even if email aliases are used, people who sign up might receive abusive or obscene emails (you may think this unlikely but, sadly, it can happen). At best, a person who has signed up may get questioned or teased by their friends, at worst … **General point in recruitment: care must be taken not to reveal participants' identities.**

2 **Benny's study.** Benny is expecting to hear some fairly 'harmless' stuff, about what it was like to move away from home and, at most, a little bit about homesickness. What if a participant reveals that they are is suicidally depressed because they have not managed to make friends? Or that they have found it hard to mix because they have experienced discrimination? Benny must not attempt to offer counselling, psychotherapy or any kind of advice for which he is not qualified. It might be useful for him to have an approved debriefing pack, which contains information on sources of help, that is given to all participants. Benny must also retain confidentiality, even for sensitive material that he had not anticipated discovering. **General points: be aware that unexpected topics may be raised in research, especially in interviews. Prepare for 'worst case scenarios'. Have appropriate information available in your debriefing pack. Do not offer advice. Retain confidentiality.**

3 **Cathy's study.** Although the internet is essentially a public medium, communities and special interest groups develop that may have their own identities and resent what they see as exploitation. There is a certain 'netiquette' that permits people to 'listen in' on discussion groups (such people are known are 'lurkers'), but great thought and sensitivity are needed before intruding into groups with vested interests. Members of discussion groups may welcome your interest and volunteer to take part in your study, but they might equally feel you were proposing to exploit them. Not only might they refuse to take part in your study (which is, after all, their right), but they may form a very poor impression of psychology students, psychologists and researchers in general, making them unwilling to cooperate in any future work. **General point: always approach prospective participants with sensitivity and respect.**

4 **Dennis's study.** Dennis might be expecting employers to talk about their beliefs on the extent to which depression affects workers' productivity. Suppose an employer reveals prejudice towards depressed people and people with mental health problems in general? Or if they start talking about women and how they are more of a 'problem' because they get depressed and 'go a bit mad' once every month? Or if they reveal that they are currently taking anti-depressant medication themself? Confidentiality is extremely important here. The participants' views must not be attributed to them by name, or even to the company they work for. The people interviewed might lose their job for embarrassing the company, or be discriminated against on the basis of their own mental health history. Finally, of course, Dennis must not give diagnosis or advice for

which he is not qualified. **General point: be aware that participants may bring up unexpected material and ensure confidentiality.**

5 **Ellie's study.** Interviewing people that you are close to is always a little risky. The intensity of a semi-structured interview can raise issues that friends, relatives or close associates have (perhaps subconsciously) avoided in the past. If conflict does arise, it may affect the relationship long term and cause friction in the household. **General point: beware of disrupting close relationships by 'using' friends and relatives as research participants.**

6 **Frank's study.** Friday nights in the student union bar may seem an ideal place to recruit participants for this topic – it is convenient and naturalistic. However, people approached may already have consumed alcohol, which may compromise their competence to give informed consent. If the interviews are carried out in the *bar while alcohol is consumed*, it might be argued that participation encouraged people to consume more alcohol. Supposing they suffer alcoholic poisoning, fall and injure themselves, drink-drive, or do badly in an exam the next day because of a hangover? You might find that you were judged partly responsible for their actions. **General point: participation in research must not lead people to take risks that they would not normally take in their everyday lives.**

7 **Gillian's study.** Two problems here. If people have volunteered for an interview of up to an hour, they should not be kept waiting or detained any longer than that. Perhaps, more importantly, being asked to wait should not create a situation where people can identify other participants (unless it is a group interview, in which people should have been clearly briefed in advance that this was the case). Participants with radically opposing views could come into conflict with each other in ways that would never have happened if it was not for your research. You might be held partially to blame for any conflict that arises. **General point: try to think through all the practical details of your study. Visualise what will happen at each stage, and try to prevent the 'worst case scenario'.**

8 **Hussein's study.** Bearing in mind that this is an interview study, if participants are free to bring up related topics of their choice, a participant might happen to mention that he or she take illegal substances to enhance their performance (say, for example, certain types of steroid). Confidentiality is an issue in this case, just as much as in the previous examples, and in a potentially much more complicated way. Should participants reveal to you any form of illegal activity, you could be forced to reveal this to law enforcement agencies. As a consequence, any promise of anonymity made in the participant briefing and research agreement would be rendered false. **General point: do not make promises of confidentiality that you cannot keep, especially if it is possible that participants may bring up illegal activity.**

INDEX

A-B design, 59
abstract, 183–4
  length, 184
accessibility in thematic analysis, 161
action orientation, 157
after submitting report, 31–2
allocations to supervisors, 15–19
  project proposal, 15
ambiguous referent, 176
American Psychological Association (APA), 5, 92,
        145, 171, 173, 184, 192, 194, 196–7
analysis of variance, *See* ANOVA
'analytic units', 157
analytical themes, presenting, 163–4
  data extracts, using, 164
  described theme, 163
  diagram, 164
  listed theme, 163
  tables for themes, using, 164
ANCOVA, 150
2×2 ANOVA, independent groups, 148–9
  lineplot, 149
anonymity, preserving, 106
ANOVA, 147–8
  calculation, 55–6
  error rate, 148
  factorial ANOVA, 148–9
  one-way ANOVA, 147
  t-test, 147
appendices, 187
archival data, 135–7
  broadcast media, 135–6
  documents, 136–7
  hard copy material, 136–7
  print media, 135
  publicity material, 135
  traditional media, 135
  web-based data, 136
  web-based material, 135
archival data, analysing, 63
arguments, analysing and evaluating, 48–9
associations, 144
audacity, 90
audio editing software, 90
availability, assessing, 78–9

backup, 92
balancing, 56–7

being evaluative, 47–8
belief, 122
between-groups, 53
blocks, 146
Bonferroni correction, 58
book chapter, referencing, 185–6
book, referencing, 185
briefing, 95
  briefing sheet, 99–102, *See also* participant
        information sheet
    basic information, 100
    subheadings, 100
  when working with children, 113–14
British Psychological Society, 95, 98–9, 104, 116
broadcast media, 135–6

captures, of individuals' lived experience, 63
career aspirations, 9
category saturation, 167
Celebrity Worship Scale, 143
central focus of experience, 63
checking, 56–7
children, research with, 111–14
  briefing, 113–14
  consent when working with, 112–13
    'opt in' procedure, 112
    'opt out' procedure, 112
  debriefing, 113–14
  practicalities of working in schools, 111–12
  watching children's behavior, 114
chi-square analysis ($\chi2$), 150
citations in the text, 184–5
closing paragraph, 175–6
closing statement, in report, 173
clubs, 78
Code of Ethics and Conduct, British Psychological
        Society's, 95, 98–9, 104, 116
codes, 73
communication, 76–8
  general rules, 77
    acknowledging and addressing
        concerns, 77
    with admin staff, 78
    applying rules to stakeholders, 78
    being deferential and respectful, 77
    being explicit, 77
    gratefulness, 78
    with people in organisations, 77–8

communication (*continued*)
   politeness, 78
     visiting relevant locations, 78
  issues, working off campus, 140
completion date of activity, 82
confederates, 134
confidentiality, preserving, 106
confounding variables, 54
consent when working with children, 112–13
constant comparison, 167
construct validity, 133
content analysis, 153–5
  deductive, 153
  inductive, 153
contingency table, 150
controlling variables, 134
conversation analysis, 160–1
  designs using, 72
  presenting, requirements for, 166
conversation, study designs based on, 62
conversational interaction, 72
'cooling off' period, 116
copyright issues, 110–11
correlation, 143–7
  correlation matrix, 144
    emotional intelligence, 144
    graphology, 144
    job performance, 144
    sample of work, 144
    spatial intelligence, 144
correlational design, 59–61
  cross-sectional study, 60
  longitudinal study, 60
  multivariate designs, 61
  types of, 59–61
    criterion variable, 59
    predictor variable, 59
counterbalancing, 56
criterion variable, 59
cross-sectional study, 60
current journals, 5

data analysis and presentation, 142–69,
    See also qualitative methods; statistical
    methods
data analysis phase, 27–8
  supervisor's help with, enhancing, 27–8
  feedbacks, using, 28
  giving sufficient time to supervisor to look
    at data, 28
  need to be prepared to have a go, 28
data collection, 62–3, 120–41, *See also* archival data;
    experiments; observation(s)
  data collection phase of project, 25–7
    confidentiality considerations, 26

    supervisor's presence, 26
  existing measures, using, 128–30
    source reference, 129
  focus groups, 121–5, *See also individual entry*
  interviews, 121–5, *See also individual entry*
  naturalistic data, 125
  original measures, designing, 130–2
  questionnaires, 128–34
  reliability, 132–4
  scales, 128–34
  survey, 131
  validity, 132–4
  working off campus, 139–40
data extracts, using, 164
data preparation, 180
data protection issues, 114–16
  fair collection of data, 114–15
  right to withdraw, 116
data saturation, 167
data sharing, 92
data storage, 92
databases, research, 40–1
debriefing, 104–5
  information/support sources, 104
  when working with children, 113–14
deception, 98
  versus withholding information, 98
deductive content analysis, 153
deductive/hypothesis driven approach, 65–6
described theme, 163
design of report, 177
design phase of project, 22–5
  availability of specialist materials, 24
  changing project plans, reasons, 22–3
designing the study, 52–74, *See also* correlational
    design; observations(s); phenomenological
    designs
  archival data, analysing, 63
  discourse analysis (DA), 69–70
  experimental design, issues in, 53–9, *See also*
    individual entry
  focus groups, designs based on, 62–3
  grounded theory (GT) designs, 73–4
  hypothesis testing, 58
  initial decisions about, 53
  interactions, designs based on, 62–3
  interpretative phenomenological analysis
    (IPA), 68–9
  interviews, designs based on, 62–3
  narrative designs, 70–1
  participants, number of, 57–8
  phenomenological designs, 67–8
  qualitative data analysis, 63–7
  single-case experiments, 59
  two-tailed hypotheses, 58

using conversation analysis, 72
using thematic analysis, 72
diagram, 164
'disclosure', 111
discourse analysis (DA), 157–8
  designs using, 69–70
    social action, 69
  interpretative repertoire, 158
  permissive discourse, 158
  requirements for presenting, 166
discussion, 181–3
  accounting for findings, 181–3
  closing remarks, 183
  discussion forums, 88
  opening paragraph, 181
  suggestions for future research, 183
  theoretical implications of findings, 181
disseminating the results, 190–201
  media, 199–201
  outlets, 191–2
  publishing in an academic journal, 192–7, *See also*
    journal publication
DMDX, 134
documents, 136–7
doing projects as a team, *See* teamwork
doubtful projects, 8
drafts
  feedback on, reasons for, 29
  submission, best time for, 29–30
dress codes, in working off campus, 140
Drive for Muscularity scale, 143
Dropbox, 92
duration of activity, 82

eigenvalue, 151
emails
  for feedback, 30
  use in research, 108
employability, 202–7
  applying for jobs, 203–4
  'graduate level' job, 203
  job interview, 207
  mapping skills onto a person specification,
    205–7
  person specification, 203
  shortlisting, 204
  transferable skills from project, 205
eprime, 134
ERIC, 40
error rate, 148
essential documentation, preparing, 99–105
  briefing sheet, 99–102, *See also individual entry*
  debriefing, 104–5
  obtaining consent, 103–4
ethical scenarios, 118–19, 211–12

ethics in research, 94–119
  materials, 110–11
  principle of 'no harm', 95–9, *See also individual entry*
  recruitment, 106–9, *See also individual entry*
  research with children and other vulnerable
    groups, 111–14
ethnography, 62
event sampling, 139
experiences, 122
experimental design, issues in, 53–9
  balancing, 56–7
  between or within, 53–5
  checking, 56–7
  counterbalancing, 56
  factorial designs, 55–6
  latin square, 57
  manipulation check, 57
  measuring interventions, 54
  participant recruitment, 53–4
  potential confounds, 54
  pretest-post-test design, 55
  random assignment, 55
  repeated measures, 53
  research question, 54
experimental work, 89–90, *See also under* online
    resources
experiments, 134
  confederates, 134
  controlling variables, 134
  running trials, 134
  specialist equipment, 134
    DMDX, 134
    eprime, 134
    mathlab, 134
    psyscope, 134
    SuperLab, 134
explanations, 122–3
external reliability, 133
eye-catching title, 186
Eysenck Personality Questionnaire (EPQ), 143

F ratio, 150
face validity, 133
factor analysis, 151
  principal components analysis versus, 151
factorial ANOVA, 148–9
  2×2 ANOVA, independent groups, 148–9
factorial designs, 55–6
factors, 55
fair collection of data, 114–15
'false positives', 58
feedback
  asking for, 30
  benefits of, 31
  on drafts, reasons for, 29

feedback (*continued*)
emails, 30
hand-written comments, 30
making sure to get feedback in a helpful way, 30–1
non-verbal behavior, 30
fieldnotes, 62
Fisher's notation technique, 48–9
fishing, 182
flexibility in thematic analysis, 161
flyers, recruitment, 108
focus groups, 121–5
distinctive features of, 125–6
study designs based on, 62–3
focused coding, 162

G*Power, 107
Gantt charts, 80–2
advantages, 81
completion date of activity, 82
duration of activity, 82
start date of activity, 82
gap in the literature, 43–5
index cards, 43
sifting through the pile, 44
sorting the cards, 44
sorting within a spreadsheet, 44
gatekeepers, contacting, 108–9
generating stimulus materials, 110
Goldwave, 90
good project idea, 2–3
rooted in psychological literature, 2
something new being added to literature, 2
something one can understand, 2
something that is achievable, 2
Google Scholar, 87
'graduate level' job, 203
grounded theory (GT), 73–4, 161–3
codes, 73
cyclical 'art' of, 162
research versus analytical techniques, 73
group-based quantitative projects, 107
group interaction, 138–9

hand-written comments, 30
hard copy material, 136–7
harm through carelessness, 98–9, *See also* principle of 'no harm'
hierarchical regression analysis, 146
hypotheses, 45–6, 65–6
testing, 58
Bonferroni correction, 58
two-tailed hypotheses, 58
Type 1 error inflation, 58
'Hypothetico-deductive' versus inductive qualitative designs, 65

idea for a project, coming up with, 1–10, *See also* good project idea; topic selection, strategies for
image editing software, 90
impact ratings, journal publication, 193
indexing extracts, 165
using line numbers, 165
using participant numbers, 165
using pseudonyms, 165
inducement, 97
inductive content analysis designs, 66–7, 153
non-numerical data form, 67
numbers form of data, 67
predetermined coding categories, 66
inductive versus 'data driven' design, 65
inferences, 66
information/support sources, 104
informative title, 186
interactions, study designs based on, 62–3
internal reliability, 132
International Personality Item Pool (IPIP), 91
internet, 41–3
using wisely, 41–43
key terms search, 41
web addresses, 41
'wiki', 42
interpretative phenomenological analysis (IPA), 156–7
analytical process in, 156
codes, 156–7
designs using, 68–9
'real' analysis, 156
interpretative repertoire, 158
realist repertoire, 158
romantic repertoire, 158
inter-rater reliability, 138
interviews, 121–5
bad questions, 124
duration of a good interview, 124–5
establishing trust, 121
leading question, 123
obvious questions, avoiding, 123–4
online resources, 90–1
pacing the interview, 122
schedule, 122–3
belief, 122
experiences, 122
explanations, 122–3
paranormal topics, 123
religion, 123
study designs based on, 62–3
transcription, 126–8

job interview, 207
jobs, applying for, 203–4, *See also* employability
journal article, referencing, 185

journal publication, 192–7
  challenges in, 192
    hard work, 192
    payment, 192
    rejection rate, 192
  impact ratings, 193
  order of authorship, 193
  publication process, 193–4
  review process, 194–7, *See also* reviews, journal
    publication
  submission, 194

kwik survey, 91

latin square, 57
leading question, 123
line numbers, 165
lineplot, 149
listed theme, 163
literature review, 22–5, 38–51, 87
  in report, 173
  research question, identifying, 38–51
literature search, conducting, 39–45, *See also* research
    question; theoretical framework
  finding the gap, 43–5
    index cards, 43
    sifting through the pile, 44
    sorting the cards, 44
  general knowledge of work in the area,
    building, 39
    textbooks, 39
  internet, using, 41–3
  originality, 44
  research databases, 40–1
    ERIC, 40
    key terms search, 40
    Medline, 40
    PsycINFO, 40
    Web of Science, 40
local dissemination strategy, planning, 84
locating stimuli, 90
log linear analysis, 150
longitudinal study, 60

making assumptions, 46
managing supervisory relationship, 11–37, *See also*
    allocations to supervisors; troubleshooting
    supervisory relationship
  expectations from, 14–15
  importance, 12–14
  working independently versus working alone, 13
manipulation check, 57
MANOVA, 151
materials, 110–11, 178–9
  copyright issues, 110–11

generating stimulus materials, 110
  psychometric tests, using, 110
mathlab, 134
matrix, correlation, 144
mean, 151
measures, 178–9
measuring interventions, 54
media coverage, 199–201
  press release, 199–200
  published reports, 199
mediation/moderation analysis, 152
Medline, 40
'mental state' references, 66
'middle range' theory, 73
'minors', working with, 112
monitoring and maintaining progress, 83–4
multi-part questionnaires, 130
multiple baseline design, 59
multiple regression, 145
multivariate designs, 61

narrative designs, 70–1
  pragmatic factors, 71
  theoretical significance of, 71
narrative psychology, 158–60
  as constructions, 159
  as descriptions of lived experience, 159
  stages within, 159
naturalistic data, 125
non-numerical data form, 67
non-verbal behavior, for feedback, 30
notation technique, 48–9

observation(s), 61–2, 137–9
  group interaction, 137–9
  inter-rater reliability, 138
  participant observation, 61
  remote observation, 61
  sampling issues in, 139
  schedule, 137
    developing, 138–9
obtaining consent, 103–4
omnibus F test, 151
one-way ANOVA, 147
online resources, 86–93
  backup, 92
  data storage, 92
  Dropbox, 92
  experimental work, 89–90
    Audacity, 90
    audio editing software, 90
    Goldwave, 90
    image editing software, 90
    locating stimuli, 90
    paint.net, 90

online resources, (*continued*)
    Praat, 90
    video editing software, 90
    Wax, 90
  Google Scholar, 87
  literature review, 87
  recruitment and project management, 88–9
    discussion forums, 88
    project management tools, 89
    social networking sites (SNS), 88–9
  sharing, 92
  surveys and interviews, 90–1
    International Personality Item
      Pool (IPIP), 91
    kwik survey, 91
    QDAP Coding Analysis Toolkit, 91
    Skype, 91
    Survey Monkey, 91
    Survey Share, 91
  Writing Up, 92
open coding, 162
opening paragraph
  of discussion, 181
  of report, 173
'opt in' procedure, 112
'opt out' procedure, 112
oral presentations, preparing and
    submitting, 197–8
order, 163
order of authorship, 193
organisations, 78, 174
original scale construction, 132
outlets, dissemination, 191–2
overambitious projects, 8
ownership, 76–9

pacing the interview, 122
paint.net, 90
paranormal topics, 123
participant information sheet, 101
  in case something goes wrong, 102
  confidentiality, 102
  funding, 102
  organiser of research, 102
  participation, 101
    benefits, 101
    question of, 101
    reason for, 101
  purpose of study, 101
  reason for being approached, 101
  reviewing, 102
  study title, 101
participant numbers, 165
participant observation, 61
  disadvantages of, 61

participant recruitment, 53–4
participants, 177–8
  number of, 57–8
path analysis, structural equation modelling
    versus, 151
permissive discourse, 158
person specification, employability, 203
personal data, 114–15
phenomenological designs, 67–8
  first-person accounts of experience, 67
  using interpretative phenomenological
    analysis, 68–9
phenomenology, 155–6, *See also* interpretative
    phenomenological analysis (IPA)
  steps recommended for, 155
    giving overall shape to meaning units, 155
    reading the entire description given by
      participant, 155
    segmenting the data into 'meaning units',
      155
    transforming meaning units to published
      reports, 155
physical harm, 95–6
pilot studies, 180
planned comparison, 58
planning project schedule, 80–2, *See also* Gantt charts
poster presentation in conference, 191
  preparing and submitting, 198–9
posters, recruitment, 108
post-hoc significance tests, 58
potential confounds, 54
'power analysis', 107
Praat, 90
pragmatic factors, 71
predictor variable, 59
  time in, 60
present study, in report, 173–5
pretest-post-test design, 55
principal components analysis, factor analysis
    versus, 151
principle of 'no harm', 95–9
  deception, 98
  harm through carelessness, 98–9
  physical harm, 95–6
  protecting oneself, 99
  psychological harm, 96–7
principle of constant comparison, 162
print media, 135
procedure, 179
process, 166
project management tools, 89
project planning and management, 75–85, *See also*
    Gantt charts
  assessing availability, 78–9
  clubs, 78

communication, 76–8, *See also individual entry*
local dissemination strategy, planning, 84
monitoring and maintaining progress, 83–4
organisations, 78
ownership, 76–9
resources, 79–80
risks, 83
schools, 78
stakeholders, 76–9
project proposal, 15–16
projects to avoid, 8
doubtful projects, 8
overambitious projects, 8
simply replicating well-established effects, 8
not sufficiently researched before, 8
unethical projects, 8
protecting oneself, 99
pseudonyms, 165
psychological harm, 96–7
The Psychologist magazine, 5
Psychology Experiment Building Language (PEBL), 89
psychometric tests, 110
PsycINFO, 40
psyscope, 134
publication process, 193–4, *See also* journal
    publication
publicity material, 135
publishing the results in an academic journal,
    192–7, *See also* journal publication
PubMed, 40

QDAP Coding Analysis Toolkit, 91
qualitative data analysis, design decisions in, 63–7
captures, of individuals' lived experience, 63
central focus of experience, 63
deductive content analysis designs, 65–6
'hypothetico-deductive' versus inductive qualita-
    tive designs, 65
inductive content analysis designs, 66–7
inductive versus 'data driven' design, 65
qualitative methods, 152–68
content analysis, 153–5
conversation analysis, 160–1
discourse analysis, 157–8
grounded theory, 161–3
indexing extracts, 165
key issues, 155
narrative psychology, 158–60
overview of sample, 165
phenomenology, 155–6
presentation of qualitative findings, 166–8
    using published examples, 166
    ways to show that analysis is rigorous, 167–8
    writing for assessment versus writing for
        publication, 166–7

presentation of, 163–6
    analytical themes, 163–4
    tables showing themes across participants, 165
    thematic analysis, 161
questionnaires, 128–34
    multi-part questionnaires, 130

R^2 statistic, 147
random assignment, 55
realist repertoire, 158
recruiting participants, 88–9
recruitment, 106–9
    email use in research, 108
    flyers, 108
    gatekeepers, contacting, 108–9
    group-based quantitative projects, 107
    number of, 106–7
    participants, 107–8
    posters, 108
referencing, 184–6
    book, 185
    book chapter, 185–6
    citations in the text, 184–5
    journal article, 185
reflexivity, 167
regression, 143–7
    blocks, 146
    designs, terminology in, 60
    hierarchical regression analysis, 146
    multiple regression, 145
reliability in data collection, 132–4
    external, 133
    internal, 132
    test-retest reliability, 133
religion, 123
remote observation, 61
    limitations of, 61
repeated measures, 53
report, preparing, 170–89, *See also* sundries
    ambiguous referent, 176
    appendices, 187
    data preparation, 180
    discussion, 181–3, *See also individual entry*
    four part format, 176
        design, 177
        participants, 177–8
    main body of report, 172–83
        closing statement, 173, 175
        extensive literature review, 173–4
        opening paragraph, 173
        present study, 173–5
    materials or measures, 178–9
    method, 176–80
    pilot studies, 180
    procedure, 179

report preparing (*continued*)
  referencing, 184–6
  report writing style, 171–2
  results/analysis, 180
  schedules, 179
  settings, 179
  subsection, 177, 179
  titles, 186
report writing phase, 28–31
  after submitting report, 31–2
  best time to submit drafts, 29–30
  feedback on drafts, reasons for, 29
research databases, 40–1
  ERIC, 40
  Medline, 40
  PsycINFO, 40
  Web of Science, 40
research ethics, *See* ethics in research
research evidence, evaluating, 49–51
  students criticising research, 50
research predictions, 45
research question, 45–7, 54, *See also* literature search,
    conducting
  identifying, 38–51
  importance, 45
  making assumptions, 46s
resources, 79–80
respect and patience, in working off campus, 140
results/analysis, 180
reverse-keyed items, 144
reviews, journal publication, 194
  APA style, 195–6
  reading and responding to, 195–7
    for papers accepted outright, 195
    paper accepted subject to major revisions, 195
    paper accepted subject to minor revisions, 195
    paper rejected, 196
    rejected but a resubmitted version considered, 195
reward, 97
right to withdraw, 116
risks, 83
romantic repertoire, 158
running trials, 134

sampling issues in observation, 139
  event, 139
  time, 139
scales, 128–134
  original scale construction, 132
schedules, 179
  observation, 137–9
schools, 78
  practicalities of working in, 111–12
scree plot, 151

scrutinizing proposal, checklist for, 117–18
separate model, 147
settings, 179
shortlisting, employability, 204
signposting, 174–5
single-case experiments, 59
  baseline phase, 59
  multiple baseline design, 59
  treatment phase, 59
skills and employability
  mapping skills onto a person
    specification, 205–7
  transferable skills from project, 205
Skype, 91
social action, 69
social networking sites (SNS), 88–9
source reference, 129
specialist equipment, 134
specialist expertise, 18–19
stakeholders, 76–9
start date of activity, 82
statistical methods/techniques, 143–52, *See also* ANOVA
  ANCOVA, 150
  associations, 144
  Celebrity Worship Scale, 143
  chi-square analysis ($\chi2$), 150
  correlation and regression, 143–7
  Drive for Muscularity scale, 143
  factor analysis, 151
  log linear analysis, 150
  MANOVA, 151
  mediation/moderation analysis, 152
  omnibus *F* test, 151
  reverse-keyed items, 144
  structural equation modelling, 151
  t-tests, 150
  variables, 143
stimulus materials, generating, 110
structural equation modelling, 151
  path analysis versus, 151
subheadings, in briefing sheet, 100
subsection, 179
sundries, 183–4
  abstract, 183–4
SuperLab package, 89, 134
supervisor
  choice of, unavailability, 19
  in data analysis phase, 27–8
  in data collection phase, 26
  first meeting with, 20–2
    items to take, 20–21
    things supervisor want to find out, 20
  negotiating supervisory contact and style, 21–2
    meetings, 21

practical ethics associated, 25
support, 21
selection criteria, 16
established or high status researcher, 17
specialist expertise, 18–19
working relationship with, 11–37, *See also*
managing supervisory relationship
Survey Monkey, 91
Survey Share, 91
surveys, 131
online resources, 90–1

tables
showing themes across participants, 165
for themes, using, 164
teamwork, 7–8
advantages, 7
difficulties in, 7
test-retest reliability, 133
thematic analysis, 161
accessibility factor in, 161
designs using, 72
flexibility factor in, 161
theoretical framework, 47–51
areas to consider, 48
quality of argument, 48
quality of evidence, 48
arguments, analysing and evaluating, 48–9
being evaluative, 47–8
building, 47–51
Fisher's notation technique, 48–9
theoretical significance of narrative features, 71
time sampling, 139
time, as key predictor variable, 60
titles, 186
eye-catching, 186
informative, 186
topic selection, strategies for, 3–7
flaws in earlier studies, identifying, 4–5
'hot' research area at the moment, 5–6
current journals, 5
meeting to discuss ideas, 6
personal web pages of psychologists, 5
'The Psychologist' magazine, 5
published papers, accessing, 6
identifying the area, 4
personal interest (Approach 1), 3–4

projects to avoid, 8
scope for future research, 4
traditional media, 135
transcription process, of interview, 126–8
troubleshooting supervisory relationship, 32–6
help from other staff, 36
no help from supervisor, 34–5
personal and academic issues get muddled
together, 36
research interests mismatch, 33
talking in meetings, 33–4
when student cannot get in touch with
supervisor, 35–6
t-tests, 147, 150
two-tailed hypotheses, 58
Type 1 error inflation, 58

unethical projects, 8

validity in data collection, 132–4
construct, 133
face, 133
variables, 143
variations, 163
video editing software, 90
vulnerable groups, 121, *See also* children
definition, 111
naming as, reasons, 111
ability to comprehend research, 111
power imbalance, 111
research participation effect on, 111
research with, 111–14

Wax, 90
web-based data, 136
advantage, 136
limitation, 136
web-based material, 135
Web of Science, 40
'wiki', 42
withholding information, 98
working independently versus working alone, 13
working off campus, 139–40
communication issues, 140
dress codes, 140
respect and patience, 140
Writing Up, 92

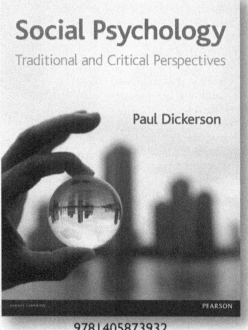